AF663206

Fifty Years of Tryst with Destiny

L P S Shrivastava

ARAVALI BOOKS INTERNATIONAL
W-30, Okhla Industrial Area Phase-II
New Delhi - 110020

First published 1997
Aravali Books International
W-30, Okhla Industrial Area Phase-II
New Delhi - 110020

© 1997 L P S Shrivastava

ISBN 81-86880-26-7

Price : Rs. 350/-

Designed, Typeset & Printed at New Printindia, Pvt. Ltd.
8/4B, Shahibabad Industrial Area, Site IV,
Sahibabad, Ghaziabad (INDIA)
Ph : (011) (91) 8-770112, (011) (91) 8-770997

CONTENTS

FOREWORD

Every statement about India is true. So is its opposite. One can make a good case for Indian Democracy, one can also make an equally convincing case against Indian democracy, particularly the type practised in India's most populous state. However, we must dispassionately analyse the totality of the Indian secular democratic - pluralistic experiment. That this experiment has worked is one of the political miracles of the 20th century. That a country so diverse, so varied, so linguistically unique, inhabited by about a billion people, is, with all its failings, a going concern is a matter of rejoycing.

Shri L. P. S. Shrivastava in his thoughtful book has summoned his vast experience to address India's major achievements, failures and concerns during the past 50 years. This stock taking has produced a useful book. No major area has been left untouched. Foreign policy is examined minutely as is the new economic policy. The judiciary is given detailed treatment. The summing up is not altogether pessimistic. The author is not reluctant to praise, where praise is due. He does not hesitate to criticise where a rap on the national knuckles is required.

I do not subscribe to all that he writes, but broadly speaking it is a constructive and satisfying book, written by a man who feels deeply about India, who shares N. A. Palkhivala's view, that, "We have too much government and too little administration ; too many public servants but too little public service." When all is said and done, when the pluses and the minuses are put under close scrutiny, the pluses out-number the minuses. That, if I have read him right, is also L. P. S. Shrivastava's view.

K NATWAR-SINGH

New Delhi
15th August 1997

MAHATMA GANDHI THE FATHER OF NATION.

Introduction

Fifty Years of Tryst with Destiny

August Fifteen is a day of national rejoicing. It is a day for the Indian people to redeem pledge and to re-dedicate themselves to the service of their motherland and to the cause of freedom.

The wave of decolonisation originated on Indian soil on **15 August 1947** and changed the entire political map of the world. India's freedom and the ideals it symobolised revolutionalised human thinking and ushered in an age based on universality of peace, freedom and respect for human values. The late Nagendra Singh, the then President of the International Court of Justice at The Hague, in his book (1986) "Enforcement of Human Rights," wrote "India's independence was by far the most momentous event of the current century. It was an unparalleled joint exercise, in which the conqueror and the conquered collaborated in a peaceful transfer of power by an unique Act of Parliament at Westminister (London) which gave India and Pakistan in 1947 their cherished Independence. It showed the harmonisation of spirit which set an example for other colonisers to follow. Recognition of the fundamental rights of man to be free, which flowed from India's independence in 1947, synchronised with the UN Charter of 1946, which ushered in a new era heralding a better future for the mankind."

India has proved its capability of vindicating a threatened identity, in the evolution of an ideology and civilisation of its own which will stand the country for generations to come. In the face of threats constantly confronting the national identity, Indians have shown wisdom in keeping themselves together in one State.

It is reasonable, therefore to ask why the euphoria that Independence Day used to evoke seems to be missing now. This is an occasion, therefore, that needs introspection about the functioning, commitments and the governance of this great country. In the pursuit of power of the political clans, the vision of the great leaders of the past seems lost. Inevitably the politicians are blamed for all the ills. Still they have not changed. Rajiv Gandhi gave the slogan, *"Apna Desh Mahan"*. He sought to create an urge to serve the nation which needs most, for everything seems to have gone wrong and there is much that is unethical in Indian political and social life. In this situation, how could one enthuse the people about the vision and the dreams of Gandhi, Nehru, Pal, Bal as well as Tilak, Subhas, Vinoba, Jaiprakash and others. Trends in the governance of the nation are depressing. Even the dignity of the office of Prime Minister has suffered. The President suffers criticism. Governors are shouted down.

August 15 is just not "one more day" in national life. Otherwise, the nation would not be celebrating the 50 years of Independence. Doubtless, the country has an unending galaxy of men and women of high calibre talent and brilliance and who with honesty and sincerity devote themselves to the cause of their motherland. Even so, millions wait all along to get two meals a day, shelter, medicines, clean drinking water and a job for living. These basic needs could not be met even in 50 years.

Legislators go to the people only to seek their vote and they, in turn, wait in vain for the realisation of their hopes and fulfillment of their minimum aspirations. Where is equity when the bulk of the people have little share of the wealth and property generated in half a century?

Is it not sad and demoralising to find that even sacred rivers have been gravely polluted and silted up so much so that even boats cannot navigate them? Our thinking, beliefs and the sense of values have all been distorted. People seem to have lost even a sense of balance and cohesion.

The entire system is being subverted for partisan politics. There is a decline in standards in the functioning of the Parliament and the State Legislatures. In Nehru's words "All our institutions including the Parliamentary institutions are ultimately the projection of a particular character, thinking and aims. They are strong and lasting in the sense that they are in accordance with the people's character and thinking. Otherwise, they tend to breakup". Has the country reached that last stage? Nehru and the founding fathers of the republic believed in democracy because democracy means an attempt at the solution of problems by peaceful methods and not by violence and 'hulla bol'. It was because of their tradition, culture and values that the Indians, secured all their democratic rights enshrined in the Constitution which ushered in the new Republic.

Even as the stalwarts of the freedom struggle were framing the Constitution they were faced with the trauma of partition. The whole of the north was engulfed in a holocaust of a scale never witnessed on the birth of any nation. C. Subramaniam, who was a member of the Constituent Assembly reminisces. "The demons of religious chauvinism have devoured the apostle of peace and non-violence. The premptive sister nation of Pakistan had unleashed hordes of raiders into the Kashmir valley in a bid to project a fate accompli by grabbing valley by force. Internally and externally the perils confronting the nascent nation seemed almost insurmountable. Dark and ominous shadows of a country being shattered into fragments at the very moments of its 'tryst with destiny' encircled the process of Constitution-making. Being liberal democrats and several civil libertarians, India's founding fathers were torn between their innate urges impelling them towards a true federation and the onerous responsibility they bore for strengthening the fragile edifice of a nation whose very survival with its unity and integrity in-act was hanging in the balance. A strong centre in these circumstances was, in their judgement, the only surest guarantee for the nation." Even today, India faces the challenges of hostile environment, with some of its neighbours abetting terrorism and separatism. Preservation of the unity and integrity and security continues to be a major challenge for national leadership. The three organs of the Indian State viz. the executive, the legislature and the judiciary should generate hope and dispel despair.

After 50 years of Independence and democracy the Indian electorate has proved its maturity in spite of the many and continued failings of the political class. One also cannot ignore the fact that the electors have become more assertive about their aspirations and concerns. The politicians must keep themselves abreast with these concerns and feelings of the people. Time is of the essence and the next few years may not be as smooth, as perhaps, the rulers think. The President, the Prime Minister and the Speaker must combine to ensure smooth and effective functioning of the executive and Parliament. They should ensure orderly functioning of all institutions and governance of the country.

Almost three generations of freedom fighters, liberals, reformers and idealists and anti-colonialists worked continuously to create a national consciousness and the non-violent movement to attain our freedom which finally came in 1947 without much bloodshed. Democracy has taken roots and the masses increasingly get themselves involved in the system through elections, governance and economic development. Besides, our spiritual life, has reinforced the concept of the unity and confidence and prevented any collapse. The Indian way of life is deep in harmony with the belief that all pervasive is not destroyable. Dr. Sachchidanand Sinha, the first President of the Constituent Assembly concluded his speech by quoting the poet Iqbal :

"Yunan-o-Mishra-o Roma Sab mit gaye Jahan se
Baki abhi talak hai nam-o-nishan hamara
Kuchch bat hai ki hasti mit ti nahi hamari
Sadio raha hai dushman daure zaman harmara."

English Translation

"While Greek, Egyptian and Roman empires
vanished from the world, India firmly
stood its ground and survived as a nation"
The poet further says "There is an eternal
element in us which had frustrated
all attempts at our obliterations."

When reservation was provided in the Constitution for scheduled castes and scheduled tribes it was hoped that gradually its need will get diluted with socio-economic development. Once during Nehru's tenure both the founder President of the Jharkhand Party Jaipal Singh and Jagjivan Ram asked each other in the Lok Sabha to agree for the ending of reservation for the scheduled castes and scheduled tribes and not to extend it further as was being done then by an amendment to the Constitution. However, they were persuaded not to insist and the matter ended there. Now in the past few years the reservation move is on the reverse gear.

In the name of social justice casteism has been invested with respectability. Reservationists have become bellicose and more and more castes are being wooed by political parties, each outdoing the other in support of rabid casteism.

Now there is also a demand for 33% reservation for women in Parliament and in the State Assemblies. Already, under the Panchayat and Municipal Acts, on the basis of Constitutional amendment, 33% reservation has been provided for women. No political party is in a position to openly oppose the move for 33% reservation of seats for women. But there are sharp differences among them. However, one must accept that this is a revolutionary change being brought about in our political and legislative system which may be first of its kind in the world.

The security of the country has acquired paramountcy. The arms build up in our neighbouring countries pose rising threats. The need to go in for nuclear tests and development of Prithvi and Agni missiles has become imperative. China and Pakistan both have developed advanced type of missiles, reportedly with nuclear warheads. India cannot postpone its own decisions any further. People need to be assured on this count.

There are other areas of concern too. A recent development in which not only the judges of the Supreme Court but even the Chief Justice of the Apex Court himself have been telephoned to act in a particular way in the Jain-Hawala case is illustrative of this situation. The Chief Justice J. S. Verma has said : "efforts are being made by people to say that we recluse ourselves from the case. These things are not going to work". It may not What has happened is sheer disgrace. Nothing seems to be sacrosanct. There has been talk about judicial activism which has been dealt with in a separate chapter in this book. The shocking developments referred to by the Chief Justice should not recur. The Government will do well in taking appropriate measures. Apart from judicial activism, all the major topics of current concern has been discussed in the book. As the country completes 50 years of Independence and is on the threshold of the next millennium, it is everyone's business that issues relating to national unity, administrative integrity and security environment are effectively tackled keeping in view public interest as paramount.

In 1918, Lionel Curtis in a report on Constitutional Reforms in India suggested that India should be divided into racial and linguistic groups. But the then Secretary of State for India, Edwin Montague opposed this report and said in the House of Commons that it would mean the end of the United India. Therefore, he presented his own plan in the House of Commons which provided for provinces as units under the strong Central Government of the Crown. Now we by our acts of omission and commission are leading the country towards instability and division on the basis of caste, creed and religion. More dangerous is the slide down in the ethical standards of politicians, administrators and press. The situation is best summed up when N.A. Palkhivala says "We have too much government and too little administration ; too many public servants but too little public service." Now every Institution created under the Constitution seem helpless. The previous President S. D. Sharma called a meeting of the Governors in which he also invited the leaders of the political parties to participate. This proved a bold step as the issues discussed were of paramount importance i.e. the role of governors in a situation which we face at the Centre after the elections to the Eleventh Lok Sabha and in U.P. In his view, Dr. Sharma said, "It is of the utmost importance that in the given situation the Constitutional Head functions with due impartiality, independence, constitutional propriety, transparency and upholds national interest paramount."

A new President has taken over. Every Indian will wish Kocheril Raman Narayanan success. While he is universally liked his tasks may be difficult given the current political scenario. There will be occasions when the President will have to exercise moral pressure over the Prime Minister and his Council of Ministers. All executive powers are vested under the Constitution in the President. But he has to act on the advice of the Council of Ministers which is collectively responsible to the Lok Sabha. The President has, however, "discretionary" powers on which opinion is still divided. Even in the early fifties India's first President had raised the issue of defining the powers of the head of State. But Prime Minister Nehru shrugged his shoulders and disagreed with Dr. Rajendra Prasad.

None can afford to ignore that freedom has set in motion a process of social, political and economic development. The Indian Experience has been closely watched by the newly liberated societies in Asia and Africa. Five Year Plans, industrial development, large infrastructure and huge technical manpower, self-sufficiency in most consumer items and agricultural products testify that notwithstanding the colossal bottlenecks, India has achieved a great measure of success. In fact, there is a lot to be proud about. As the same time, a land-mark year, like the 50th anniversary, should be an occasion of introspection and review. This book is an attempt in this direction. Solutions, to pending problems are urgent to restore confidence among the people in the legal, political and administrative set up. Only a good and responsible government can restore this confidence.

The lives and achievements of great leaders should inspire the nation and its leadership in facing up to the current issues. In paying tributes to the leaders of the freedom struggle the country should not forget patriots & freedom fighters like Khan Abdul Gaffar Khan, the Frontier Gandhi, who could not Parttake of the fruits of India's freedom. In the life sketches of our past leaders, published in the book, lot of information is available about the freedom struggle.

Along with India, Pakistan also celebrates 50 years of its creation. Its former President Zia used to say that building a 'nationhood' was still in process in Pakistan. I asked him at one of his meetings with visiting Indian Journalists, "you have taken over 40 years or so but are still trying to build Pakistan as a nation". He explained that people there still called themselves Delhvi, Jalandhari, Rampuri etc. He was right. Pakistan is still a divided nation. So problems of unity confront Pakistan. By fighting India all the time, they cannot maintain their unity and build a nation. India wishes them well and only wants peace in the sub-continent.

I am grateful to Kunwar Natwar Singh for having agreed to write the Foreword for this book. I want to acknowledge with thanks to his review of my last book 'Nepal at the Cross Roads'. He has always been kind and helpful while he was a diplomat, secretary and Minister of State for External Affairs. I have always been impressed by his intellectual acumen in policy-planning and decision-making.

I am also thankful to S. Dharmarajan former Head of the Times of India News Service for editing the book. He had edited my book on Nepal also. I am also thankful to Gopal Dass for providing me Secretarial assistance in this venture.

I have sourced material for the book from the writings of many eminent persons, Parliament Library Research Reference Section as also published official reports. Most of the material relating to the Parliament has been taken from Parliament Publications, also the Publication Division of the Ministry of Information and Broadcasting and its Research and Reference Division Library. India 1995 have been a great help to me. Other valuable reference material has been "Introducing India" a book by G.N.S. Raghvan and the History of South India written by P.N. Chopra and colleagues. I have also taken points and quotations from a Parliament publication "Nehru & Parliament" to which I had also contributed a paper. I found two articles by A.G. Noorani lawyer and commentator useful. The past 50 years are an epochal period in world history.

India became independent on 14/15 August 1947. It was closely followed by the end of colonialism in most of Asia and Africa. A little earlier on 24th October, 1945 the United Nations came into being established by 50 nations. Today the UN is an association of 185 nations. Also, post-war recovery of Europe began in 1947 when the Marshall Plan was launched for rebuilding of the economy shattered by Second World War.

I am thankful to Aravali Books International for the support and encouragement they gave me in writing this book. I have made an earnest effort to provide a useful book to readers.

Thanks

(L.P.S. Shrivastava)

To sum up the book writer says : "the state of the nation is worry-some. But our march towards 'Tryst with Destiny' is definitive. Only our leaders must serve the nation, for that is their pledge. We have many successes and have failures. Only the three organs of the Constitution viz. the executive, legislature and the judiciary must function in harmony and obey the provision of the Constitution in unison."

PT. JAWAHAR LAL NEHRU DELIVERING HIS ADDRESS TO THE MIDNIGHT SESSION OF PARLIAMENT ON AUGUST 15, 1947

PRESIDENT DR. RAJENDRA PRASAD SIGNING THE CONSTITUTIONS.

was the voice of self assertion which we followed up in the Constituent Assembly and drafted the Constitution for the Indian Democratic Republic. The process of making the Constitution had begun along with the movement for Independence. Under the inspiration of Bal Gangadhar Tilak, the Constitution of India Bill was drafted in 1885. As the freedom movement went ahead and gathered momentum and as the prospect of India's Independence seemed real thinking on the Constitution of free India began taking shape. Our leaders and lawyers took a lot of inspiration from the Constitution of the United States of America as also from the unwritten British Constitution with which our leaders had experience.

The Government of India Act 1935 was the base on which the clauses were drafted and redrafted to meet our own beliefs and disbeliefs. In the Constituent Assembly, members faced the same challenges that confronted the members of the Philadelphia Convention in 1787, where the problem was more to reconcile between liberty and authority; freedom and the government. Our Constitution makers were committed to provide for building a nation-state which would not be weak in maintaining its security concerns, while still it would preserve the right of liberty for its people.

The Constituent Assembly of India was elected in 1946. Sir Benegal Narsing Rau was its Constitutional Adviser. He prepared a collection of brief studies entitled, "Constitutional precedents to assist the Members in preparing themselves for participation in the debate on various proposals and clauses."

The Constituent Assembly held its first meeting on December 9, 1946 and its oldest member, an eminent jurist of Patna (Bihar), Dr. Sachchidanand Sinha presided over the session as a temporary Chairman. The Assembly had met in an atmosphere of hostility created by the Muslim League and its leader Jinnah. In his address, Dr Sinha said: "there is an external element in us which had frustrated all attempts at our obliteration." He dwelt at length on the constitutions of some of the leading Republics of the world and asked the members of the Constituent Assembly to weave a fabric for the Indian Constitution which suited to India's genius and needs.

We won Independence following the philosphy of non-cooperation and non-violence under the leadership of Mahatma Gandhi. Even our freedom movement generated admiration and even respect from the alien rulers. Otherwise, Lord Mountbatten could not have become the country's First Governor-General.

Dr Rajendra Prasad was elected the President of the Constituent Assembly on December 11, 1946. On December 13, 1946, Jawaharlal Nehru moved a Resolution in the Constituent Assembly which defined the aims and objectives of the Constitution of free India. Moving the Resolution, he said: "Whatever system of Government we may establish here, it must fit-in with the temper of our people and be acceptable to them. We are going to make constitution for India and it is obvious that what we are going to do in India is going to have a powerful effect on the rest of the world, not only because a new and free Independent nation comes in the arena of the world but because of the very fact that India is such a country that by virtue not only of her large size and population but of her enormous resources also and her ability to exploit those resources, she can immediately play an important and vital part in the world affairs. Therefore, it is right that the framers of our Constitution should always bear this larger international aspect in mind." The Resolution which was in the nature of a pledge laid down the principles as also the form of the Indian Constitution. It guaranteed social, economic and political justice, equality of status and opportunity and freedom of thought and action. Nehru wanted for India its own place in the world politics and for this a modern Constitution and a well thought out foreign policy was to be a beacon light.

It was this Constituent Assembly led by Nehru and Patel that devised a constitutional plan for the merger of the princely States into the Indian Union. India was indeed fortunate in being endowed with the leadership of these great men in bringing about integrity and stability to the new nation born amidst strife. The making of the Constitution was completed on November 26, 1949. On Nehru's suggestion it came into force on January 26, 1950. The country with all castes, religious prejudices and social tensions and a record of gory violence attending on Partition, adopted with one voice the most secular Constitution in the world. It upheld the principles and ideals which our visionary leaders had cherished and practised all their life with devotion. And, India was declared a Republic.

Earlier, in January, 1948, a dispute arose between Nehru and Sardar Patel on the powers of the Prime Minister. Nehru thought that in the type of democratic set up envisaged in the Constitution, the Prime Minister was to play an outstanding role. He is responsible more than anyone else for the policy and for coordination among various ministries. The final authority necessarily is the cabinet itself. But Patel thought Nehru's conception of Prime Minister's duties and functions would raise the Prime Minister to the position of a virtual dictator. To him, this was contrary to the democratic and cabinet system. Nehru, however, adopted caution and avoided controversies as far as possible, although he did become almost the sole authority in decision-making. As thinking grew later on among the political leaders that the Opposition in India must also grow along with the functioning of Parliament and the State Assemblies, Jayaprakash Narayan even suggested to Pandit Ji to help build a strong Opposition. Though surprised at the proposal, Panditji seemed to agree that there should be a strong Opposition. But how could he as the Leader of House in the Lok Sabha and of the Ruling Party assist in uniting small groups into a single coherent party. The situation continued for a long time and ultimately Dr. Syama Prasad Mukherjee became the first leader of Opposition with 50 members belonging to groups joining to vote together. Incidentally, the subsequent experiment that was made with the Sanyukta Vidhayak Dal since 1967 failed mainly because small groups could not be united into one coherent party.

The Indian constitution has been the guarantor of the rule of law and perhaps, for this reason it has been described by many eminent men and women around the world as an unique document and constitutionally a democratic Bill of Rights and Magna Carta. However, the present political leadership have shown little respect for the provisions of the Constitution in managing the affairs of the country. This has resulted in a demand for amending the Constitution and even for the creation of a second Republic. But any step in this regard will only unsettle the faith of our people and destabilise the nation. The need is to change ourselves to a new and stable code of conduct and not for changing the postulates of the Constitution.

It will be worthwhile to recall some of the things which happened and were said during the making of our Constitution. Nehru pleaded for preserving the unity, stability and security of India. He was opposed to inducting factors in our Constitutional machinery which would tend to disrupt unity by the frequent recourse to elections, which he said disrupted people's mind.

In November 1951, on the eve of the first general elections, Nehru said: "Hundreds of millions of people in India shall determine the future of our country. They will put their voting papers in terms of thousands of ballot boxes indicating their choice and will run it and do so peacefully. Of this voting papers will emerge the Members of Parliament of India and the State Assemblies and we will accept the results of this election without question." He further said, "In democracy we have to know how to win and also how to lose with grace. Those who win should not allow this to go to their heads; and those who lose should not feel dejected."

On the Election of the President of India and his role as the Head of the State, Pt. Nehru said: "President should not function as party man after he is elected. He should function completely impartially when he is in high office."

An important question arose in theConstituent Assembly whether the Governors in the States should be nominated or elected. Nehru took a clear and firm view that "if we have elected governors, that would to some extent encourage separatist provincial tendency than otherwise.There will be far fewer common links with Centre. It would encourage a rather narrow provincial way of thinking and functioning in each province... After all what is the test of a democracy? Carried to the extreme it may be perfectly democratic in the sense of election everywhere but this may produce conflicts, with the result that the machine begins to crack. He asked : "How many governmental machines are working smoothly and how many are cracking and how many are cracking all the time, for political and economic reasons? There are very few stable democratic machines... It is important for us not to take any step which might tend towards loosening the governmental machinery and thus producing conflicts. We have passed through very grave times and we have survived them with a measure of success. We should thus always view things from the context of preserving the unity and stability and the security of India."

Through theConstituent AssemblyNehru worked to create political institutions which would sustain the unity of India and give the nation a stable government committed to rapid socio-economic progress. He pleaded for reforms in our political and social life and told the Members of the Constituent Assembly that what they create must stand the test of the time when future generations will take over the government of the country. He thought of generations ahead and sought to establish a political and economic system that would also survive upheavals and pressures.

Late in 1947, Sir Benegal visited the USA, Canada, Ireland and Britain for personal discussions with experts in these countries. The record of his meeting with President Hary Truman deserves to be quoted: He said "On November 19, 1947, I had the privilege of seeing President Truman at the White House. Almost the first thing he said was: "Whatever else you may copy from our Constitution, do not copy our provisions for mid-term elections." (A.G. Noorani, Making of Indian Constitution - Span - August 1987, vol. XXVIII and Span No. 8 published by the US Information Services K.G. Marg, New Delhi).

The issue of Centre-State Relations came in for discussion in the Constituent Assembly. On this subject Dr. Ambedkar had said: "The Constitution established a dual policy with the Union at the Centre and the States during the periphery - each endowed with sovereign power to be exercised in the field assigned to them respectively by the Constitution. The Union is not a league of States united in loose relationship nor are the States, the agencies of the Union deriving powers from it. Both the Union and the States are created by the Constitution; and derive their respective authority from the Constitution. The one is not subordinate to the other in its own field; the authority of one is to coordinate with that of the other." He went on: "A serious complaint is made on the ground that there is too much centralisation and that the States have been reduced to Municipalities. It is clear that this view is not only an exaggeration but is also founded on the misunderstanding of what exactly the Constitution contrives to do. The chief mark of federalism lies in the partition of the legislative and executive authority between the Centre and the units of the Constitution. There can be no mistake about it. It is, therefore, wrong to say that the Sates have been placed under the Centre. The Centre cannot by its own will alter the boundary nor can judiciary."

As we went along, in later years, with the working of the Constitution and through the functioning of Parliament and the State Assemblies, States seemed, however to be got treated like subordinates. The centre did exercise extraordinary powers at least in dismissing duly elected State Governments. The governance became a ploy in the hands of political executive at the Centre.

The sanctivity of the border demarcating the executive authority and that of the ruling party got eroded as the same party was in power for most of the time both at the Centre and in the States. This created the problem that we face today. C. Subramaniam, a Member of the Constituent Assembly and later the Finance Minister in an article contributed to a book published by Parliament of India, "Constitution of India and Practices" says: "A Centralised Party which for most part did not practise internal democracy was an anchronism in a federal set up. The Party High Command superseded mechanisms and safeguards set up under the Constitution. Constitutional functionaries like Chief Ministers had to take orders from the High Command even on matters like cabinet making, and since they themselves were often not democratically elected but imposed by Centralised Party headquarters were inhibited in taking bold initiatives. Lacking correctives against absolutism the State Governments had been for long periods under their thumb. The Centralised Party High Command if it was also ruling at the Centre, developed aversions to letting other parties come to power. This is what is at the root of its proneness in going to any length to dismiss the duly installed governments of those parties. Things have not been helped by some governors construing their role to be the agents of the political party (or combination of parties) in power at the Centre instead of being the friends, philosophers and spokes-persons, of State Governments and bridge-builders between them and the Centre, looking at the interest of the nation as a whole."

The result was that most of the decisions of State policy – economic, political, security or foreign affairs were taken outside the Cabinet Secretariat and the Central Government. The Working Committee of the Congress or such other bodies took decisions which were supervised and or even prepared in advance by the Prime Minister or under his guidance. These decisions were then put in a formal shape which were approved by the Cabinet or the Ministers concerned. As a result the Planning Commission and even the National Development Council functioned only as rubber stamp of the Government or of the High Command of the Congress Party.

We as journalists were often told after the meeting of the National Development Council that the only other person who spoke in the meeting was the Chief Minister of West Bengal, Dr. B.C. Roy. All other Chief Ministers only accepted the prepared decisions of the National Development Council by voice vote. So there was no difference left between the executive which had a Constitutional authority to function and the Congress Party which was in power at the Centre and in most of the States. The problem arose only when the non -Congress Governments started coming into power in the States and they expressed their own views on major issues and wanted their suggestions to be accepted by the Central Government. That is how the conflict arose and States started asking for autonomy and for changing the pattern of Central-State Relations as provided in the Constitution.

Even on Parliament, the provisions of the Constitution were drafted carefully to assign an overriding role to Parliament and to establish its supremacy. Patel in consultation with Nehru had also ordered that the independence of Parliament Secretariat will be maintained under the authority of the Speaker. This single order however helped greatly to the development of sound Parliamentary practices as the officers and staff were free to discharge their functions unfettered by any thought of accepting or violating the Government law. Nehru himself showed great respect to the House and the Speaker by his conduct as Leader of the House, which we as reporters have seen for many years in the Lok Sabha as also in the Rajya Sabha. The Speaker was treated as the spokesman of the House and given the respect by the Prime Minister which the House itself received.

When Panditji was on his seat or spoke in the House he seemed to be all the time aware that there was a need to make healthy conventions within the framework of the Constitution, for want of which the institutions built in India or the Constitution itself could not function. He not only accepted the authority of Parliament but also showed all respect to it. However, the decades following his passing away witnessed disquieting features in our Parliamentary functioning. That situation still persists. Further, there has been a lowering of standards.

PT. JAWAHAR LAL NEHRU BEING SWORN IN AS PRIME MINISTER OF INDIA ON AUGUST 15, 1947

PARLIAMENT HOUSE

II

Destination Unclear

After 50 years of freedom and democracy, interrupted by a short spell of emergency, our electorate has demonstratedly become wiser, articulate and assertive in exercising its rights and voicing its concern about problems facing the country. The political class has, however, not yet risen to the occasion and reformed themselves in responding to the people's aspirations and the need for good governance. Adventurism in politics has run its course perhaps, and may be, has reached the point of diminishing returns. The question, however, is still being asked: "Have they?". In Asia, may be Japan and South Korea, they have learnt their lessons quicker than we in India. They also suffered humiliations. We suffered humiliations in the hands of our subjugators. Our freedom fighters, reformers, idealists and others fought for their rights and created a national consciousness and pride and eventually we won our freedom under the leadership of Mahatma Gandhi in 1947 without bloodshed and war. When Tilak was provided with a copy of the blueprint of Gandhiji's non-cooperation movement, he said, "Either this man is insane or great. If he succeeds in this I will have to play second fiddle to him and I shall do it."

India's journey towards freedom and democracy has been unique in all respects. A country as large as ourselves in area and population has survived all ordeals that came in its way. Often people in the world wonder how we survive. People forget that economics is not the only thing on which human beings survive. Of course, India is known to have trade with the rest of the world thousands of years ago and it must have been based on large economic activity. And our people, in spite of poverty have been votaries of democracy even when rajas and maharajas ruled various regions. Even then people talked of elections and various types of Pratinidhi Sabhas existed. This entrenchment of democracy in India had made our journey towards modernity easy in many ways.

India continues to offer spiritualism and a spiritual life style which is practised even among the rational and highly educated persons.

This has given confidence to our people to face the world of today full of conflicts and disharmony and the will to exist and sustain ourselves. The Indian way of life is already making strong appeals to sizeable sections in the western world and thousands of young men and women pour into this country seeking a way of life other than their own. India's persistence with democracy and spiritualism has continued to the point that "the Indian way of life is secure and continues to survive in the face of materialism which has made the world often cruel, ugly and vulgar. May India lead the light and at the same time secure for herself a place of pride in the democratic world and in a capitalist society. In its diversity, the Indians will continue to maintain amazing unity and purposefulness which makes the world wonder and ask "how do we survive."

India's journey towards political freedom and thence economic development has been unique. Under the leadership of Gandhiji our fight for freedom was by and large non-violent which interested the whole world in its form and methodology. After freedom, India has made rapid strides in its quest for economic growth, democracy and social well-being. Though still a poor country, the definition of poverty and backwardness has changed. We are called a developed country among the developing ones. Along with this, however, our attachment to Swadeshi has been sustained and maintained through our policies and programmes through these years. Since the launching of the Five–Year Plans and mixed economy we have continuously worked for a self-sustaining society and indigenisation of our product base, although most of our heavy industries were set up with foreign assistance, mainly from the former Soviet Union in the beginning. We have generated financial resources internally and that is why the country has been able to claim before the world that for our development plans 90% resources have been provided through our own savings. Today our industrial base is very large, wide and varied.

There was a time when the Government had to feed its people on the wheat imported from the USA under the PL-480. But this country launched a vigorous programme of agricultural growth and over the time brought about the green revolution that had made India self-sufficient in mainly wheat and rice and later, in other crops as well. That Green Revolution sustains our economy and economic development. India is self-sufficient in all agricultural products, industrial goods, including plants, equipment and machinery and consumer durables, fruits, oils, vegetables, textiles, building materials and even hard drinks. How many countries have achieved this growth in fifty years? This is particularly laudable in the context of the trauma of Partition that left India broken and weakened.

The people meanwhile started voting for the regional parties. Then all the non-congress governments got de-stabilised and went out of power. In the late seventies, United Front, or the Janata experiment also failed. Like Congress, most other parties also suffered from dissent and disunity. Even politics is an art of possible. But the personal ambitions failed to help the parties that later on came to be born and sustain.

During the last 50 years in spite of all political and economic developments, greed for self and power has made our leaders corrupt and undependable. Allegations of bribery, forgery, conspiracy, murder, tax evasion and even black mailing of political opponents have been made and in some cases, proved. Police and CBI investigations are going on in a number of cases against VIPs, leaders of trade and industry, bureaucrats, police officers and others. Constitutional propriety, principles, party ideologies, national interests and security have been undermined. Therefore, many eminent persons have started asking for constitutional amendments. People like Vasant Sathe have been suggesting the Presidential system while others like the former President, R. Venkataraman are pleading in favour of a national government. A suggestion for appointing a Constituent Assembly to draft a new Constitution has also been made in this, so that we could elect a new Parliament under the new Constitution heralding a second Republic. This would be a drastic step that may affect national unity and pride. Most people will prefer some amendments to the Constitution so that stability could be brought about in the political system and in the functioning of the Government and Parliament. During the last several years, the functioning of the executive and the legislature had been weakened so much that the Supreme Court had to intervene and advise the government to move in a certain direction, which the executive should have done on its own. Then, there could not be an occasion to complain about judicial activism. The people seem to feel, however, that the courts are the only refuse where they could get their grievances redressed and issues of law and Constitution could be addressed and settled.

The concept of secularism in the sense of tolerance of different religions and modes of thought has been another issue in focus. This is something inherent in our culture. But politicalisation of the voting system on the basis of caste, language, religion and even region is now playing havoc with parliamentary democracy and the Constitution. Still the situation does not warrant total pessimism about the future of the country. The period since 1974 has seen the weakening of the Union Government and its authority both in the economic and political arena. Regional parties have grown in strength and the use of Article 356 by the Centre against non-Congress Governments in the States has weakened our will to govern faithfully and honestly.

In a country as big as India, both in size and population, we cannot but have a strong Centre and also equally strong States. The end of one party rule at the Centre and emergence of new national and regional parties as strong political organisations has created divisions at all levels in the States and at the Centre. Regional and caste influences have become dominant and the United Front Government at the Centre has been sustained mainly on the support of the regional parties in Tamilnadu, Andhra Pradesh and Assam and organisations drawing strength from their caste base. Their role in politics, instead of being positive, has become negative. It is this which weakens the will to survive as a united nation and solve our problems in amity and strengthen our political structure to maintain our nationhood. Opportunism, expediency and narrow party interests have divided society and disrupted social and political order. Could it have been possible in any democratic society to postpone the formation of a government for nine months after elections in Uttar Pradesh, the most populous and politically more important State of India?

The new India must be built on our traditions of togetherness and faith in ourselves, our system, our culture and our Constitution. Unless this is done, the rise of separatism, terrorism and caste fanaticism may continue to grow and endanger the unity and integrity of this country for which many freedom fighters had given away their lives. The hopes and aspirations of our people must be sustained at all costs. The voice of the people is for unity and not for any division of mind and soul, and for not exploitation and loot. Today, our women-fold are asking for 33% reservation in the legislatures and no national or regional party is able to resist the demand. This reflects a big change in the mind of our people. When he spoke of the 'tryst with destiny', Panditji obviously was hopeful of laying the basis of a new socio-economic order and democracy. The question to be asked is: are we going to sustain this or destroy his vision? That will be the moral of the 50 years of our society as a free and democratic nation. The Constitution of India provides for government of laws and not of men and material, meaning thereby that no party or individual is above the law of the land.

III

Political Double Speak

We have a functional democracy, strong and vibrant, though of late, we encountered difficulties, which are deep and chronic. Still we are able to hold fair and free elections. However, there have been more mid-term polls both for the State Assemblies and the Lok Sabha than the founding fathers of our Constitution had ever imagined. This understandably is a cause for concern as it has aggravated our political problems and endangered the future of parliamentary democracy in this country.

There is even talk of a second Republic for the reason that the present constitutional provisions do not seem adequate to remedy the deteriorating political situation. The question often raised is whether our country could afford a General Election every now and then. The answer is obviously 'No'. But a solution to the problem has not been attempted so far.

This may erode ultimately the faith of the electorate in the present system and thus create a crisis which may become insurmountable. Constitutional provisions have often been misused in the past. Since the end of the Nehru era, governments have been falling and the Lok Sabha and the Prime Ministers have been finding it difficult to carry through the process of governance and even holding the elected Members of the House together. It was, however, for this reason that during Rajiv Gandhi's times the Anti-Defection Law was enacted. Earlier his mother Mrs. Indira Gandhi herself had become so desperate that she imposed an emergency even taking away the right to live. The courts became helpless in preventing her from imposing herself both on the party and government. Since then, governments have fallen one after another and mid-term elections have been held almost every two years barring an occasion or two.

Rajiv Gandhi was the only Prime Minister who in 1984 won 401 seats out of 508 contested in the Lok Sabha, a position which even Nehru could not achieve. It may be surprising but true that after the Nehrus it was only by sheer luck that Narasimha Rao completed the five-year term as Prime Minister. His was also a majority built by paid-for-defection. Cases have since been launched against him and some of his ministers.

Vasant Sathe, an Ex–Congress Minister at the Centre and a seasoned politician, had been advocating a Presidential system. This issue was discussed in the Constituent Assembly but was not accepted. Atal Bihari Vajpayee has also been asking for a change in the law and to amend the Constitution to provide for an alternative system.

There is even talk of the President himself taking an initiative to form a national government to end the impasse created by fractured votes from time to time. The former President, R. Venkataraman has been talking about it for sometime and only recently he has made an appeal for the formation of a national government. Extreme situation call for extra ordinary remedies and the President has the authority under our Constitution to use his own discretion. The former President, Late Sanjiva Reddy used his discretion liberally in 1978 when the Janata Party Government turned into a minority government.

So far as the government of Deve Gowda was concerned it came into existence because the second largest party in the Lok Sabha, that is the Congress, decided in its wisdom to support it from outside. It may look strange that the biggest and the second largest party in the Lok Sabha supports the 13-Party United Front government from outside. The third largest group, CPM is in the United Front but not in the Government. The minority government is still at the helm of affairs. This is an unreal situation with an uncertain future.

There have been coalition governments in most West European countries and they also face uncertainties and similar problems from time to time. In fact, the situation in Italy became so ridiculous and untenable that a new Constitution had to be adopted to provide for a somewhat stable government in Rome.

As already mentioned, that we should constitute a new Constituent Assembly so that a new Constitution could be framed and a second republic is born with better stability both at the Centre and at the States.

At an informal chat at a dinner party, I once asked Rajiv Gandhi whether the present situation of holding frequent elections for State Assemblies and the Lok Sabha separately creates problems of stability and governance. Promptly, he reacted saying that this was a grave situation and efforts should be made to prevent a political crisis. We should try whether it would be possible to hold elections both for the Lok Sabha and most State Assemblies simultaneously. In any event his own government could not last long.

In an address towards the end of the Constituent Assembly, Ambedkar said: "On 26th January we are going to enter into an era of life of contradictions. In Politics we will have equality and in social and economic life we will have inequality. In politics, we will be recognising the principle of one man, one vote and one value. In our social and economic life we will continue to deny the principle of one man, and one value." This contradiction in our social and political life has since taken its toll. V.P. Singh became Prime Minister on the slogan of ameliorating the conditions of the backward classes by implementing the Mandal Commission recommendations. But terrible things happened during his regime when young men in different parts of the country and in the capital city of India, Delhi, burnt themselves alive protesting against the Mandal recommendations. V.P. Singh did not shed even crocodile tears. Madal had submitted a long and detailed report to Mrs. Indira Gandhi to improve the lot of backward classes. Mrs. Gandhi kept the report with herself and did not release it. A copy of the Report was, however, sent to some selected top officials in the Government and Dr. Manmohan Singh, the then Deputy Chairman of the Planning Commission also received a copy. He later, referred to the Mandal Commission Report when Mrs. Gandhi arrived in Yojana Bhavan to preside over the meeting of the Planning Commission. Dr. Manmohan Singh told me sometime later that he had asked the Prime Minister whether there was anything that the Planning Commission could think and do about it. Mrs. Gandhi curtly said 'No'. Please leave it at that, "If this Report is released", she said, "there would be bloodshed on the road." How true she was. She had foresight. V.P. Singh, perhaps wanted to be known as 'Messiah' of the downtrodden. He not only got the report released but also announced programmes for action to implement the reservation system as suggested by Mandal. Mrs. Gandhi wanted to bring B.P. Mandal born in Madhipura, in Saharsa District of Bihar, where I was also born, in the national politics as a backward leader. My Uncle Late Keshab Prasad Singh and Mandal were close friends and Congress workers who went to Jail together. My father Jagannath Prasad Singh was a non-cooperative. But he was not allowed to join politics.

Later, B.P. Mandal became a socialist leader and also the Chief Minister of Bihar for a brief period. Mrs. Gandhi, perhaps, thought that he will fill in the gap of a backward leader in her party replacing Babu Jagjiwan Ram who had left her and formed a separate party and then joined the Janata Party. But the Report which Mandal submitted frightened the Prime Minister and, hence she did not act on this report as the policy of reservation had created divisions in the society on caste lines. Regional parties drawing strength from their caste base both in the South and in the North, had gained strength and importance enough to overawe national parties and dictate terms to them. Most Indian people, however, staunchly adhere to the democratic system and also to the Constitution which created the first Republic on January 26, 1950. Our experiment with democracy has not been a failure and the whole world has often praised our functioning and called it a great successful experiment.

The electoral verdicts seem now to mean little to parties which form the government at the Centre, be it with a majority or a minority. But the question remains : Why a minority government at the Centre did not allow or advise the Governor of U.P. to invite the largest single party in U.P. to form a popular government. The pseudo-secularist government decided that "communalists" like the BJP should not be allowed to form a government. Even when the elections had been held, the newly elected members were not even allowed to take the oath.

But what happened in a few months? The Congress party itself got divided and demanded the dismissal of Romesh Bhandari as Governor of U.P. After a succession of developments the BJP ultimately succeeded in forming a government in cooperation with the Bahujan Samaj Party, whose General Secretary, Mayawati became the Chief Minister, in a power sharing agreement.

In another case of political irony during the Gowda Government the BJP suffered a crisis in Gujarat and there also Governor was used to install a minority Government in Ahmedabad under the leadership of Vaghela who had defected from his parent party the BJP. Some claim a matured democracy for Britain and immature one for India. Perhaps, it is true that Indian democracy has fallen in bad days. The pledges taken and promises made to the people lost their meaning with the lesser mortals after Nehru in power. The rhetoric and promises made at the time of the polls lost relevance. Dr. Ambedkar, wanted the principle of one man and one value to be the guiding principle of running the State. But this was used later to divide the people on caste lines and create political uncertainty. As much as 40% of our countrymen live below the poverty line, as determined by the Planning Commission under the guidelines prepared by Prof. Lakadawalla who himself was once the Deputy Chairman of the Commission. Today, after 50 years of Independence in spite of all the Minimum Needs Programme and the 20-Point Programme of Mrs. Indira Gandhi, even drinking water is not available to a majority of people who live in the villages.

We have failed not only to provide drinking water to our people but also allowed our rivers to silt to such an extent that they have become foul and turned into *Ganda Nallas*.

The electoral system in our country had also degenerated. And politics got perverted to such an extent that even known criminals and Mafias and hawala tainted can get elected and become heroes. Thanks to T.N. Seshan, many corrupt practices have now been removed.

This has been one great achievement during the last five years which a fearless man like Seshan could bring about and achieve success. About electoral system, Mahavir Tyagi, formerly Minister of State at the Centre raised the question of adult suffrage. During the debate on the subject, in the Constituent Assembly, his view that this could not work and hence any experiment in our country has to be a failure. But Dr. Rajendra Prasad, the then President of the Constituent Assembly, persuaded him to accept the provision and included it in the draft constitution.

In his address to the Constituent Assembly, Dr. Rajendra Prasad said, "I am very doubtful about the wisdom of adult franchise personally, although I look upon it as an experiment, the result of which no one can forecast today. I am not dismayed by it. I am a man from the village, I therefore know the village people who will constitute the bulk of our vast electorate. Our people still possess the common sense and I have no doubt in my mind that they will be able to take this measure in their own interest and in the interest of the country at large, if things are explained to them."

There has also been a talk of a care-taker government independent of the political parties. In Bangladesh, the 13th amendment to the Constitution passed in March 1996 provides for a care-taker government to hold all future elections. Such a care-taker government will perform rest of the work and will not take any policy decision and they will be accountable to the President. The General Elections in Bangladesh were held in 1996 under the supervision of a care-taker government and it was accepted around the world to be a fair election. The President in our system can, perhaps, constitute a council of ministers from the party legislators for a short period as suggested by Rajindar Sachar, formerly Chief Justice of Delhi High Court, only for conducting the General Elections. After all, we have had and we have Prime Ministers from the Rajya Sabha though not directly elected by the people to the lower house of our Parliament. There have been Prime Ministers under the Constitution who have, without being Member of either House, been sworn as Prime Minister. It may not, however, be very credible. Our politicians seems to have lost the will to sustain our democratic fibre. Instead greed for power and money through manoevours and scandals has grown. Not a day passes when we do not hear CBI unveiling some scandal somewhere.

IV

Cooperative Federalism

A dangerous situation seems to be emerging in the current Indian polity. It has been long accepted that the unity of India is not negotiable at any cost even if the central-state relations need to be improved or corrected and some more autonomy be given to the States. In fact, it has been a miracle that in all its diversity democracy has survived for the last five decades. The structure of the democratic Government laid down in the Constitution of 1950, has been preserved in toto.

Talk of 'cooperative federalism' that we now hear is against the very spirit of the Constitution and unity of the country. Regionalism which meant, perhaps, to take a special care of Regional needs, and nationalism which protects and promotes interest of the nation as a whole of which the States are an integral part are to be harmoniously reconciled. The Indian Constitution is a blend of federal and and unitary features meaning, a strong Centre on an overall basis. The capability of the Union Government to promote balanced regional development and assist the States through the transfer of resources and advice on a national basis must not be eroded. In our pattern of planning, all the States have their annual plans prepared and finalised in consultation with the Planning Commission. This enables the country to maintain and strengthen the naional fabric and distribution of resources after determining the priorities of development in the developed as well as backward areas.

Recent statements by some of the United Front leaders on "co-operative federalism" is, however, a dangerous trend as it may undermine the unity of the country. No one can deny that India is a nation and this canot be diluted in any manner. If regionalism is to lead to fragmentation then the notion has to be alerted. May be, the Akalis do believe that India exists in the States and the Centre is only a united administrative set up for linkage etc. The DMK, in the early days of its movement and the Telegu Desam Party led by late

N.T. Rama Rao believed in strong regionalism and even described the Centre as a myth. The Asom Gana Parishad has also been talking of Assamese entity. The Communists, after many years of Independence accepted India being a nation; a united nation. Now even the United Front at the Centre has raised the issue of 'cooperative federalism. If the future Governments of the Union are going to be dependent on the regional parties for their existence, the national parties and national perspective are likely to weaken. One should not forget that India was divided on the basis of the two-nation theory advocated by the Muslim League and its direct action led to bloodshed and partition.

Jawaharlal Nehru himself was not in favour of even the linguistic States but after Andhra Pradesh was formed, the creation of the States Reorganisation Commission thereafter led to the formation of the States mainly on a linguistic basis. Since then, the cry of smaller States has grown. Uttarakhand movement has almost succeeded in influencing the Centre in its favour and the demands for Jharkhand or Vananchal in the South of Bihar still persists, though, an advisory council has been set up at Ranchi for the Jharkhand areas where Advasis are prominent by their presence from time immemorial.

The river water dispute among the Southern States continues to worry the Centre. There has also been a talk of dividing Uttar Pradesh which during the British times was called United Provinces. This is a sentimental problem for the people of U.P. and there is a strong feeling to maintain its unity. The trends towards creation of more States are not desirable and the national leaders must come out in the open and denounce such trends. India's unity and democracy must be maintained at all costs.

There is no need for radical revision of our Constitution and most of our problems can be solved by amendments and adjustments in policies and programmes. The problem today is not that of the Constitution but of opportunism and deterioration in the national outlook and national vision. Corruption and dishonest methods by the political class undermine the moral fabric of the nation. It has demoralised our people. A great India needs great leaders and not puny & unfit or immature men pursuing petty ideas and differences.

People themselves must come forward and lead the nation to revitalise their democracy and strengthen unity. A commitment to national well–being can alone restore faith in leadership and ensure integrity of the nation.

The Presidential System may not work in a country of India's diversity. Even Amercia, in the past and today, has been beset with many problems. Some people from the rural background told me that if you are to have a Presidential dictator then why not revive monarchy. After all, the ex-rulers still command respect among the people. At the time of the transfer of power, there were 565 princely States; but they were part of the Dominion of India. Their total population then was over 93 million. Hyderabad was the largest ruling State. British paramountcy over these States was to lapse with the withdrawal of the British from India. Lord Mountbatten had made it clear to the princely States that they would not be permitted to become members of the British Commonwealth and that each ruler should accede to either of the two new Dominions *i.e.* India or Pakistan. Initially, this accession was limited to three subjects; defence, foreign affairs and communications.

By the time India became Independent on August 15, 1947, all the geographically contiguous States had chosen to accede to the Indian dominion. But Hyderabad and Junagadh and Jammu & Kashmir were still undecided. It was Sardar Vallabhbhai Patel, the iron willed man, India's first Home Minister who after Independence, integrated them with the Indian Union.

The Nawab of Junagadh and its Diwan Shah Nawaz Bhutto father of Late Zulfikar Ali Bhutto announced the State's accession to Pakistan on August 15, 1947. But the people protested and ensured that Junagadh stays as part of India. The Nawab and his family members fled to Karachi.

The Nawab of Hyderabad first wanted to become independent but Lord Mountbatten told him that Hyderabad could not become a dominion.

Nizam's supporter Kasim Razvi and his armed volunteers called Razakars decided to fight and challenge the authority of the Indian Government. Simultaneously, the ban imposed on the Communist

Party in 1943 was lifted by the Nizam. The Razakars and the Communist combined to create problems which resulted in the breakdown of law and order in the State. Indain troops were sent inside the State in September 1948 and in a police action Hyderabad fell in line. The Nizam was allowed a large privy purse and privileges after his proclamation of Hyderabad's accession to India. The Maharaja of J & K also aspired for an independent Status. In October 1947 raiders, organised and equipped by Pakistan attacked the border town of Muzaffarabad and advanced into the Kashmir valley. Maharaja Hari Singh then acceded to India and handed over the administration to an interim Government headed by Sheikh Abdullah.

When India went for its first General Elections in early 1952 on the basis of the universal adult franchise, many people abroad wondered whether democracy would work in a country with a low level of literacy and of economic development apart from diverse religions and languages. But their doubts were dispelled and India has held ten general elections. After the death of Pandit Jawaharlal Nehru the state of the nation, however, had not always been of glory. Congress was broken in 1969 and since then the party has been losing its strength and popular support. The Congress Party was in power at the Union and in a majority of States continuously after Independence, from 1947 till 1977. Since 1977, the experiments of coalition Government has been going on. It has not met with much success either. Still the fabric of democracy and its structure as well as all the institutions created under the 1950 Constitution remain strong. Regional and national parties are struggling hard to function within the ambit of Constitutional framework in the new set up. Some of the biggest challenges stem this process of government.

Obviously, the founding fathers of our Constitution had not envisaged such a situation featuring the current crisis. Political uncertainties and the weakening of influences of national parties have given rise to many apprehensions. The caste system giving advantage to some parties has acquired new political dimensions tending to destabilise India. This requires a solution and may be the electorate will decide the issue sooner or later. For, that is the way democracy funtions.

Jagjivan Ram who had served as the Union Minister longer than others had once said: I was a born Hindu and I am proud to be one. I have read Hindu scriptures with various commentaries and have come to believe that Hinduism as revealed in the Vedas and Upanishads is such as can claim to be a religion of eternal modernity. A fascinating feature of Hinduism is that it is not dogmatic and authoritarian... The greatest merit of Hinduism is its catholicity and spirit of accommodation. ....Hinduism conceives of the world as one family and each individual is part of the indivisible Divinity with all its attributes and hence the equality of all inmates. (From Introducing India by G.N.S. Raghavan - pp. 84-85, published in 1976). Dr. Ambedkar rejected Hinduism and embraced Budhism. But this assertion did not settle the issue of Hinduism. The Congress peristed in its secular theory to win votes of the Muslims and continued its front in Kerala with the Muslim League. There has been a demand to discuss the issue of secularism and communalism in depth in Parliament since the Partition of India has not been taken as a lesson in some quarters. The partition and tragic events, before and after, had hurt the sub-continental ethos and its cultural synthesis. Independent India however quickly recovered from the shock and aberration as it moved forward to build for itself a new India of peace and prosperity and secularism.

But today again the concept of unity of the nation is being challenged. Deve Gowda in his address to the Inter-State Council meeting on October 15, 1996 laid stress on greater consultations with the States and on a new style of governance by the United Front Government. He also talked about confrontationist approach based on protection of interests of either the Centre or the States, which he emphasised could weaken the fabric that has held together Independent India. He said: 'I want to strengthen the sentiment of cooperative federalism which in the Indian context means a strong Centre and strong States and viable local Governmental institutions. After 50 years doubts are being expressed in the corridors of power about our nationhood itslef'.

It is very well known that since the promulgation of the Constitution in 1950, the Centre and the States have always maintained a cooperative and partnership relationship. At the apex level, we have the National Development Council, the Finance Commission and the Planning Commission which assist in the formulation of the Central and State Plans and in the distribution of resources between the Centre and the States. There has also been zonal Councils consisting of four or more States, to sort out their individual and regional problems. The meetings of these councils are presided over generally by the Home Minister of India.

The Ministeries of the Central Government have also maintained close liaison with the States and from time to time regional problems like the river water disputes have been settled with the good offices of the Central Government. But the Union and the States never came into confrontation. There have been annual meetings of the Chief Ministers and Ministers of State Governments and officials on specific issues.

Suddenly, we now find the need for the creation of new institutions and a new framework for Centre-State consultations. The concept of cooperative federalism is not based on regionalism and its growth. This is highlighted only now when at the Centre, there is a Government whose main constituents are the regional parties, ruling some of the States. Recently, the Chief Minister of Kerala,, E.K. Nayanar stressed the need for the restructuring of the Centre-States relations in the context of decentralised planning process and hoped that cooperative federalism would not remain a pious wish.

Cooperative federalism has been discussed in the past also by some eminent persons. But it has also been said that the Planning Commission, the Finance Commission, National Integration Council and some other national bodies serve the purpose of promoting consultation and cooperation among the States and between the State and the Centre. One cannot forget that if there is an unstable Government at the Centre, as at present, the concept of the Union and the States can be weakened. The concept of nationhood at this point of time needs to be strengthened. If national parties, national organisations and the national government weaken the institutions created under the Constitution, the integrity of the nation will also weaken.

Therefore, one has to be cautious while discussing her relationship between the Union and the States. After all, the Union has no territory of its own. It is India which is its territory where it functions and operates. All the national projects/schemes are implemented only in the States in addition to their own plans and projects. So far as the devolution of resources is concerned, its methodology has also been changed by the successive governments. Over 50% of the total resources available for the plans now go to the States.

The emerging balance of forces can have dangerous consequences for the Republic. We have a multi-party system but we are not a multi-national country. Our tryst with destiny lies in free and united India, and single nationhood. Our forefathers laid down their lives at the alter of freedom so that we could live in unity and peace. Our unity was tested in 1962, 1965 and 1971 and the world applauded us. Unity like life is not divisible for we will perish without it.

India's journey towards freedom and from freedom towards economic development has been unique. Under the leadership of Mahatma Gandhi our fight for freedom, in spite of poverty and social weaknesses, India made rapid strides in the growth of democracy and social well-being. Though, still a poor country, the definition of poverty and backwardness has changed. We are called a developed country among the developing ones. Our attachment to Swadeshi may have changed in concept but it has been maintained through our policies and programmes. Since the launching of the Five–Year Plans and mixed economy we have continuously worked for a self-sustaining society. Although most of our heavy industries were set up with foreign assistance, mainly from the former Soviet Union in the beginning, we have generated financial resources of our own and that is why the country has been able to claim before the world that in our development plans 90% resources have been generated internally.

Our experiment with democracy has varied results. We had a stable government during the period Jawaharlal Nehru was the Prime Minister. It was during this period and because of his vision that India's planned development succeeded and set the pace for economic growth with confidence. After his departure India has faced problems of governance continuously. The Congress Party has ruled this country since Independence but it broke into pieces in 1969 when Mrs. Gandhi was in power.

During the last many years Constitutional proprieties, party ideologies, national interest and security have been undermined and that is why many eminent persons, have started asking for Constitutional changes.

There is a visible change in the mind of our people, and the women folk which may lead us to light and bring about cohesion in our society and political life. Panditji when talked of the 'tryst with destiny' obviously was hopeful of laying the basis of a new and sustainable socio-economic order and democracy. The question to be asked is : are we going to sustain this or destroy his vision? That will be the conclusion of the 50 years of our social and political functioning as a free and democratic nation. The Constitution of India provides for government of laws and no more, meaning thereby that no party or individual is above the law of the land. Only the people are supreme and for whose welfare all the policies were framed and structures built.

V

Judicial Activism

A look back at the proceedings of the Constituent Assembly shows that many of the problems and issues that are now being faced, were also discussed at the time of the making of the Constitution. This included the role of the judiciary and its functions.

Once Nehru said: 'our right on ex-propriation of land could not be considered wrong as there was no moral right attached to property'. The question under discussion was the right to property and whether it was not in consonance with the prevailing western democratic thought. He could not, however, persuade public opinion to wholeheartedly support him on his policy of land reforms. Many years later, eminent persons like Prof. N.G. Ranga resigned from the Congress and joined the Swatantra Party on the question of collective farming to be introduced as part of the land reforms.

Nehru depreciated the tendency of the judiciary to function as a kind of third chamber often undoing the efforts of the legislature in matters of social reforms. On a reference to the issue in the Constituent Assembly on September 10, 1949; he said: "Ultimately the fact remains that the Legislature must be supreme and must not be interfered with by the courts of law in measures of social reforms." That was the time when some of the Land Reform Acts had been declared unconstitutional by some of the High Courts. These Acts were later put in the Ninth Schedule of the Constitution so that their validity could not be challenged in Court. Issues relating to the judiciary have also been raised and discussed elsewhere as in the U.S. Congress. On many occasions and on many of the cases when they were discussed in the Constitutent Assembly, there was a reference to the American system and their experience.

Many would remember that Chief Justice Earl Warren who presided over the U.S. Supreme Court during the period October 1953 to June 1969, made many path-breaking pronouncements and became a controversial figure. There was also a controversy whether, 'courts ought not to enter the political arena'. Judges in the United

States also raised the issue of self-restraint and debated judicial activism. Strongly agitated over the restraint shown by the executive and legislature they asked if unconstitutional use of power were violative of the Constitution and, therefore could be raised in courts. When, however, the question of the welfare of the people arose, Justice Warren himself agreed to follow the rule of self-restraint in the field of economic development and people's welfare. Thus, the controversy which has arisen in our country is nothing new. However, when the executive becomes non-functional and issue of public welfare continues to get ignored, they become substantive issues of law. We now find the courts have started listening to people's demand for justice and good governance.

When the Cauvery dispute became a grave issue between Karnataka and Tamilnadu during the premiership of Narasimha Rao, the matter was raised in the Supreme Court which advised the Prime Minister to call the Chief Ministers of both the States for a tea meeting and assist in resolving the crisis. Even when Mr. T.N. Seshan was unhappy with the appointment of two more Commissioners in the Election Commission and declined to give them work, the Supreme Court gave the same advice to the Chief Election Commissioners to organise a get-together with the newly appointed commissioners and thrash out the problem. The Supreme Court has for the first time even fixed dates for the cleaning of garbage in the capital city of Delhi. In December last year, the Court directed the closure of aqua farms in coastal areas except those which followed traditional methods of fish farming. The Court also ordered that over 100 million children employed in the hazardous industries should be freed and compensation of Rs. 20,000 each be paid to every child employed in those industries. These are welfare issues. But the Government of India or the State Governments gave scant attention.

The Supreme Court also put curbs on running of saw mills and mining in forest areas. It also has banned tree felling in forests. Telephone tapping was another issue raised in the Supreme Court and the Court ruled that it was violative of the Right of Freedom of Speech and the Right to Privacy. Thus we find that today judicial 'activism' has become a part of our functioning insofar as the protection of people's rights, welfare are concerned and perhaps a necessity. These instances have firmly established the principle of judicial supremacy although the politicians are calling for judicial restraint. But for the order of the Delhi High Court, even the Haveli in which the literary poet Mirza Ghalib lived in the 19th century could not have been restored.

Along–with the judicial reviews and orders the question has also arisen about public interest litigations. This concept has spread like fire and often courts are persuaded to hear these petitions which have emerged as an apparent important innovation in the practice of freedom rights. But the Government feels harassed.

The Constitution provides for judicial review of legislation, as to its conformity with the statute. This, however, seems to have been enlarged in its concept and coverage. In the case of Kesavananda Bharati case, the Supreme Court stuck down a Constitutional Amendment Bill on the ground of its being violative of the basic structure of the Constitution and now as part of the new concept of litigation not only the aggrieved person but also anyone can move the court in public interest for the redressal of citizen's grievance.

Article 141 of our constitution says: 'the law declared by the Supreme Court shall be binding on all courts within the territory of India'. Article 144 enjoins that all authority, civil and judicial in the territory of India shall act in the aid of the Supreme Court'.

Fundamental Rights are guaranteed to the Indian citizens and they have the right to move the Supreme Court for their enforcement. Thus the principle of judicial supremacy has been firmly laid down in the Constitution itself. But the word 'activisim' and the word 'restraint' are to be used with great caution. This question will continue to be debated for sometime.

The need, therefore, as mentioned earlier is that the executive should improve its performance and alertness in the governance of the country and Parliament should become active again in binding the Government to the constitutional provisions and Articles. There may also be the need for Parliament and the judiciary to improve upon the provisions of the Constitution in the administration of justice and of good governance.

During the regime of Mrs. Indira Gandhi, there was a talk of committed judiciary just as the activism of the judiciary has become a hot topic now. Lawlessness either among the people, the police, administration, executive or the legislature or the judiciary cannot be accepted and it must be checked in all its functions and behaviour. There was criticism by L.K. Advani, now the President of Bharatiya Janata Party, that notwithstanding the behaviour of some judges during the Emergency, respect for the institution of judiciary had not lapsed. He has proved it in his context of the court approach in the Havala case. The rule of law was suspended during the Emergency and the courts did not look into the petitions in *habcaus corpus* cases. The then attorney General, Niren De stated that the citizens had no claim to redressal even if their right to life was suspended at least for the duration of the Emergency. There was even a fear for the duration of the Emergency. There was even a fear that the basic structure of the Constitution may be altered whereas in Keshavananda Bharati case the court had ruled that this could not be changed. But Niren De pleaded for reconsideration which was not accepted by the Supreme Court. There have been cases in which complaints have been made about the lapse by the court. Investigation of the Bofors case was one such instance. Recently, in the case of Kalpnath Rai there was a broad degree of agreement with the Magistrate's ruling which kept Members of Parliament behind the bars. The controversy arose with the remarks passed on the general behaviour of the Parliament as a whole. The Constitution grants the judge the right to punish. But it does not give a licence to insult anyone.

It is, however, true that the judiciary has now established its moral leadership vis-a-vis the legislature and the executive. At the same time utmost caution should be exercised in the execution of judicial powers by the courts. It is true that in cases against political parties and their leaders, there is some rejoicement at the discomfiture and disrepute of the politicians. The politicians should understand the reality of the situation and remove doubts about their integrity, work and character. While judicial review has been an integral part of the constitutional system it is worthwhile to recall what Justice H. R. Khanna had said, "The courts, however, do not act as super-legislative."

The right of the legislature to decide what laws should be enacted, has never been challenged or denied. The courts function is mainly to interpret the laws and decide about their validity. The policy decisions remain with the Assemblies and Parliament. Many politicians and eminent persons have been asking for amending the Constitution on many important issues but no amendment can eliminate the basic structure of our Constitution. If that is done, then the first republic will seem to be ending its life.

Alongwith the expansion of Legislatures and economic activities the court have also grown at all levels both vertically and horizontally. The population has increased high. Cases relating to claims and violation of various enactments have increased the work load of courts. Economic offences have grown in volume far and wide. The result is that the backlog of cases has tremendously increased. Abhishek Singhvi, the Addl. Solicitor General of India in an article in the '*Times of India*' dated April 25, 1997 says, 'it is more than a little ironic that in a country with over 25 million cases pending in the High courts and lower courts, the substance and content of law and sophisticated legal doctrines continue to fascinate while administrative and managerial arrangements of the legal system is generally overlooked. Even the limited debate on the elimination of delay and backlog of Indian courts had rather stopped and the need is being ignored'. The use of computers has been advocated for the quick and smooth functioning of the courts. This work should be given high priority because thousands of people are languishing in jails in different parts of the country without their cases having been heard. If they have completed a period of jail-term that could have been awarded to them under the law then all such cases should be considered at a fast pace and their release ordered without delay. There is a need to improve the administration of courts at all levels and this could not be postponed any longer. Justice delayed is justice denied.

The way laws are being enacted in State Assemblies and in the Parliament makes it difficult for the courts and lawyers to keep a track of them. Sometimes even copies are not available. This is another cause of delay in the administration of justice. The Law Commission has been giving reports to the Government on the reforms that should be carried out. The Law Commission also revises, consolidates and brings all Central laws up-to-date, because of delays there is no doubt that people are losing faith in the system.

The Law Commission has taken up a detailed study of the procedures and the reasons for delay and lapses. There is also a proposal to establish one or more separate investigative agencies for the judicial system. This has become necessary because often Police reports are not being believed and in many cases they have not been found to be correct in the courts and seem to be tutored. However, people continue to suffer because the Police FIR (First Information Report) once written cannot be changed. Thus ordinary persons cannot do anything to get their grievances redressed in the hands of the Police and even in the courts because nobody listens to them. Therefore, devotion to duty, integrity and character is a requirement for all in our institutions and organisations in various fields.

The nexus between the crime and politics has reached alarming proportions. Since Independence not only the civil administration and the police but also the judicial administration has deteriorated. Often people say that it is beyond repair. But this affects day-to-day life of our citizens who cannot be allowed to suffer because the system has degenerated. Therefore, the system has to be changed or improved at a rapid speed and solutions found to bring about reforms in the criminal law, Police working and introduction of modern techniques of management in the judiciary. The system must serve the public interest in whose name it functions. The judiciary cannot be accepted as an aristrocracy of the robes & it is not so, as Justice H.R. Khanna points out.

Justice A.M. Ahmadi, formerly Chief Justice of India said in the courts of an interview (Hindustan Times, New Delhi April 27, 1997) I have always said that the courts should exercise restraint in the exercise of their judicial power and it should not project itself as a crusader for a certain cause. It must not give an impression that the judge or judges have pre-determined the issue. Such a conduct impinges on the credibility of the courts and its impartiality.

The rule of law must be accepted and respected. The rule of law has to subserve the interest and welfare of the people and it should protect them from harassment and injustice as also against the misuse of law, power and authority. The institutions which have been created under the Constitution must abide by law. A 'date' may be pleasant in love-making but a 'date' and another 'date' in the courts makes life difficult and intolerable.

GANDHIJI ADDRESSING A PUBLIC MEETING DURING THE FREEDOM STRUGGLE.

SUBHASH CHANDRA BOSE, JAWAHAR LAL NEHRU
AND OTHER LEADERS IN A PENSIVE MOOD.

VI

Good Governance

The question of good governance was discussed in the Constituent Assembly and Jawaharlal Nehru himself spoke on many occasions on the subject. He tried to visualise and evolve, what he considered to be the most appropriate structure of governance. It had been democratic in content and accord primacy to the concepts of social thought and secularism. He was convinced that this system with all its imperfections was most suited to India's ethos and expediency. Moving the objective Resolution in the Constituent Assembly on December 13, 1946, which was the fifth day of its first session, Nehru observed: "Whatever the system of government we establish here must fit in with the temper of our people and be acceptable to them." Ten years later, Jawaharlal Nehru speaking at a Seminar on parliamentary democracy on February 25, 1956 remarked "Democracy is a means to an end, the end we aim at. What is the end, we aim at? I don't know if everybody will agree with me but I would say the end is the good life for the individual. What form it should take could be argued about but the good life must imply certain satisfaction of the essential economic needs which will release him from continuous oppression and which will give him a chance to develop his creative faculties." Again in his inaugural address at the seminar on parliamentary democracy on December 6, 1956, Nehru said: "Parliamentary government is a democratic concept. It means the actual providing of the franchise and thus it becomes an adult franchise. The effects of Franchise are being felt in full only now. This political change has fully established itself and it has become obvious that a political change by itself is not enough. From parliamentary democracy we advance to the concept of economic democracy. First of all, that means working for a certain measure of well-being of all, call it a 'welfare state'. Secondly, it means working for a certain measure of equality of opportunity in the economic sphere." Nehru gave shape, meaning and content to the provisions of the Constitution guaranteeing parliamentary system, social economic and political justice, liberty, equality and dignity of the individual, as well as unity and integrity of the nation.

A 'no confidence' motion was brought before the Lok Sabha by the Opposition during the fifth session of the Third Lok Sabha. Replying to the discussion, Nehru said: "Personally I would welcome this motion and this debate and have almost felt that it would be a good thing if we have a periodical examination of this kind." Later he admitted that the problems of the government have grown so enormously that sometimes one begins to doubt whether parliamentary provisions are adequate to deal with them. But he always felt and said: "If the economic problems are not solved the political structure tends to weaken."

About individuals and parties, Jawaharlal Nehru said in Madras in 1951: "Individuals howsoever able and efficient, they do not represent or are not in touch with the people while an organised party, by the mere fact of its functioning, as a party is in contact with the large masses of people whom it guides, whose thinking it influences and which in turn is effected by the people's wishes." He always believed in the party system but emphasised the need for a strictly disciplined party for the smooth functioning of the parliamentary governance of the country. He often said in the Parliament, "We should not set up wrong precedents for that would damage our system and will go against the concept of good governance which can only be established and protected if there is peace and harmony in the Society and the country at large." In the AICC Economic Review of 1958, Nehru explained, "In any aspect of our programme, we have always to remember the basic approach of possible means and, perhaps, we might also keep in view the old Vedantic ideas or the life force which is the inner base of everything that exists." He agreed with Gandhiji that the old Panchayat system of village democracy in India was actually the base on which our parliamentary democracy flourishes.

Governance of a vast country like India has always been beset with many difficulties. But every time one realises that the needs of the system created by the Constitution and even aspirations of the people have changed. However, even four wars, one with China and three with Pakistan and the vast changes that have taken place within and outside our borders have not deterred our people to continue to believe in the adult Franchise.

Though coalition governments have failed to last their very formation and existence for a period has brought about significant changes in the nature of governance. There is a growing demand for greater transparency in governance and tolerance in our democratic system which never happened during the status quo regimes of the Congress. Emergency ended in 1977 when Morarji Desai was sworn in as the Prime Minister of the Janata Party Government. Civil liberties and right to live were restored which had been suspended during the Emergency.

The concept of unitary form of Government also has got diluted to federalism and further decentralisation of authority, from the two tiers of the Centre and the States to lower levels. The experience of the short-lived experiment with Sanjukt Vidhayak Dal has, however, led to the loss of faith in the party system and its relevance. The Party system and coalition governments have in essence, little to offer to the mass of our people who continue to suffer poverty and humiliation. The new rulers continue to divide the people so that they could impose their will and authority over them. The other most dramatic change that has come about during the last two and a half decades is the surge of a popular will to share power with the oppressed from the Panchayat to the State and Central level.

This explains how Mandalisation of politics has become a compulsion for all the parties to adjust themselves and to declare their commitment to the poor and down-trodden and help them share power and authority. The fall-out has been that it has enchanced chances of success in the search for an alternative system of governance. May be some new political models emerge and develop from the ground level and replace in opportunistic alliances and authoritarianism as was seen in the state of Uttar Pradesh after the Assembly elections.

The masses are looking for new ways of governance and development which will bring about stability as well as fulfill their aspirations and make them partners in progress and prosperity. This would not be possible without making amendments in the Constitution. This reinforces the demand for a new Constituent Assembly consisting not mainly of politicians but an assembly of intellectuals and eminent persons from all walks of life to bring about the requisite changes.

We are thus in a transitional phase of politics. The current political turmoil has thrown a challenge which the people must grasp and give an answer—maybe through upheavals or through the ballot. Surely, not through "chaos, destruction and anarchy." No

There is also a demand to change the bureaucratic apparatus. The Late Rajiv Gandhi during his premiership took two welcome steps. One, he brought about a Constitutional Bill to transfer power to the Panchayats and to local bodies — both administrative and financial. The second was his travel to the State capitals and meet collectors and discuss with them the ways to improve the administration at the district level free from political pressures and to make them accountable for all acts of ommission and commission. Later, a Collectors' Committee drafted a report and made recommendations which were widely discussed and welcomed. But after his loss of power and subsequent death, this report was given a go by. No successor government has showed any interest in the report. Now both the collectors at the district level and secretaries at the state level continue to be de-stabilised and transferred at will by the political masters. The result is that the concept of good governance and a permanent administrative machinery built by the British and continued by the government of free India has suffered enormously and lost their will to act.

In governance the executive has a lot of constitutional powers but for all its actions it is responsible to Parliament, more so to the Lok Sabha which is elected directly by the people. The question often asked is: "What is the mandate?" During the recent debates on the confidence or no confidence motion the Ruling Party and the Opposition gave different interpretations. They charge each other with not allowing stability in the governance which is essential to acceleration in the process of economic development. Elections are quite costly and the country cannot afford them too frequently. The chief Election Commissioner, T. N. Seshan and his colleagues sought to bring down the cost through a set of norms and compelled the political parties to follow these rules in the 1996 elections. Hopefully, these norms may stay in future.

If it is accepted that the mandate in the 1996 Lok Sabha poll was against the Congress because of the decline in its votes and seats in the lower house, then by the same logic, the big increase in the BJP vote and its strength in the Lok Sabha has also to be accepted as a mandate of the people. At the time of the elections, there was no United Front and all its partners fought separately on separate platforms. But after the Elections, small and regional parties joined together to constitute the United Front and then claimed that they had obtained the mandate. This was political expediency camouflaged as mandate. Obviously this has further eroded confidence in the system. The question of finding the solution to the problems of governance have assumed great importance. The system cannot be allowed to be perverted overlooking the goals and objectives enunciated in the Constitution. During the last many years, in the two Houses of the Parliament politics dominates to the exclusion or subservience of other important issues. Even the Budget is now hardly discussed at length. Most of the demands of grants of various Ministries are passed without any discussion at all.

The Houses do not get time to discuss the major issues like unemployment, law and order situation, criminalisation of the society and politics, and rising prices. Even poverty elimination programmes are not discussed in depth, though the Members of Parliament know very well that the implementation of social programmes is tardy. It is time that the governments concentrate on the governance of the country; law and order, security, question of good administration and economic development. We are at a watershed in our history. The world itself is changing all over. Therefore, in the context of the emerging situations and deterioration in social and political norms and values it is incumbent on our leaders to come out of their political grooves and seek a system of better governance that can take us to the next century. Is the Constitution coming in the way of bringing about adjustments in various fields or that the political class has little interest except in manouvering and power brokering. There is a general erosion of values in public life and crisis of character. The founding fathers of our Constitution did not foresee that in expedient or inappropriate or wary or undue smaller persons could come to power. We are suffering the consequences.

VII

Institution of Bureaucracy

India became free to face immediately the trauma of Partition. The direct action launched by Mohammed Ali Jinnah in 1946 had brought untold misery and bloodshed, especially in the north. It was a precarious situation and with wounded heart leaders, government and people had to stand together and share the pain of country's rebirth. The wounds were deep. Lakhs of people were uprooted from their hearths and homes and they had to be sheltered and resettled.

The British civil servants who were heading most of the Ministries/departments and organisations decided to resign and left the country along with British troops. The Government had, therefore, to face the problem of running the administration, managing law and order, looking after the security of the nation, conduct its foreign affairs and economic development. In fact when British officers left the running of the trains became a problem and Sardar Patel called a meeting of the senior most officers of the Indian Railways from all over the country from Gorakhpur, Kota, Calcutta, Bombay, Madras etc. and held a meeting with them at his residence and told them about the predicament. At that time it was the only mode of transport available to be used nationally. He asked them a straight question: Can you manage the Railways? He gave them two hours to say 'yes' or 'No'. After the time given to them was over, they stated in front of Sardar Patel with courage and conviction, 'Sir, we can manage'. And the bell started ringing all over the country. Immediately, the Home Ministry issued orders, held meetings, made organisational changes, appointed and promoted officers and thus railways continued its journey. Since then we have not looked backwards. Today the Indian Railways are regarded as the largest system of train running and management and a very efficient one at that.

As for running the administration even Lord Mountbatten gave some advice to Nehru and Patel. He himself was a great administrator. It had become necessary to reorganise the Central Secretariat and it was also important for the new rulers to know how to run the administration and order them about. There was also the question of managing the morale of the civil servants which had taken over the responsibility of managing the administration from the colonial Government. There had been a dignified and smooth change over.

In certain political circles doubts were expressed if the ICS (Indian Civil Service) recruited and trained by the colonial rulers would cooperate with the Government of free India. There was also a complaint that they treated people of India harshly at the behest of the British during the freedom movement. In fact, however, one or two ICS Officers had been killed in Bihar around the same period. But Nehru and Patel were not inclined to accept this theory and decided that the ICS will continue to manage the Secretariat both at the Centre and in the States.

Patel called a meeting of all the ICS Officers in Delhi in the North Block which was attended by Nehru as well. He appealed to the ICS Officers to cooperate with the Government and the Government will welcome their cooperation and commitment to the Indian nation. He also left them the option to go abroad and settle there with the facilities the British Government had already provided to them i.e. to get their salary, full or in parts in Pound Sterling in London.

After listening to the two great leaders of India, Nehru and Patel, all ICS Officers in one voice rose to pledge their commitment to the country and to serve the motherland and the administration with honesty and all the efficiency and experience they had both at the Centre and in the States. This brought about jubilation and a great satisfaction in realising that the country will have no problem in this regard. After all, they were all highly educated, trained and very experience people. They were all Indians and men of high calibre and understanding.

There will be no problem in running or managing the affairs of this free country. A contrasting situation emerged many years later when a meeting was organised by the Cabinet Secretary for the then Prime Minister P.V. Narasimha Rao. It was perhaps in 1995. But this meeting did not prove of much use because the Prime Minister did not make any important point in his irrelevant speech and after dinner everybody dispersed in disappointment. This meeting was also organised because there was a feeling in the Central Secretariat and elsewhere that the morale of the civil servants was no longer very high and the politics had demoralised them completely. And therefore, they were keeping themselves away from taking decisions. This situation has continued even till now.

During the British rule it was the Executive Council of the Governor General and Viceroy who were the principal authorities running the administration. Knowing the problems of Nehru, as Lord Mountbatten did, he advised him to have a secretary who would be different from the Cabinet Secretary. Panditji, however, depended mainly on the institution of the Cabinet Secretary to manage the affairs of the State in coordinating the activities of the Central Secretariat. Later, when Lal Bahadur Shastri became Prime Minister, he appointed L.K. Jha, a retired ICS Officer as the Principal Secretary to the Prime Minister. Mrs. Indira Gandhi continued with this system. Later she expanded the Prime Minister's Office greatly and the importance of the Cabinet Secretary since then, has diminished although the Cabinet Secretary has continued to coordinate the activities of Secretaries to the Government in various Ministries. The PMOs Office has become a political wing of the Prime Minister to order about top bureaucrats in the Government of India and even taking decisions which have been often critically discussed in the press and the Parliament.

Favourtism in the appointment of Secretaries to the Government and the Cabinet Secretary as also the Chairmen of the public sector undertakings has weakened the civil and police administration from the top to bottom and there seems to be no respite. The will has been lost.

The question of senior most civil servant being appointed as Cabinet Secretary has also become controversial. There have been instances when the Prime Minister wanted to appoint a particular person among the two or three top civil servants. After one was selected, the post of a Principal Secretary to the Government was given to the rest. Dr. K.B. Lall I.C.S. was made Principal Secretary to the Government and Secretary to the Ministry of Defence during the days of Bangladesh War and the post of Cabinet Secretary went to another senior most officer. Since then, however, the post of Principal Secretary has not been utilised for the purpose of removing grievances among the top officers after a Cabinet Secretary was appointed.

The Cabinet Secretary is to maintain a link between the political authority of the Government i.e. the Cabinet and other government machinery which has always been considered apolitical. However, now one cannot say that either in the State or at the Centre they have been allowed to remain apolitical. U.P. and Bihar are the worst examples.

There is a system, however, to appoint Committees of Secretaries on important subjects to assist the Government in the formulation of proposals and decisions. At one time the office of Prime Minister generated confidence and provided authority to the top civil servants in the discharge of their duties. But the situation has completely changed and now there is more fun about everybody than functioning. The trust between the political masters and the civil servants has been eroded. The Secretaries and administrators in the States are the worst sufferers. They are shunted day in and day out from one place to another either on the basis of favourtism, caste or likes and dislikes of individual political masters. The result is that the civil administration and the law and order situation continues to deteriorate. There is neither stability in the Government nor in the administration. The last few years have not been worthy of us. Otherwise, our bureaucrate and experts, scientists and others are considered best in the world. But our political masters have not only failed themselves but also failed the country. Rajiv Gandhi consistently spoke about restructuring the bureaucracy. But even he also could not improve the system and before the report of the Collectors' Committee could be implemented he had to leave the Government.

The IAS officers (Indian Administrative Service) came to replace the ICS, a British creation. But the entire system got into a rut. Morarji Desai, headed the Administrative Reforms Commission and gave a good report. But not even one of the recommendations of his committee has been implemented so far. There is also the problem of the tenure of service. Even Cabinet Secretary and Secretaries retire just after one or two years of service of less. This has done no good to the Central Administration and the system of lobbying for posts has created cracks in managing the affairs of the State and government.

The East India Company when got itself established, chose its personnel from amongst men of letters and thereby enriched itself with intellectual accumen of its employees and officers. When the Governor General was appointed, the incumbent Warren Hastings was a brilliant student of English literature as well as of Indian philosophy. He appointed Charles Wilkins, a lover cadre employee of East India Company for the translation of Bhagvad Gita which was published in 1785. A great genius, Sir William Jones had been appointed the Chief Justice of the Supreme Court of Calcutta who along with Charles Wilkins in 1784 founded the Asiatic Society of Bengal whose contribution in research was acclaimed all over the country and which for the first time revealed India's past to the world. T.B. Macaulay was also a servant of the East India Company who prepared a new history of educational system in India with English as the medium of instruction. A.B. Kieth, Member of Indian Civil Service prepared an authoritative vedic index and wrote a history of Sanskrit literature. There were several other members of the Indian Civil Service known for their contribution to Indian art, culture, and civilisation. The British Officers also prepared the gazetteers which are still a major source of history, geography, sociology, archaeology etc.

After the Indians had started joining the ICS they did not much contribute to intellectualism as started by the British Officers and now it is almost non-existent with few great exceptions. I have known persons like S.V. Sohoney and T.P. Singh (Jr.), I.C.S. Officer in Bihar service who spoke extempore in Sanskrit like a scholar. Jagdish Mathur, I.C.S. revived Nalanda and Vaishali in Bihar. But such men have become rare. They were, however, sucked in the political system which ultimately overpowered the Indian bureaucracy and made it almost subservient to the political class. The doctrine of neutrality or anonymity gradually disappeared and the civil service lost its confidence and courage to protest and resist the wrong doings of the political masters although Constitution of India provides them with safeguards in service. Like the new brand of politicians the new bureaucrats want to amass power and misuse it for personal aggrandisement endangering the very fabric and future of our democratic society. The rule of law requires a fearless civil servant who performs his duties honestly and effectively.

In France, in times of the continued instability of the coalition government under the multi-party system in the post-war period, the bureaucy ran the administration effectively as developed administrative law which supplemented the regular judicial system. Our future as a democracy also depends on the vigilance that we command day to day and not merely on adult franchise.

During the Emergency, the concept of committed bureaucracy, committed judiciary and committed police and forces was promoted. During the Janata rule (1977-79) efforts were made to cleanse and restore the bureaucracy to its original position. Later the bureaucracy mellowed down. But Rajiv Gandhi during 1985-89 showed some determination to rectify the situation. However, it will be wrong to assume that all is lost. The Indian bureaucracy has still sufficient resilience and a core of dedicated professionals. Only they should be given a tenure of survival and freedom to perform their duties under the Constitution. The people suffer because the system of the redressal of grievances has broken down and from the Patwari to the constable even a clerk in a bank and the sales-tax and income-tax inspector another the common man. Dr. Manmohan Singh once told me that as a part of the reform process, 'I will break the inspector raj'. He tried. But the power behind the functionaries at the lower level continue to rule. The rule of law is what they say and order about. The civil servant does not even present an alternative policy choice or advice to the ministers for, they know that the rule of the law is dictated by the political masters. It does not serve the country.

We have reached a very crucial stage in sustaining ourselves as a nation. It is already threatened by internal strifes of all kinds and the failure of the administrative machinery and the political system to bring about confidence in the country and among its people about the future. H.D. Deve Gowda said in his address, as Prime Minister, to the Conference of Chief Secretaries held in New Delhi on November 20, 1996 : "The very objective of creating the IAS, IPS etc. was to see that in our political system anybody or any political party may come to power and may run the country as political master but you will continue as a permanent administrative machinery for 30-35 years. You must understand that your responsibility is much more than the political bosses, who only frame the policies but the responsibility for implementing these policies is yours''.

We have seen in the last fifty years in our democratic system the tallest leaders and the tallest bureaucrats. As days pass there is a decline and we must admit that. So far as the political leadership is concerned, there is a visible change towards decline and even amongst bureaucrats, there is sufficient decline in their work. You can ask: what shall we do? If a political master wants a particular thing to be done which is not in accordance with the rules. Deve Gowda said: ''the very purpose of creating your cadres is that you can withstand any type of pressure and be loyal to the Constitution and to the rule of law. Now the main task is how to win back the confidence of our people.'' The question asked again is : 'how should we restore the confidence of the people in the very system, collectively both by the politicians and bureaucrats — it is a matter of concern to all of us. I am prepared to take your advice in this matter without formality'. I do not know how we will collectively rise to the occasion without allowing to drift further. ''Let the history not be repeated.'' He deserves praise for this remark, which it is to be hoped, he will practise in all his political tenure. If politicians intend to serve the people then they must allow the permanent machinery to assist then for their merit lies in their intellect, experience and knowledge.

MAHATMA GANDHI WITH INDIRA GANDHI

VIII

Triumphs and Tragedies

The fifty year period has seen landmark developments. We have not only undergone a political revolution but also an economic reorientation. The Constitution abolished untouchability and made its practice punishable. It provided for reservations and safeguards for the scheduled castes and scheduled tribes. The child Marriage Restraint Act was amended in 1949 providing for punishment in the case of marriages in which a male under 18 years of age and female under 15 years is involved. A succession Act gave the women the right to property.

Yet another important development was the adoption of democratic planning as a methodology for economic emancipation of our people. To give shape to this concept and focus priorities for investment, public and private, the Government decided to set up the Planning Commission which was established in 1950. At the instance of Nehru the Congress adopted a Resolution at the Karachi Session of the Congress in 1931 which said ''the State shall own and control key industries and service, mineral resources, railways, waterways, shipping and other means of transport. The Congress also set up a National Planning Committee with Jawaharlal Nehru as the Chairman as far back as 1938.

In the fifties, Acharya Vinoba Bhave, a prominent disciple of Gandhiji launched the Bhoodan Movement and toured the whole State of Bihar for its success. He promoted voluntary contribution of land in favour of the landless. The communists had launched in the Telengana region of Hyderabad an anti-landlord uprising which resulted in deaths and, created a law order problem. As a follower of Gandhiji, Acharya Binoba Bhave chose the path of discipline and non-violence and created a band of workers who travelled with him in camps as he moved from one district to the other. Jayaprakash Narain left the Socialist Party, he had helped to found and joined this movement which to him was a constructive work. He had resigned from politics.

Bihar was the first important State which after Independence enacted land reforms Acts and land ceiling Act also. But Bihar had a large number of landlords, known as Zamindars who controlled the land and the British used them for not only collecting land revenue but also as a law and order machinery. Even the Congress was infested largely by Zamindars and they did not agree to the abolition of Zamindari system. Therefore, they went to the court which upset even Nehru for he felt that social laws are not being enacted because the courts were not cooperative in social reforms and transformation. In this situation Acharya Vinoba Bhave came to Bihar and through his Bhoodan Movement collected thousands of acres of land which was distributed among the poor and the peasantry. But later this movement also died down.

Another major movement was the Community Development Projects. Nehru was very fond of this programme which was meant to ameliorate the conditions of the rural poor through various socially oriented action programmes. He made S.K. Dey its Chief Administrator and later appointed him as a Minister in the Union Council. Dey worked very hard and turned the programme into a movement and made it successful. But after some years, this programme also suffered political criticism for a new class of officers were created who spent money lavishly on transport, and salary and allowances. At least, this is what people complained about. It was this movement of community development which affected the people's thinking for a change in their living style. Many prejudices were revealed and removed. I remember that in some villages in the Adivasi area of Ranchi and other districts, the tribals were not willing to dig a well. The belief was that if a well as dug all sorts of calamity would fall on the villagers. But the officers of the Community Development Programme went ahead and provided fresh drinking water to many villages through the newly dug wells and therefore, the prejudices gradually started disappearing. However, after many years the Community Development Movement died and nobody remembers it.

Nehru also revived the old Panchyati Raj system in the rural areas and provided funds for it. Along with that, a large number of cooperative societies were opened as a part of the new rural development programmes. But many cases of corruption came to light and the programme of cooperative movement suffered a setback. In many States like Gujarat and Maharashtra, however, it proved to be a great success. During his long tenure of 17 years as Prime Minister, Nehru led the nation from backwardness to growth and development. However, the Chinese aggression shattered him so much that he fell ill at the Bhubaneshwar Session of the Congress. He died on May 27, 1964.

Then came the days of nationalisation. To strengthen herself politically, Mrs. Indira Gandhi launched a major programme of take overs in 1969. While life insurance had been brought under public ownership in Nehru's time when C.Desmukh was the Finance Minister, Mrs. Gandhi nationalised 16 major banks, took over the control of coal industry, nationalised general insurance and also some nonferrous mines.

Although this move was criticised, the nationalisation of banks made a great contribution to mobilisation of funds both for the rural and urban development programmes and the development of coal mines started apace. The money of the banks was earlier used for the benefit of the private industry. After the nationalisation, branches were expanded at a fast pace and resource mobilisation gathered momentum even in the rural areas. She also launched a large Family Planning Programme, although it became very unpopular during the Emergency, when all freedom enshrined in the Constitution were suspended.

One of the major items on the social agenda came from the Mandal Commission. It divided the society distinctly on caste basis. V.P. Singh as Prime Minister made it his mission. Young students immolated themselves at Vijay Chowk down the Raisina Hills protesting against reservation in colleges, universities and Government services. But V.P. Singh decided to go ahead.

Subsequent United Front regimes drew its strength from regionalism, instead of nationalism. This has affected our political systems and governance both at the Centre and in the States. This has also spurred the demand for amending the Constitution. It has certainly created uncertainties which need to be removed at the earliest. Corruption has become so endemic that many Ministers at the Centre and in the States and even the ex-Prime Minister and Chief Ministers are being called to appear in the courts. Surely, the founding fathers of our Constitution could not have visualised such a demoralising situation which has overtaken us.

The most tragic event immediately after Independence was the martyrdom of Mahatma Gandhi on January 30, 1948 when a fanatic shot him dead at the prayer meeting in Birla Bhavan ground in New Delhi. A dedicated life thus came to an end. But the Mahatma has lived in the hearts of his people in India and a large mass of people around the world. The Indian ethos for which Mahatma stood and worked for was embodied in the Constitution which was framed after his death.

Another great tragedy was the death of Prime Minister Indira Gandhi at the hands of assassins in her own bungalow which caused great anguish and resentment among the people. The death of Mrs. Gandhi was an offshoot to the violent movement launched by the extremists in Punjab with the support of Pakistani military and intelligence agencies This had resulted the killing of thousands in the State culminating into the military action to get rid of the Golden Temple from Bhindranwala and his followers.

Rajiv Gandhi also died at the hands of assissins who belonged to the LTTE, a Srilankan Tamil terrorists organisation. They have been fighting and are still fighting for the creation of a separate Tamil State in Srilanka. After the liberation of Bangladesh from Pakistan in 1971, Indian forces had also to be sent to Jaffna, northern province of Srilanka where the LTTE had taken control and thousands of refugee Tamilians came from Jaffna had to be given shelter in Tamilnadu (India). LTTE cadres even entered the State of Tamilnadu and operated from there. There are charges and counter charges as to who supported the LTTE. India received nearly 150 thousand Srilankan Tamil Refugees.

Thus terrorist activities have affected the political scene in India and created a fear complex among the people in various States. The Pakistan Inter-Services Intelligence Agency still continues to train and abet terrorists. They indulge in killings in various parts of India. They have been operating even from Nepal and Bangladesh.

The events which followed the partition were unavoidable and dictated to a large extent the proceedings of the Constitutent Assembly. Internally and externally, the perils seemed unsurmountable. The fear of the country being 'shattered', into fragments at the moment when we were talking of 'Tryst with Destiny' was real. In the circumstances, a strong Centre seemed to be the major consideration in drafting the provisions of the Constitution. Not only national security but even financial solvency threatened the country's unity.

It was not one but many threats to India's integrity which loomed large in the horizon. The Portuguese even after India's Independence refused to hand over Goa, to the successor government in India. The country waited for quite sometime and appealed to the Portuguese authorities to cooperate with the Government which had got its independence from the British on August 15, 1947. But there was no positive response. This resulted in many groups inside and outside Goa organising themselves to enter the torritory and make it free. Many people were injured and many died in Portuguese repression. Ultimately, on December 19, 1961, Indian Army liberated Goa from the Portuguese.

It was at the instance of Ram Manohar Lohia that in 1946, Indian nationals and Goan patriots joined hands for a non-violent struggle to free Goa from Portuguese hands. The Salazar Government of Portugal let loose a reign of terror to suppress the freedom movement. The Government of India's efforts to secure withdrawal of Portuguese rule was not heeded. In 1954, the Goa Liberation Movement took a new turn when Satyagrahis from India started pouring into Goa defying the ban imposed by the Government of India. Nehru made it known to Lohia and other sponsors of Satygraha agitation that he would not be in a position to take any drastic action against the Portuguese Government. The Portuguese military killed many Satyagrahis and nationalists in Goa and committed untold barbarism aginst them.

The firing on Indian passenger ship and the firing on Indian fishermen and peaceful border villages in India and the mining of Indian waters and the importation of white African troops and the violation of Indian territory and coastal waters came as a shock and posed grave provocation. Nehru, in the circumstances, could not continue his old policy and at last took the decision to send Indian troops to liberate Goa from the despotic colonial rule. it had become a historic necessity. Thereafter even Deman & Diu also were merged into Goa as a Centrally administered territory. On May 30, 1987 Goa was granted full Statehood and Daman and Diu were separated from it to continue as a Union Territory. At that time in 1961 the Soviet President Mr. Brezhnev was on a visit to India and before the Indian Army entered into Goa at a meeting in Bombay, he gave full support to India in its right to liberate Goa.

The French also had a territory in the East coast in Pondicherry which was closer to the State of Tamilnadu. The French who had colonised this territory cooperated with the Government of India and handed over Pondicherry to it.Their only condition was that French culture and language will be maintained in this territory which the Government of India accepted willingly.

Another major development in the sub-continent took place in 1971 when the territory of East Pakistan was liberated by the Mukti Vahini (of Bangladeshis) which was supported by Indian Armed Forces with men and material. A movement of separation from Pakistan which ruled over East Pakistan almost as a colony, since Partition in 1947, had been launched years before 1971. India had all the goodwill for the people of East Bengal. Mrs. Indira Gandhi was the Prime Minister then and she visited Britain and America and pleaded with the leaders of the Governments of these two nations to support the liberation movement in East Pakistan which had been launched by Mujibur Rehman and to a large extent she did received a good measure of support. However, the American administration was not in full agreement with India on this issue and even took some hostile action. But the sufferings of Bangladeshi people and the cruelty perpetuated on them by Pakistani army created a stir both in Britain and America. In Britain with a large population of Bangladeshis, it was easy to enlist the support of the British people and the Government. In the meantime the Pakistani authorities arrested Mujib and took him to West Pakistan. There was an effort by the then Government of Pakistan to eliminate Sheikh Mujib. But world opinion stood against any such move and his life had to be spared Ultimately, when the tyrany by the Pakistani troops increased Indirajee as Prime Minister ordered Indian troops to enter the then East Pakistan and assist the Mukti Vahini in their struggle for freedom.

This, however, unleashed a war between India and Pakistan in November 1971 and Pakistan was defeated. Over 90,000 Pak troops and their officers were arrested and kept in various camps in India. In the process Pakistan lost East Bengal which became an independent 'Bangladesh'.

This war had shattered Pakisan so much that its people and leaders feared that in a very short period the West Pakistan itself will disintegrate. It was in this background President Zulfikar Ali Bhutto pleaded for talks and the summit between Mrs. Gandhi and President Bhutto was held and the Shimla Agreement was signed. There is a recorded evidence of what was said and talked about between the two leaders at Shimla. President Bhutto had agreed for a quick solution of the problem of Kashmir. However, on his return to Islamabad he reneged completely. He had never been reliable either as a leader or a friend.

It is perhaps necessary to recall that in 1951, there was an insurrection movement organised by the Nepali Congress for changing the feudal Rana rule in that country. Even in this case some military assistance had to be provided to the Nepali Congress and ultimately the Ranas surrendered and a democratic Nepal was ushered in. King Shri Tribhuvan had with the support of our then Ambassador in Kathmandu, C.P.N.Singh escaped to Delhi and sought shelter for himself and his family. Nehru not only gave him his goodwill and willing support and also agreed to provide financial support to the democratic Government as also to assist him in modernising the administration in Nepal and also for the setting up of its first permanent army.

In the history of Independent India, 1962 will go as the blackest period when the Chinese attacked India both in the Western Sector (Ladakh) and in the North-Eastern Region. India had constantly been led by China to believe that she accepted the traditional Indian alignment of the border in the Himalayas and on the other hand she kept undisclosed claims to about 50,000 sq. miles of our territory. They even declined to accept the McMohan line agreement which established the India's norhtern boundary with Tibet. But nothing deterred China to attack India in 1962 in which she annexed a large part of the Aksai Chin area in Ladakh and parts of Indian territory in the Eastern Sector from which it, later unilaterally withdrew.

After Independence, India had to face and still continues to face insurgency problem in the north-eastern States. In fact, to assuage the feelings of the tribals in that region that they had been ignored in their political and economic development both by the British and Independent India that Nehru agreed for the creation of Nagaland as a State. Another State called Mizoram was also established. Since then, situation has improved in the Region. However, insurgency in some form or the other continues and Inter Services Intelligence of Pakistan has become overactive in this area both through Bangladesh and Burmese border to train insurgents for terrorist activities.

India perhaps is the only country in the world which after Independence and partition has part of its territory under alien occupation by people's Republic of China both in the Eastern and Western Sector and some areas even in the Middle Sector.

At the time of the Independence Indian economy had not only been ravaged by the Second World War but also disrupted by the Partition of the Sub-continent. It had to face a very serious problem of re-settlement of lakhs of refugees who came from West Pakistan and also from East Pakistan. The refugees needed immediate shelter which was provided in a large number of improvised camps. Mehar Chand Khanna, the then Minister of Refugees Resettlement will be remembered in the Indian history for his remarkable services in settling these refugees and providing them shelter and relief. This was a very difficult task but was accomplished with care and devotion. And the miracle of rehabilitation was affected in a manner which turned out to be a national asset. Punjab was turned into a granary and in many parts of the country new enterprises, small, and medium, were started by these displaced persons. They built their life with hard work in addition to the relief provided to them by the Government. In a few years time these uprooted people became indistinguishable from their brothers and sisters spread over the country. However, refugees entering India have not stopped even yet. People from East Pakistan, now Bangladesh, both Hindus and Muslims have been coming and settling in Assam and also in West Bengal and East

Bihar. A large number of them in recent years have even come to Delhi and reached Mumbai in search of jobs and livelihood. Earlier, mainly Nepalese used to come and settle in India. But now the Bangladshis are pouring into this country ceaselessly. This has been causing concern. However, the influx continues unabated.

Independence brought with it a complicated problem for the Indian Armed Forces. The migration of a large number of Muslim officers and 'Other Ranks' to Pakistan on a territorial-cum-optional basis and sudden departure of a number of British Officers to UK created an unprecedented difficulty. To this was added the task of dealing with large scale movement of population on both sides of India-Pakistan border. It may be stated to the credit of our Armed Forces that they successfully coped with this situation. Within six weeks they escorted 15 lakh of Muslims to Pakistan and a larger number of Hindus, Sikhs and others from Pakistan to India.

There was no respite, however, for the soldiers and airmen who were soon called upon to drive back the raiders from Kashmir and Jammu. Thereafter, they also had to undertake 'Police Operation' in Hyderabad to elimnate Razakar menance which had assumed alarming proportion.

Our Armed Forces since Independence have been asked time and again to protect the territorial integrity of India and safeguard its interests. They have fought three major wars with Pakistan with success and even helped the Mukti-Vahini in East Pakistan to win their freedom from Pakistan oppression and thus, a new nation 'Bangladesh' was created. It was only in 1962 that we suffered a major defeat at the hands of the invading Chinese forces. This, however, was the defeat of our political beliefs, foreign policy and betroeyal by china in the name of CHINI-HINDI BHAI-BHAI.

The influx of refugees both from West Pakistan and East Pakistan in 1947 a situation of crisis created almost in the country and posed a formidable problem both for civilian and military authorities. Hundreds of thousands of homeless men, women and children had streamed into India from Pakistan. The total population of displaced persons in India, as recorded in the All India Deciminal Census of 1951 was 74.80 lakhs. Of this, 49.05 lakh came from West Pakistan and 25.75 lakh from East Pakistan.

Displaced persons were provided rehabilitaion facilities in most States of the country. Upto 1952-53, 9.1 lakh displaced persons had been provided with accomodation and 14.7 lakh have been given evacuee houses etc. So about, 23.8 lakh persons had been provided houses. In West Bengal also houses were built and land was given to resettle the refugees coming from East Pakistan. Employment exchange were opened to assist them to get jobs. Vocational and technical training was also provided and free were offered for education to the children of the displaced persons. In addition, shops and industrial sheds were also provided so that they could start their own work. Camps for the displaced persons from West Pakistan were closed down in 1952-53. In West Bengal, however, relief camps continued owing to the rise of influx of Hindus from East Pakistan. Altogether, the post independence years have been marked by several notable triumphs but marred by a few tragedies.

IX

Southern Line-Up

For over 50 years events and developments affecting national politics have been mainly confined to the Northern and Western parts of the country. Even the 'Quit India Movement' and the aftermath of the partition mainly concerned these regions. However, the fact remains that parallel developments in South of Vindhyas have the same relevance to Indian polity as the events in the North.

In more recent times, the States of the South have come on their own and influence in making and un-making of the Government in New Delhi. Mrs. Indira Gandhi had to go to Chikmanglur in a by-election to win a Lok Sabha seat. She used to visit Southern States often to gain the support of the people there. So was Rajiv Gandhi. With the advent of the United Front Government at the Centre, the South holds the key to its survival. It was by sheer chance that G. K. Moopanar, President of Tamil Mannila Congress, could not become Prime Minister after the fall of the Deve Gowda Government. But his failure this time will strengthen claim when occasion arises.

Thus, there is a shift from the north to the South in the balance of political power. Without the support of Chandrababu Naidu, Chief Minister of Andhra Pradesh and his party, Telugu Desam, and the Dravida Munetra Kazhagam leader Karunanidhi and the leader of Tamil Mannila Congress, Moopanar, no Government could hope to last at the Centre as of now. That is why the Bharatiya Janata Party is also trying to make inroads in the South. In Karnataka, the Janata Dal is in power and H.D. Deve Gowda still seems to have the State people's support. Their influence soars as in view of the developments in the North mainly in Uttar Pradesh and Bihar.

The experiment of the United Front Government started in Uttar Pradesh and Bihar before it spread to other States through Kerala and West Bengal have had different coalitions led by one strong party. The other Southern States have been electing governments of majority parties. Sometimes it is the Congress and another party, on another occasion. In Tamilnadu, however, either the DMK headed by Karunanidhi or Anna DMK headed by late M.G. Ramachandran continued to be in power for a long time. In any case, the political situation in the South has been marked by reasonable stability. Even in the economic development and running the administration the performance of these States have been comparatively better than some of the Northern States.

Pan-Indian nationalist sentiment took place in South India in the 19th century when Madras Native Association and the Madras Hindu Debating Society came into existence and demanded administrative and political reforms from the British. In 1852, they petitioned to the British Parliament asking for direct rule by the Crown and removal of misrule and oppression of the existing East India Company Government. All this happened in 1852-1855. Their view was that the people of this country were educated enough to administer their country and that they should be given Constitutional responsibility.

However, the princely States in the South like the North stood behind the British Government and even helped them by sending voluntary contributions even during the time of the 1857 rebellion. The Queen later abolished the Company Rule and established direct rule by the Crown. This encouraged the nationalists in Madras who made a strong plea for a responsible Government. The Madras Mahajana Sabha was established in 1884 and various forms of agitations were launched. After the formation of the Indian National Congress, the nationalist movements got further encouragement and the third Session of the Congress was held at Madras in 1887. This promoted political education among the people. The Press also started taking interest in supporting nationalist movements and people joined the Congress in larger numbers. The Congress organised District Conferences in which Swaraj, boycott of foreign goods, encouragement to Swadeshi, revival of Panchayats etc. were discussed and this created awareness of national ideas among the people about their rights.

Later, the Partition of Bengal provoked extremism in Indian politics and this affected the South also. Bipin Chander Pal visited Madras in 1907 and he was given a rousing reception. The British got worried and ordered the closure of Swadeshi Organisations like Swadeshi Steam Navigation Co. started by V.O. Chidambram Pillai. This encouraged people to take to violence and the agitation became intense and the detonation of Tirunelveli occurred in 1911. The Collector of the place RWDE Ashe was shot dead in a rail coach. The key figure in this conspiracy was Nilkant Brahmachari who was a political preacher and anarchist. He worked as a journalist at Pondicherry. He formed a Society with some of this friends and worshipped Goddess Kali. They took the oath that the life and property of those who took it would be dedicated to the ideal of Swaraj. And that any one divulging the secretes of the Society would be done to death.

This was the time when Brahmin and non-Brahmin controversy had emerged in the fore in Madras. The grievance was that the high caste group got benefits of the Western education and jobs at all levels in the organisations and departments keeping out he backward communities poor and helpless.

The backward castes initially joined the Indian National Congress in large numbers in Madras Presidency but found Brahmins dominant in the party. This widened the gulf between Brahmins and non-Brahmins in the South. Even the formation of Home Rule was opposed by the so-called low caste people because they thought that it would mean only high caste rule. Gradually these communities opposed the Congress as they thought that the party was also a organisation of Brahmins. Gandhiji appeared as a social reformer and insisted for social development and uplift of the masses as a precondition for the attainment of Swaraj. This brought about some change in the situation and the attitude of the backward communities.

The Home Rule League, however, spread in many parts of the South which had been started by Mrs. Annie Besant. The Home Rule movement became popular in all the districts of Madras Presidency. But the Home Rule League did not support reorganisation of India according to linguistic affinities. This was resented by Telugu speaking people, Malaylese and Kannadigas and led to the growth of regional rivalary on the basis of regional languages. On November 20, 1916, a Conference was held to start a company for promotion of the cause of non-Brahmin communities as also a political organisation for safeguarding their political interests. As a result, a South Indian People's Association was formed which brought about a daily newspaper with Tamil and Telugu editions. A non-Brahmin manifesto was issued in December, 1916.

The Justice Party was formed as a party of the Non-Brahmins. It accepted office when the reforms of 1919 were introduced and it wanted communal representation in the services.

Later the Home Rule Movement got merged with the Non-cooperation and Khilafat Movement. By then, Gandhiji had assumed the leadership of Indian National Congress and he gave the party a broader base and converted it into a mass organisation. He also made removal of untouchability a national programme and promoted Hindu-Muslim unity. He became the spokesman of the weaker sections all over the country. In 1920 Gandhiji came to the South and received enthusiastic receptions everywhere. He wanted to make the Civil Disobedience Movement a success. He was accompanied by Muhammad Ali and Shaukat Ali who exhorted Muslims to cooperate with the Congress. This brought about a great awakening and non-cooperation agitation became popular among the masses. Hartals, meetings and processions and boycott of Legislative Assembly councils became a part of he movement which brought about a great change in the political atmosphere in South India. The leaders of the movement were: Kasturi Ranga Aiyangar, Srinivasa Aiyangar, C. Vijayaraghavachariar, S. Satyamurthi, V.O. Chidambaram Pillai, kalyanasundara Mudaliar, Yakub Hasan, Singaraveluchetty, E.V. Ramaswamy Naicker, Dr P. Vardarajulu, Naidu and C. Rajagopalachari.

The Khilafat movement became popular in the South but it took a violent turn in Malabar. Gandhiji visited Malabar in August 1921 after which Khilafat committees were formed in different parts of the country. It ushered in Hindu-Muslim fraternity even in areas where the relations between the communities had been strained. Mapolla groups (as rustums are generally known in Malabar) were essentially landless farm labour nursing a lot of grievances. British repression on Khilafat Committees triggered violent reactions. Railway lines were torn up, stations attacked and telegraph wires were cut out. For one week at Thirurangadi and Malappuram were ruled by the rehels and one Kunhammod Haji even assumed the title of king. Efforts to establish peace by Congress leaders were in vain. The Mopallas suspected that Hindus were informing the Police about their activities and their wrath turned on Hindus and the entire agitation assumed communal colour. Many people fled their homes. The British clamped martial law and suppressed the movement by force. As a result, Congress activity in Malabar was affected. The joint movement failed but it had aroused the masses. Meanwhile, a movement for social reform caught. The Vaikkam Satyagraha campaign against untouchability was launched in 1924-25 in Travancore. A key participant was the Tamil leader E. V. Ramaswamy Naickar.

Untouchability was prevalent in many areas in Kerala. The so-called untouchables could not even walk along public roads. The cry for social justice gathered ground and the Congress took a strong stand on the issue. This enraged caste Hindus. However, after one and a half years of struggle an agreement was reached between Gandhiji and the Police Commissioner Mr Pitt as a result of which the Satyagraha was withdrawn. The Government allowed the untouchables to use the roads beside the Vaikam temple. The nationalist movement acquired a new stranger.

At its Lahore Session in 1929 the Congress launched the Civil Disobedience Movement which created a stir in the South as well. In every district of the then Madras Presidency the call for Civil Disobedience echoed and people joined in vociferously until, the movement was called off as a result of the Gandhi Irwin Pact. The Congress movement spread to the princely States as well. In Cochin and Travancore, agitations were launched for political democracy against the autocratic rule of the Maharajas. In Travancore, an agitation was lauched on the model of non-cooperation movement of 1932. Later on, Travancore State Congress was formed with Pattom A Thanu Pillai as its President. In Cochin, the Cochin State Congress led this movement. The failure of the Round Table Conference in London again made people to start Civil Disobedience in January 1932 which, however, was called off. Meanwhile in Madras, E.V. Ramaswamy Naickar started his 'Self-Respect Party'. Though he had been a prominent Congress worker he left the party alleging that its leaders had a bias in favour of upper castes.

He started a campaign to banish Brahmin leadership in all spheres and declared that his movement was atheist. He attacked Brahmins as the authors of the caste system. In this situation, the Communist ideology got roots and the party denounced the Congress. In 1934, the Government of India banned the Communist Party and the Madras Government declared the Young Workers' League which was in touch with the Communist International as unlawful.

The Congress Government came into power, in 1937 under the Government of India Act 1935 with C. Rajagopalachari as the Chief Minister. Thereafter, the Communist Party revived its activities. But Ramaswamy Naickar led a massive movement against the Congress Ministry and opposed introducing Hindustani as a compulsory subject in schools curriculum. The Dravadian movement added the anti-Hindi campaign as one of its plank. The Congress Ministry resigned in 1939 protesting that India had been dragged into the Second World War without consulting its people.

Then came the Quit India Movement which began in August 1942 after the British Government arrested all Congress leaders. C. Rajagopalachari had his reservations on the movement, and left the Congress when it was banned by the Government. Madras became the scene of hartals, strikes, riots and some violent incidents. The students of Annamalai Univesity took prominent part in organising strikes and processions and hartals. Telephone and telegraph wires were disrupted at many places in the South. A train carrying ammunition from Cochin consisting of two engines and 44 wagons was de-railed by sabotage between Podanur and Singpnallur Railway Stations. Many municipal councils were suspended for six months by the Government. Students participated in full measure in the Quit India Movement. The Communist Party totally opposed the Movement and even obstructed the nationalist activities by aligning themselves with the imperialist forces on the plea of 'people's war against fascisim'. South India returned to normalcy by the end of December 1942.

Jinnah's insistence on Pakistan caused a great Hindu-Muslim divide. Muslims in the South also became enthusiastic about the formation of Pakistan. They took out processions and held public meetings with vigour in Malabar and elsewhere which often resutled in violence.

The tensions continued even as the Congress accepted the Cabinet Mission's Constitutional proposals which led to the holding of General Elections and the formation of the Interim Government at the Centre. A Congress Government was also formed in Madras. However, communal squabbles were both in the North and South and the anti-Brahmin activities of Dravida Kazhakam against the Brahmins produced uneasy political situation. At the same time before the dawn of independence the communists organised violent strikes and armed uprisings in many parts of South India. The Congress Government in Madras had to enact the Maintenance of Public Order Act of 1947 which provided for preventive detention, imposition of censorship, control on meetings, processions etc. Hundreds of communists were arrested and sent to jail under the Act.

The Dravida Kazhakam led by Ramaswamy Naicker continued with its movement against Brahmins. Later, the D.K. split and the new party DMK was elected to power in Tamil Nadu. The breakaway pary, led by the redoubtable C.N. Annadurai, was one of the most charismatic leaders. He evoked respect all around. His successor M. Karunanidhi, a staunch follower of Annadurai and scholar could not keep the flock together. There was a further split and M. G. Ramachandran used his charisma to dislodge Karunanidhi from power. Karunanidhi was first dismissed from the office by Mrs Indira Gandhi and when he came to power after 13 years, he was dismissed by Chandrasekhar Ministry. Mrs. Gandhi took action against him for his support to anti-emergency forces and the second time he was displaced for his alleged support to LTTE. Now he has come back to power with greater support and is a powerful force behind the UF Government.

During the recent weeks there have been caste violence in the Southern districts of Tamilnadu like Kamarajar, Chidambaranar, Nellai, Kattabmnman and Alagumuthu Kone etc. The names of these districts have been changed to eminent public figures. In continuation of this re-naming the DMK Government recently gave a new name to a section of the Tamilnadu transport plying in parts of Southern districts after Sundaralingam who was a Dalit Lieutenant of Kattabmnman. This area is dominated by Thevars or Maravars who claimed that the Lieutenant was one of their heroes. The Thevar community had another charismatic leader known as Muthuramalinga, a famous freedom fighter. This area has a large number of Dalits. But in social life the communities have much different status. The Dalits are still living in isolated areas.

In 1996, a severe outbreak of violence took place in Chidambaranar district where the Thevar community played havoc with the Dalits. But in some villages there are a large number of affluent Dalits who are working in the Gulf countries. So the Dalits also retaliated and this led to an outbreak of violence. The Police also acted against the Dalit community. A branch of the transport company was named after a Dalit leader. Thereafter, both the communities decided not to travel in the buses named after each other leaders. A number of buses were burnt and Dalits were beaten up.

The Thevars are backward castes and there is a feeling in Tamilnadu that unless these are prepared to give up their aggressiveness, caste violence will continue causing political and social upheavals. It may be surprising to many in the North. But in Tamilnadu where the social justice movement got strength several years ago Dalits are being subjected to the worst type of discrimination.

Before the States Reorganisation Commission was set up, there have been demands for creation of linguistic States in the South. Madras Presidency covered a very large area which include some part of the present Kerala, Karnataka and Andhra Pradesh. In between there were some princely States also. In 1955-56 even before the SRC was set up the demand for a separate State for the people of Andhra was conceded after Potti. Sriramlu fasted unto death because the Congress was not agreeable to the creation of linguistic State. His death provoked a great upheaval in the Andhra area after which the Congress yielded and the new State was set up. T. Prakasham became the first Chief Minister of the newly creatred State Andhra Pradesh on October 1, 1953. The Congress continued to rule Andhra Pradesh for many years till the rise of film celebrity. N.T. Rama Rao in 1980 in politics. M.G. Ramachandran, another super star had become the Chief Minister of Tamilnadu in 1987. The first Chief Minister in Madras (Tamilnadu) after reorganisation of the State was Anna Durai on March 6, 1967. He died within two years time due to Cancer. Karunanidhi succeeded him on February 10, 1969. Then DMK split and M.G. Ramachandran formed his own party known as Anna DMK. He became Chief Minister on June 30, 1977. On June 10, 1980 he again became Chief Minister. N.T. Rama Rao formed his own party in Andhra Pradesh called Telugu Desam Party. Because of films in which he played mythological roles he commanded great respect in the whole State and the masses accepted him. He became Chief Minister on January 9, 1983. With this, the Congress lost power both in Andhra Pradesh and Tamilnadu.

In Andhra Pradesh the Congress lost power in 1980 and N.T. Rama Rao became the most popular Andhra leader. This is how both in Tamilnadu and Andhra Pradesh, regional parties became popular and powerful and Congress lost its majority. In Karnataka, the Congress continued to run the administration for a longer time. Later, Ramakrishna Hegde resigned from the Congress to form the Janata Dal in the State and became its Chief Minister. But he also lost power and Sri Moily formed congress Government in Karnataka. The political situation had been changing very fast and soon he was out of power. Since then Janata Dal has been ruling party in Karnataka. The State of Karnataka was formed in 1956 on the basis of the report of the States Reorganisation Commission. Earlier this was Mysore State and was under British Rule till 1947. In 1947 Congress had formed Government in the State with K.C. Reddy as the Chief Minsiter. He was sworn in on October 25, 1947. K. Hanumanthaya was the second Chief Minsiter of the State. It was at his behest that the Vidhan Soudha, one of the great monumental edifices of modern India was constructed in Bangalore to be a Parliament House. He remained in office from March 30, 1952 to August 19, 1956. Later S. Nijalingappa became the Chief Minister. Ramakrishna Hegde became Chief Minsiter much later.

Kamraj became Chief Minister of Tamilnadu in 1950. He was the first non-English speaking person to head the administration in any part of the country. He gave up office in 1963 as a part of the plan known after him. The Kamraj Plan required senior party men to leave administrative responsibility and strengthen the Congress Party at the grass root level. Nehru and Kamraj had agreed on this plan before it was put into operation. Jagjivan Ram also resigned from the Government as part of the Kamraj Plan.

The State of Kerala was formed on November 1, 1956 and was put under President's rule. Elections to the State Assembly were held in March 1957 and on April 5, 1957 EMS Namboodripad formed the Government. This was the first directly elected Communist Government under the Parliamentary system in the world. But soon after a movement was launched against him. A leader of the Nair community led by Mannmath Padamnabham launched a revolt against the Communist Government alleging collapse of law and order in the State. The Central Government dismissed the Namboodripad Government on July 31, 1959. Mrs. Indira Gandhi was then the Congress President. Thereafter, Pottam Thanu Pillai (PSP) supported by the Congress and the other parties formed a Government in February 1960. He, however, resigned and was sent to Punjab as Governor and R. Shankar of the Congress became the Chief Minister on February 2, 1962. Later, in the new elections for the Assembly in 1965, no party secured a majority and so President's rule was imposed in the State. Elections were again held in 1967 and Namboodripad again won and became the Chief Minister. This was the time when the CPI in Kerala split and the CPM became a separate party. As a result, the Communist Government fell and Achuta Menon of the CPI formed new Government in 1970. since then the Congress Front and the Left Front have been forming Governments in Kerala alternatively.

In the North too the regional parties were ascending at the cost of the Congress. In Punjab, Akali Dal has become a predominant party and in Haryana, Vishal Haryana Party is in power today. In U.P. Mulayam Singh has formed his own party known as Samajwadi Party. Kanshi Ram has also formed a separate party known Bahujan Samaj Party. Samajwadi Party has its base mainly in U.P. But Kanshi Ram is trying to spread his influence in other States also. In Bihar, where the Congress ruled for many years it has now become a third party while the Janata Dal led by Laloo Prasad Yadav has been ruling the State. In Bihar Janata Dal has also split and a separate Samta Party has been formed. The Bharatiya Janata Party has become the second largest Party in Bihar. In Assam also, the Congress has lost power and the Asom Gana Parishad, a party of youngmen has emerged as a great force and has the support of the people and is now in power for the second time.

The national parties have become weaker and the regional parties have increased their influence at the national level. The only national party which has grown in strength all over the country is the Bharatiya Janata Party. Congress, the oldest party has been relegated to the second position as national party. It, however, has the potential of re-emerging as a new force.

X

Foreign Policy – Reappraisal

There have been suggestions by experts on foreign affairs and other eminent persons that there is a need for a fresh-look on India's foreign policy or even to change it to the extent that it serves the national interests. There has also been criticism that India's foreign policy has served many regions of the world and a number of countries but her own interests got ignored not once but on many occasions. Even during the Chinese aggression in 1962 India looked almost friendless. We involved overselves as a matter of policy into the affairs of the West Asian countries who have, however, also shown closeness with us, while Pakistan always used some of the Islamic countries of the Region sometimes to pressurise India and sometimes to embarrass our country at various international fora. The Organisation of Islamic Countries also often supported Pakistan by issuing statements on Kashmir critical to India and in matters of Indo-Pak relations. In times of war we have received threats of crude oil supply being cut off.

There has been, however, restructuring of our China Policy and mutli-faced programmes of cooperation has been launched to promote goodwill and bilateral economic cooperation. There has also been adjustment in policy towards West Asian countries and as a result of which India recognised Israel as a nation State and established full-fledged diplomatic relations. Our relations with Russia has also been re-designed to promote political, economic and defence cooperation in the changed context after the demise of the Soviet Union. India after many long years has re-formulated its policy towards South East Asian nations and as a result of which economic and political cooperation has expanded and exchange of views at political level have been resumed after many years of uncertainty and even lack of interest.

Nehru organised the First Asian Relations Conference in 1947 which laid great stress on bringing the countries of Asia closer to each other and working for political and economic development in cooperation and in conjunction with each other. Nehru thought that the people in Asia were closer and nearer to India than the other parts of the world. In Asia India occupied a pivotal position – 'pivot of Western, Southern and South East Asia, on one side and Afro-Asian and the Arab world on the other hand had been forged. He said "all along we have been passive spectators of events and plaything of others. The initiative comes to our people now and we shall make history of our choice." Later, 2500 years of Lord Buddha was celebrated in India and Buddhist monks and leaders from Buddhist countries were invited in large numbers to participate in the functions organised as part of the celebrations. However, after 1962, our relations with the countries of South East Asia suffered a setback.

In foreign policy initiatives, India started with Asia. The Bundung Conference of Afro-Asian nations was held in Indonesia as a part of the policy to bring the countries of Asia and Africa together which had emerged as free nations from colonialism and many in Africa were still struggling to get out of the colonial rule. The Chinese Prime Minister Cho En Lai was introduced to the leaders of the Region at Bandung. Nehru took personal interest and care to bring Chou closer to the nations of the Region.

As of now India's decision to open full scale diplomatic relations with Israel did not surprise many for the demand for the same had been made in Parliament and outside a number of times. But the Government of India has been delaying the decision for the fear of annoying Islamic countries of West Asia. India had always worked to promote the creation of the Independent State for the people of Palestine. The State of Israel later recognised the need to accept some formula wherein the State of Palestine could get recognition and a territory for self-governance, Apart from Russia even the Chinese Government had already recognised Israel and therefore, there was nothing new that India had also re-adjusted its policy and established diplomatic relations with Israel. In fact, it was a delayed decision. India had vigorous economic, political and cultural relations with West Asia which we tried to maintain as much as we could.

Later the American offensive against Iraq changed the whole situation in West Asia. The disintegration of Soviet Union made the West Asian countries helpless and friendless. The offensive against

Iraq by America was supported by the countries of the Region also and thus West Asia stood as a divided Region in which every country was struggling to subserve its own national interest. Not religion but national interest determined the policy formula in each of the West Asian nations.

India's foreign policy makers were obliged to re-thinking and re-shaping the country's foreign policy because they did finally realise that an astonishing change has come about in the world which has become unipolar, although Russia still claims and maintains that it is the second world power in spite of the end of the Soviet Union. On the other hand, the Chinese People's Republic also claims to be the third world power with all its nuclear arsenal and Inter-Continental Ballistic Missiles.

India, however, has always felt humble to claim anything for herself. But slowly it has started asserting its claim to a permanent seat in the Security Council. India's economic strength is no longer small and it is a self-sufficient nation in many respects. Militarily also it is a power to recokon with and Pokhran (Rajasthan Desert) nuclear device on 18th May 1974, gave a big boost to India's image in the world. I remember when many top bureaucrats on returning after a visit to Moscow after the Pokhran Test looked happy and smiled when they were asked about the visit to Moscow. They said that the Soviet authorities smiled when they met them at Kremlin or outside and shook hands warmly. They even said : "You are now a mature and powerful nation". This proves that without being a military power, India can't achieve much in the world affairs. Even today China does not relish India being called a power, equal in any sphere, compared to herself. But India has to persevere with its policy in the changed context and the fast changing world. India has also its national and international interest, its susceptibilities which it has to serve and protect. India has to safeguard its sovereignty, territorial integrity and its economic well-being with devotion, and all its might. India's foreign policy must serve to protect these interests or it will loose its importance. The old Indian Policy of faith in others and goodwill for all alone can no longer promote or protect its interest. Foreign policy is not a one-sided affair. Every nation serves its own interests first and last.

With faith in Panchsheel we promoted and established close relations with the People's Republic of China but we suffered at the very hands which we had been shaking with for a very long time. Faith turned into faithlessness. We become victims of our foreign policy and suffered at the hands of our enemies.

On October 20, 1962, the Chinese Armed Forces started military operations against India at Ladakh and Arunachal Pradesh to teach India a lesson. This is what the Chinese leaders and the General Secretary of the Chinese Communist Party Deng Xiao Peng had said. The scattered small Indian Army posts were thus wiped out. Our men did not have winter clothings or even shoes and the latest equipment to fight highly trained Chinese forces. In fact, with the advance of the Chinese forces we lost all control of the situation. Nehru, through a broadcast over All India Radio had to say Goodbye to the people of Assam. What would have happened if the people of that State who had started fleeing from their homes and the people of India who have been fed on the slogan of 'Bhai Bhai' for many years since Independence. Even after 50 years the Government of People's Republic of China still occupies a large part of our territory in Ladakh.

When China's surreptitious intrusion into Aksai Chin came to the knowledge of the public, there was a furor in Parliament. Nehru tried to pacify members by saying that the area was arid and barren, and not even a blade of grass grew there. Nehru was, however, keenly aware of the dangers posed by China's aggressive posture. He was apologetic for keeping away certain facts about the disturbing border disputes from Parliament initially and later on furnished full information to the House as the situation took more and more ominous turn. Chinese incursions into the Indian territory and the Western sector first started in 1957 The clearing of the Aksai Chin Road was the first step. In 1959, China questioned the established boundary alignment and claimed about 50,000 square miles of Indian territory. Pandit H. N. Kunzru, a veteran parliamentarian, who was always listened to with great respect, in his speech in the Rajya Sabha was highly critical of the way in which the border problem was dealt with. He expressed his astonishment that China could lay claim to such large areas of Indian territory.

If Nehru had earlier kept parliament somewhat in the dark, it was probably because the Prime Minister had hoped that with the Chinese Premier, Chou En Lai, he would be able to settle the border issues amicably without raising any public controversy. After the singning of the Tibet Agreement in 1954, Nehru had thought that there was no more border problem left between India and China. He also felt that the Panchsheel was a guarantee for peaceful relations with China. The euphoria of 'Hindi Chini Bhai Bhai' was a manifestation of the newly forged friendship between the two countries. Nehru felt distressed beyond measure in the background of all these when China suddenly came out with such large territorial claims on India.

Prime Minister Nehru's long letter of September 26, 1959 addressed to Premier Chou En Lai on the Chinese incursions and border incidents is very revealing. Nehru wrote: "We did not release to the public the information which we had about various border intrusions in our country by the Chinese personnel since 1954, the construction of a road across the Indian territory in Ladakh, the arrest of our personnel in Aksai Chin area in 1958 and their detention. We did not give publicity to this in the hope that peaceful solutions of the disputes could be found by agreement between the two countries without public excitement on both sides. In fact, our failure to do so has now resulted in sharp but legitimate criticism of Government both in Parliament and in the Press in our country. Far from using force, we sought a peaceful settlement of the disputes."

"Despite regrettable happenings on the frontiers of the two countries, we in India have conducted ourselves with great restraint and moderation. At a number of places your forces assume a threatening attitude. At others they actually came into our territory. Such incidents, concerning as they did the integrity of India, are very serious, but in our anxiety not to create feelings against your Government we deliberately avoided giving publicity to them. Questions in Parliament had, however, to be answered and the facts could not be with-held. When the facts thus became known, the reaction both in Parliament and among the public was one of dismay and great resentment. There was criticism of our Government both in Parliament and the Press for our failure to give publicity to these developments at an earlier stage. Under the Indian Constitution, Parliament is supreme and India has also a free Press and the Government could not restrain public criticism''.

This reveals that Nehru confessed to a sense of guilt in not keeping Parliament duly informed about happenings on the Northern border in time. He also categorically declared that under the Indian Constitution Parliament was supreme and the Press was also free.

China has still not changed its tactics towards India. In February this year, armed Chinese intruders were seen deep in the Indian territory in the Central Sector of Indo-Tibetan border. This is a repetition of the like they did in Ladakh and later in the Eastern Region during the life-time of Nehru. In this intrusion, Chinese troops equipped with binoculars, cameras etc. surveyed the area, made notes and sketches and also took photographs, surreptitiously and returned. Our border security had found them and asked them to get back. This information was not given to the Parliament then but the Correspondent of The Statesman broke the news.

On the border talks China has mentioned about 'mutual understanding and mutual accommodating' knowing that India is not in possession of any Chinese or Tibetan territory. It is only the Chinese who have occupied by force our territory in Aksai Chin in Ladakh and in the Eastern Region and now in discussion they talk in terms of 'line of control', which is not known for what reason the Indian Delegation has accepted and agreed on troops withdrawal on both sides of actual control. This is obviously a policy measure by the Chinese to dilute the importance of McMohan Line. India is only getting assurance of peace and harmony while the Chinese in the negotiations are trying to get concessions in the name of "the line of actual control." This would mean that they are trying to legalise occupation of the areas they took control in the 1950's and 1962 aggression. This is an alarming situation in the present context. There is obviously no need to rush for settlement in the border negotiations. But India could still prefer to wait. But if our Defences are not improved and the broder security not ensured by all means India may have to pay a very heavy price, in its relations with China.

It is already known that the Chief Minister of Arunachal Pradesh Geogong Apang was denied a visa by the Chinese authorities for they do not recognise Arunachal Pradesh as Indian territory even today. These are not the portents of friendly relations of even reaching a just solution of the border issue.

From this it is clear that India followed weakened policy in its foreign relations for long many years. Mrs. Gandhi realised that she had to be realistic in her policy formulations and protect the interest and prestige of India without giving too many concessions. While she signed the Indo-Soviet Friendship Treaty in August 1971 she did not agree to allow the Soviet Union to open their bases on Indian territory. We have been often and too long apologetic in our foreign policy dealings. Mrs. Gandhi brought back India's pride to play its leading role in the foreign relations. On Bangladesh issue she herself travelled to London and Washington and got their direct and indirect support in what India did to assist the Bangladesh Mukti Vahini initially in its war with the Pakistan army which resulted in a full-fledged war with Pakisan. It was not a small thing that 90,000 Pakistani troops men and officers surrendered to the Indian Forces who were brought to India and kept in various camps under protection and care. But for His, Pakistan President Zulfikar Ali Bhutto would not have come to Shimla and signed the famous 'Shimla agreement' with Mrs. Gandhi and almost on her terms. In fact President Bhutto and his ministers pleaded with the Indian ministers and Prime Minister in Shimla to help Pakistan save itself from disintegration and sign the agreement and also save their face and pave way for the return of their soldiers home from Indian military camps. India had always been helpful to Pakistan. Service before self and self-sacrifice has been the motto of the South Block at the Raisina Hill where our Foreign Office is proudly housed.

India has suffered a lack of will on many occasions in the past fifty years. In regard to China our policy proved to be a dismal failure. In Tibet we had a trade representative and we also managed the P&T facilities there. But this had to be dismantled and withdrawn the moment Chinese entered Tibet in October 1950 and her troops came very close to our Northern border.

On Middle East we felt free to criticise the Western-policy of aggression and interference in the internal affairs of the countries of this region. But when in Hungary in October 1956 Soviet troops suppressed national uprising Nehru ignored the incident and though perturbed could not criticise the Soviet Government. About recognising Israel we always felt weak because that would have disturbed India's policy in regard to the Middle East.

Mrs. Gandhi, however, proved to be a different person and she did what she thought was the correct attitude in regard to India's foreign policy. On the question of Missile development India had dragged its feet for many years. There has been delay in the Prithvi Missle test. Prime Minister P.V. Narasimha Rao was to leave for U.S.A. and, therefore, some plea was taken to postpone the test. We have often forgotten that on the question of India's security decisions have necessarily to be taken at New Delhi and not in other country's capital, even if it was Washington. Even on the testing of Agni missile and its further development, Narasimha Rao went on postponing and even Mr. Deve Gowda did not show the will to decide on its development and deployment. Chinese have often made it known that they cannot be pushed around on their national policies—either economic or security. But we have always felt weak on the crucial issues of our economic and security interests. The Chineses have all along managed to hold on to their self-respect and self-assertion. The question often asked is : can India also manage to protect its self respect and pride in its foreign relations. It is difficult to be emphatic in our answer.

It is a known that during the bilateral talks with the Government of the Chinese People's Republic we had hardly mentioned to the Chinese our concern on their continued supply of arms to Pakistan. Our political will is weak and we frown at the talk of national assertion.

When after Independence, the Americans took advantage of the British withdrawal from the India Ocean to develop their own area of influence and promoted NATO in Western Europe. Pakistan joined both the Baghdad Pact in the Middle East and SEATO in South-east Asia to promote her foreign policy and security interests against India. At that time, John Foster Dulles, the US Secretary of State was a great promoter of the military pacts and called the non-aligned movement dishonest. But Nehru, Marshall Tito of Yugoslavia and Naser of Egypt stood firmly together and did not allow the Non-aligned Movement to falter in its effort to promote and protect the political and economic interests of the countries of Asia and Africa. The Latin American countries joined the NAM much later. In the years to come the military organisations set up by the USA gradually disappeared and America launched a bilateral Defence treaty policy in which Pakistan was always an eager participate. NATO, however, continued in Western Europe and now in spite of all great talk of peace and harmony in the world, the USA and the Western countries, are as a policy measure, extending NATO to the borders of Russia. This is a threat not only to Russia but also to the whole of Middle East and South Asian countries. India has opposed the extension of NATO to the countries of Eastern Europe. But now Russia has joined hands with NATO countries to allow the extension of NATO into East Europe which they say 'brings the end of Cold War'.

The end of cold war has been acclaimed by the West as a triumph of a single ideology, that is America as the only super power left in the world. The defeat of Iraq in the Gulf War further demonstrated that the American might can easily distress and suppress nationalism anywhere. After the collapse of the Soviet State, all the countries of the Middle East felt that they have lost their protection shield and threat loomed large over their national security.

In the meantime, the world has moved towards trade blocks which has developed multi-polar economic centres in which Japan and Germany have also joined in an aggressive manner. This has resulted in the weakening of the American economic power over the world. In addition, in all the developed countries, expansion of economic growth has slowed down. As a result, they want to expand in the developing regions of the world on which India and China, they find, offer greater scope because of their geographical size and large population. In the circumstances, the political motive to rule the world has weakened for their economic interest could not be protected otherwise. This is a major development from which the developing countries can unitedly bargain and benefit. Both the developed and the developing countries are living in a competitive world where cooperation, instead of confrontation, can alone serve their national interests — economic or security or both.

Our experience and knowledge required a faster movement in policy making and quicker response to situations and opportunities that unfold before us day-to-day and from time to time. India has been slow in responding to the changing times and even on deciding where its national interest lies and in what form and ways we need to promote and protect them. It looks sometimes strange to hear that a country has to deploy a public relations firm in Washington or New York to promote its foreign policy interests with the U.S. Congress and the State Department and Pentagon. That is the real situation in the USA and even India has attempted to do so. It is business all the time. One should, however, realise that in matters of protection of our national interest it is the nation's strength and will that matters. India today is not a weak nation economically and why should we respond to challenges meekly – China is a challenge. But it is a lession in self-assertion and national pride.

Even in the matter of defence we are relatively strong but needs to develop and deploy our missiles including Agni and the ICBMS. That alone can give strength and pride and will to promote the country's political and economic interest and well being. That is why as people say, there is a need for rethinking on foreign policy. Even on the question of permanent membership of the Security Council one hears that unless you are a big economic and military power it may be difficult to get the support of the West and specially that of USA. This is a question on which we have to assert our right. I was told by a Foreign Secretary that we should build and test our nuclear weapons and then sign the N.P.T. Yes, why not.

We have often heard of foreign pressures on almost every economic and political issue that crops up from time to time. India needs to demonstrate to the world that it will not submit to any outside pressure. This has gone on for a long time. It is not a question of bravado but of self-assertion and self-respect. Every nation worth the name does so. Foreign policy is not a philanthropy nor is diplomacy jumble of words.

There is a process of re-alignment on in the world mainly because of the demise of the Soviet Union and the post-Gulf War situation in which the developing countries are struggling to look for friends and establish close cooperation among themselves and others, in various fields and in various forms. The countries of the East Europe, on the other hand are keen to become part of the Western world for the sake of their economic development and political stability as Russia herself is finding it difficult to sustain itself both politically and economically. The United State has increased its sphere of influence in the Middle East and even in the Latin American countries. Now USA is trying to engage China in various ways on issues of trade and investment, liberalisation, human rights and the like. The developing countries are also reorienting themselves for enlarged economic cooperation between themselves and joint various trading blocs round the world.

The ASEAN (Association of South East Asian Nations) countries viz. Malaysia, Singapore, Indonesia, Thailand, Philippines and Brunei are exploring the possibility of a new ASEAN Economic Grouping with Japan, China, Vietnam, Taiwan, Hongkong and South Korea. America, Japan and Germany are also finding in this region their own areas of influence and efforts are on to join these new trade blocs in terms of trade and economic cooperation. These, however, have their political ramifications.

South Korea and Japan are preparing themselves to put in investment in the former Soviet Union areas. On its part India is also exploring the possibility of joining ASEAN countries and their new groupings in the Indian Ocean and Pacific area. These trading blocs look important in view of the increasing realisation of the dangers of the America led unipolar world. India has to take advantage from this situation to secure for itself a place in the new and emerging grouping and promote economic cooperation with the Asian nations and thereby promote its political and security interests also, for friendship and cooperation has no boundary of its own. In the case of India these interest have continued to be of great importance for the war cry from Pakistan has never ended and on China we have moved toward enlarging economic and political cooperation. Progress has been also reported in bilateral talks in spite of reservations.

Our problems are different from most of the countries of the world. We cannot afford to maintain a low profile posture. One cannot ignore the fact that terrorism and secession are still being promoted from across the border both in the East and in the West and there are people around us who enjoy India's predicament.

The strategical environment around the world because of the new economic imperatives and expansion of regional groupings has lessened tension around the world. Military blocs have been loosened in most parts of the globe except the decision to extend NATO upto the borders of Russia. But the developing countries are not cut of the woods. There is still tension in the Middle East, in Afghanistan, in Latin America, Russia and also in Africa. In these conflicts and tensions it is the developing countries that are mostly involved and concerned and they suffer the worst.

India has always worked for peace around the world and it goes to its credit that India has always tried to bring about peace, even while conflicts and wars have continued. It proved during Iran-Iraq War in Afghanistan and in Gulf war also. India, since Independence, has sent its Military Missions in Korea, Loas, Vietnam and Congo in Africa as also in the Middle East. It has been possible mainly because the host countries have always welcomed the deployment of Indian troops in peace-making processes.

The issue of nuclear non-proliferation treaty has also been raised and discussed while both China and USA have continued to improve their nuclear weapons capabilities. India has, however, stuck to its stand that it cannot sign any such treaty unless the nuclear powers agree to eliminate all their nuclear weapons in a time frame. Perhaps no other country is so critically placed as India is in regard to its security. Therefore, no Government of India can agree to self immolation and sign the Treaty. India cannot accept any obligation under the Treaty of a privileged class of nuclear powers. We are under threat from the North and the West of our borders.

It has been suggested that India should undertake nuclear tests, become a nuclear power and then sign the treaty. It, however, requires the political will of the nation to go ahead with this alternative. We should have the wisdom to re-assess the new world situation and follow imperatives of our security threat. We need to become a nuclear power.

We have often heard about neighbourhood policy in our foreign relations. The new Government at the Centre in Delhi has professed and promised to follow and implement the neighbour-hood policy for bringing about cohesion and enlarging cooperation among the countries of the region. But Pakistan has always been a stumbling block and as a result of which even the implementation of the decisions taken at the SAARC are often not implemented. The Janata Government in 1977 also projected a peace offensive and the then Minister of External Affairs, Atal Bihari Vajpayee visited Bangladesh, Nepal, Sri Lanka and Pakistan. His meeting with President Zia in Isalamabad opened ways from liberalising the policy in regard to the exchange of visits by the nationals of the two countries and also start bilateral cooperation in the economic and cultural fields. Indira Gandhi and later Rajiv Gandhi ought to dramatise their policy in regard to cooperation among the countries of the South Asian Region. We are still hoping for the best.

In between arose the problem of Afghanistan where Soviet Union interfered by sending its troops at the invitation of the then Government of Kabul. India had also to send troops to Jaffna to assist President J.R. Jayawardene's Government in maintaining Sri Lanka's territorial integrity.

Afghanistan in the meantime, in spite of all the peace efforts, continues to suffer and all the old Mujahidin leaders have been thrown out of power. Pakistan-backed Taliban have captured most parts of the country. In Nepal, Pakistan has become active and its Intelligence Agency ISI is reportedly training Talibans and other territorist groups through 'Madarasa' in the Terai and hill areas bordering U.P. and Nepal in spite of all its goodwill for India, has not found it possible to control the ISI and other terrorist groups in their territory who have been conducting subversive activities inside our territory.

Our problem with Pakistan runs deep with roots in the Partition. Any effort by Pakistan to promote bilateral negotiations get derailed soon after it is launched because India baiting continues to dominate in thinking and in deeds. Prime Minister, Gujral has taken upon himself to improve relations with Pakistan and hopefully it may bring about some results. Rajiv Gandhi visited Islamabad in July 1989 when Begum Bhutto was the Prime Minister. There was some effort to solve the Siachin issue but things remained as they were.

Nehru said on February 3, 1958 "We are friendly with everyone and even with those who do not like us. There is nothing wrong in being friendly with everyone. India wants her friendship with everyone to be useful to the world. We are not prepared to be told by anyone that friendship with this or that country is bad. India does not involve herself in any of the Blocs. She is a non-aligned country and she will remain so".

On September 1, 1959, the then President of Pakistan General Ayub Khan visited New Delhi on his way to Dhaka and had a very cordial talk with Nehru at Palam Airport. They discussed matters of mutual interest. The Joint statement issued on that day said : "They agreed that there was need to conduct their relations with each other on a rational and planned basis and not according to the day-to-day exigencies as they arose and that their outstanding issues and other problems should be solved in mutual interest in accordance with justice and fair play in a spirit of friendliness, cooperation and good neighbourliness."

During his talks with Nehru at the Palm Airport Ayub Khan made suggestions for solving bilateral problems. But for reasons unknown no progress could be made towards this end and General Ayub returned to his special plane tired and disappointed. As the plane took off journalists accompanying him rushed forward to his lounge and asked, "Mr. President, what happened?" General Ayub was not happy and refused to talk but after a good deal of persuasion, he only said in a loud voice: "If there was a Hindu Maha Sabha Government in New Delhi I would have solved all our problems between the two countries. But with Nehru nothing can succeed." I was given this information by an editor of a Pakistani journal who was accompanying him during his visit to New Delhi and Dhaka. But what he meant, by saying what he said, no one knows.

In December 1959 Dwight D. Eisenhower, President of the United States of America, visited India which turned out to be historical in many ways. He was the first US President to set his foot on Indian soil. President Eisenhower said : "Between the first largest democracy on earth, India and the second largest, America lie 10,000 miles of land and ocean but in our fundamental ideas and convictions about democracy we are close neighbours. We ought to be closer." His visit lasted from December 9 to 19. In the recent years, efforts have been made with a sense of achievement to bring about closer political and economic relations between India and America. President Eisenhower had long talks about developments in China and Nepal. He gave details about Chinese armed concentration and preparedness in Tibet also towards the Himalayas. It was implied that he cautioned the Prime Minister on the Chinese designs. However, Nehru did not share his view and reportedly said : "We have close and friendly relations with China and that they would do nothing to break that relationship." On this President Eisenhower did not agree with the Indian Prime Minister but extended military assistance to India to the extent necessary and without any condition. Nehru did not respond positively. India had raised the issue of supply of arms to Pakistan, on which he gave some assurance.

According to the reliable reports available then, Nehru did not feel it necessary to involve India in any arms supply deal with America and the matter ended there. But later Nehru frantically appealed for US military aid and was willing to pay a price for it. The routing of Indian forces on the border in 1962 war with China had created a situation in which India suddenly came under extreme pressure and policy in regard to arms deal had to be changed. The Chinese soon after withdrew right upto the other side of the Mac Mohan line. It was later that India did sign a peace and friendship treaty with the Soviet Union which was also a Defence treaty.

Our efforts to develop relation with America in many fields have been successful and given rise to new hopes for the future. In October 1949, Nehru stated: "It is necessary and even desirable and perhaps, inevitable that India and the United States of America should know each other more and cooperate with each other. India looks forward to continue its partnership with America in future also."

India has built a mutually beneficial relationship with all countries of the world and earned the goodwill of most nations in the conduct of our national and foreign policy.

In the situation that we are now placed politically any economically and security-wise, there is often a feeling that our Indianness has been lost. We are more a conglomeration of individuals and self-seeking leaders. So far as the sub-continent is concerned it has lost its sub-continental ness. Zulfikar Ali Bhutto once said: "Yes, he is a man of contradictions because he is a product of the Indian sub-continent which itself is full of contradictions."

Our policy of togetherness, has not brought about sub-continent ethos. Our past, our commonness, our ethnicity has also failed to promote oneness amongst ourselves. This is the contradiction.

Neighbourhood policy, though a necessity and based on goodwill has not changed the mind set of our neighbours mainly because of the fact that they have sought friendship elsewhere away from us and for no fault of ours. Nepal and Bangladesh are examples in history. In spite of our shedding blood for them, it has not bound these nations with us. Sri Lanka and Maldives received our military support to protect their security and nationhood. This was not a favour but a duty which India felt, it owned to its neighbours. But they do not even seem to acknowledge the problems of our national security. Otherwise, Pakistani intelligence agency, ISI, would not have been operating in Bangladesh and Nepal. Our policy makers are not oblivious of this situation. But the assurance we receive does not translate itself in policy and actions as warranted by the situation and expected from them.

Our contribution to world affairs has been immense and even epoch making. It was Nehru, who for the first time proposed a treaty to end nuclear testing. The dissolution of colonialism started speedily unfolding after India had won freedom. It was also Nehru who guided the Asian nations to join in a group which took a formal shape at Bandung, on April 24, 1955. It was on December 23, 1954 that the President of Yuogoslavia Marshal Josip Broz Tito and Indian Prime Minister Jawaharlal Nehru who in a joint statement proclaimed the policy of non-alignment which was later formulised into Bandung Afro-Asian Summit.

It was India where, breaking the iron curtain, Soviet leaders, N. A. Bulganin, Chairman of the Council of Ministers of U.S.S.R. and N. S. Khruschev, member of the Presidum of the Supreme Soviet visited in November-December 1955. This was their first ever visit outside their country. It made a great history and surprised the world of India's legitimacy in world affairs.

XI

Economic Policy

A major challenge as India became free was to decide the model of economic development for itself. Of the options available one was the free enterprise based on capitalism in the developed countries of the West and the other was the centrally planned economies of the communist countries led by the Soviet Union. Our leaders, however, chose their own path under Nehru's leadership that was to establish democratic socialism. In the early fifties he declared at the Avadi Congress Session that his government would work for the establishment of socialistic pattern of society in which there will be State ownership of basic industries. While the country moved towards an increasing degree of State ownership or control over means of production and distribution, a large area of economic operation was still left to private initiative. In December, 1954, Parliament adopted the Resolution which said: "the objective of our economic policy should be a socialistic pattern of society."

Opinion outside India, specially in the developed world, was divided on whether economic development without an incentive of private profit and competition could be implemented profitably. The mixed economy that was ushered in India, in spite of centralised planning, proved that India's option was more practicable and result oriented. In a society which encouraged both private and State enterprise, an industrial revolution did become possible. The State ownership and control of key industries and services like mineral resources, railways, waterways, shipping and heavy industry was considered necessary for the private sector was not in a position to generate enough resources and expertise to manage and meet the demand.

The building up of the heavy industries in India with Soviet help and assistance of the Western countries brought about a sea change in the economic situation. A large number of young men and women were sent abroad for training in the running and management of these modern industries. On their return they took control of these enterprises and made them successful. Training centres and institutions were also started under the heavy projects to train the younger generation. And that is how in 20 years India became the third largest country in trained manpower in the world after the USA and the USSR. Thus a large base of industrial growth was created and many heavy industries were set up like steel plants, electric plants, machine tools, ship building, heavy vessels and forging and foundry industries, fertiliser plants, refineries, petrochemical industries and a host of others.

The construction of the Rajasthan canal in the desert areas has been another great achievement, if not, a miracle. This has brought about great solace to the people of arid Rajasthan. The multipurpose river valley projects like Bhakra Nangal are monumental achievements. Now we live in a different world, a new world. Therefore, we have to grow and change but the change should benefit the people and not the elite alone.

In the field of agriculture many multi-purpose river valley projects were announced, constructed and commissioned. Many fertiliser plants were set up. We were lucky in the early days to find oil in Assam and Gujarat. Later, we also found oil in Bombay High, some 100 miles away from the coast of Bombay. This made India near self-sufficient in oil and gas production and imports of these items were cut down. Though our production has not grown and we are suffering shortages. Engineering industries and later electronic industries also grew very fast. Today India manufactures many sophisticated items like railway locomotives, equipment for power generation and transmission, mother mechanies for element and sugar factories, tractors, bicycles, scooters, cars, trucks, buses, electric fans, telephones, T.V. paper etc. Our mining has also developed very fast and we are self-sufficient in coal and some of the non-ferrous metals as well. How we are building our own satellites and their launch vehicles.

Our agricultural development has been so fast that even in arid Rajasthan or mountain regions, people are now growing various crops. The whole country looks more green and fertile. Many scientific institutions were set up to promote research and development on which Nehru had laid great stress from the beginning. We developed nuclear energy and set up nuclear power plants in which Dr. Bhaba became a father figure. India, thanks to Mrs. Gandhi, carried out its first underground nuclear explosion in May 1974 which made this country a front-runner state in nuclear research and development. Today, we fabricate also our own missiles. This is not a mean achievement considering that we had started as an under-developed country with the minimum of resources and technical knowhow. There is, however, one controversy, whether the public sector is good or bad, profitable or unprofitable. People ignore the fact India is today agriculturally and industrially largely self-sufficient. The policy of starting state enterprises in basic industries and the training of our men in the running of the heavy and sophisticated industries has borne fruit. In fact, even the private sector has to rely on the technology and technical personnel which have been provided by the public sector institutions.

Undoubtedly, we have reached a stage from where it is possible and necessary that the economy be opened to private initiative and enterprise. The new economic order that we are talking about may not have materalised if we did not have the structure created for it in the last 50 years of our developmental process. The changeover was brought about in 1991 by Dr. Manmohan Singh, the then Finance Minister mainly because we had built an infrastructure for the private enterprise also to join the mainstream of economic development and growth without any bottleneck and slowing down of the economy in the process of change-over This itself became path-sctting and an example to the vast world.

India, the largest democracy, symbolises the struggle of an ancient people to achieve their due place in a global economic and political order. It is the story of a country emerging from enslavement and mobilising itself to reconstruct its mind-set, resources and development effort. This has been the challenge it has had to face since the beginning. India today is riding the crest of a wave of multi-dimensional development and it has achieved enduring growth in most economic fields in its effort to secure for its people a better future.

We are now self-sufficient in our requirements of food, clothing, wide range of consumer durables and medicines. We are, by and large, self-sufficient in transport and engineering goods, heavy and fine chemicals, petrochemicals etc. Much of the technology and machinery required for manufacturing steel, cement, sugar, fertilizer, major petrochemicals, oil refinery and thermal power, is available from indigenous source. We have developed a vibrant capital market and a strong financial system.

India has also emerged as one of the largest producers of scooters, bicycles, chemicals, engineering and electronic goods and cotton yarn in the world. We occupy the first six positions in many other items on a global basis, as for example, tea, coffee, sugar, ironore and other minerals, etc. This unheralded in the world.

India today has a good R&D base as a result of which in agriculture the country has transformed itself from a major grain importer until the seventies to a net surplus producer. Energy sources have also been diversified and production considerably increased, although the demand is growing faster than supply. The composition of exports has also undergone significant change with nearly a third of our exports being non-traditional manufactured items. Although India still remains a poor country and over 30% of our population lives below the poverty line, there has been a conscious effort for raising the standard of living of our people. It has been possible to improve the quality of our life. However, the rising population continues to worry the planners and this is an area where larger efforts need to be put in.

There is a change in the outlook generally and Governmental commitment particularly to guide and control the economy itself, based on the concept of socialism, developed 100 years ago. Mrs. Indira Gandhi herself as Prime Minister, started liberalising the economy by removing many restrictions on the monopoly houses. She encouraged small and medium and inter-mediate industry to grow and also allowed the industrial houses to expand. This was necessary because after a certain scale of development, which India achieved in the first forty years of Independence, needed a surrounding for growth and expansion. Therefore, controls and 'licence-permit raj' had to be abolished. It was in this background that in 1991 Dr. Manmohan Singh, all of a sudden removed State controls and freed the economy from State intervention. He also announced a good deal of reduction in tax rates that allowed the market economy to take over the task of development and growth.

Soon, however, it was realised that in a developing country like India with a large population it was not possible to run the economy for profit alone. Therefore, State intervention in some form and some degree, was necessary. During the last three years there has been some slowing down of the economic reforms process. The new economic policy was leading towards large unemployment because the industries in the private sector were getting closed and there was no extansia of the public sector. Hence the exist policy could not be implemented and even Dr. Manmohan Singh could do nothing about it. However, the foreign-exchange regulation act was loosened and there was liberalisation in the policy of foreign exchange management. In fact, the new policy helped in the accumulation of larger foreign exchange reserve through exports, investment by foreign financial institutions and non-resident Indians in the stock market and direct foreign private investment. Today, however, the Government is facing the problem of under-utilisation of the foreign exchange reserve since it was not being used for productive purposes and we do not have many projects in hand except the power projects to utilise the reserve.

Even the policy of privatisation of public sector undertakings has slowed down because the private sector is still not in a position to take them over completely. There is also a fear that after privatisation many important public undertakings may be closed down. Investment in Central and State public sector undertaking is over Rs. 130, 000 crores. Though private sector has been permitted to set up new power plants it has not done much and the result is that there is a growing power shortage. The belief that the market economy will usher in an area of private enterprise and development has raised doubts about the mode and pace of change for the future. Already there is a lag in investment. India is self-sufficient in coal. Still the output and supply has not kept pace with the demand. This sector is being privatised slowly for the risks are mounting.

India has not only achieved green revolution and became self-sufficient in agriculture but has also recorded self-sufficiency through white revolution. Milk production has increased manifold. After long years of fundamental agricultural research. Our scientists have delivered high yielding and disease resistant varieties for wheat, rice and other crops. Even arid areas have developed methods for higher agricultural production.

However, supply of safe drinking water to every village is still a distant dream. In spite of green and white revolution the social development work in rural areas has also lagged behind. High rate of urbanisation in itself is causing great concern to our planners of economic development.

In the transport sector Indian Railways is the largest in Asia and one of the best run in the world. It carries over 10 million passengers every day. The Indian Railways have also completed many turnkey projects in countries like Iraq, Saudi Arabia, Algeria, Syria, Tunisia and Malaysia and Nigeria. Since 1950 India's road network has expanded four times in length to 1,770,00 km and while maintaining the bullock carts it has modernised its fleet of vehicles like buses, scooters, car, mobikes, trucks and even bicycles. Most of these are manufactured in India itself. Even in the field of shipping we have made achievements and at present, we are the second largest ship owners in Asia with a total of over 6 million GRT. In the field of research, Indian scientists have done pioneering work in agriculture, educational equipment, forestry, alternative energy sources and Defence. most of the research institutions are financed by the Government. We have a science and technology policy announced during the regime of Mrs. Indira Gandhi.

Antarctic oceanographic research, India is today one of the few nations which have developed capability and has her own year-around research base in Antarctica.

As for higher and technical education India has a network of 120 universities, 200 engineering colleges and 400 or more polytechnics which provide trained technical manpower for the industry and trade.

Notwithstanding these achievements there is a need, for the managers of Indian economy and industry to comprehend on how the opportunities and policy initiatives should be utilised for the benefit of the people. This could give a boost to the enormous social impact on the living conditions of our people and make India a major and strong partner in the process of economic development.

The development process that we have adopted now needs to be accompanied by an appraisal system to accurately assess our performance, potential, strengths and weaknesses. The Planning Commission Dy. Chairman, Madhu Dandavate says that the Planning Commission is working out such a methodology. Unless people found that the new policy initiatives are going to provide them with jobs and raise their living standard they will only react unfavourably to any policy and programme that the Government might think important and beneficial.

When India started on the path of planned development Prof. P.C. Mahalanobis was the Dy. Chairman of the Planning Commission and he gave the five year plan, its orientation and form. Prof. Mahalanobis said that no country of our size and at our thin level of developments, facing unemployment, poverty and ill health could develop without a clear identification of the objectives and the best use of scarce resources for the maximum benefit of the people. The planning process was oriented to this optimisation exercise.

When our new economic policy was launched in 1991, the then Prime Minister, P.V. Narasimha Rao said that while we visualise greater role for the private sector in our growth process we also emphasise the importance of the role of the State as a crucial factor in our development. The State does not wither away simply because a little more investment comes from the private sector.

There has been a controversy about privatisation of the India economy and large scale participation of foreign financial institutions and multi-nationals in country's future development. Narasimha Rao in his address to the World Economic Forum in Devos (Switzerland) on February 1, 1994 explained in detail, India's economic policy and the path it has followed to tread for the amelioration of the conditions of our people. He said: "In India we recognsie the change, but maintain a balance which has come to be known as the 'middle way'. The 'middle way' is not just a philosophical postulate enjoined by the great Buddha; it has permeated in India's life in a variety of ways. When communist ideas tended to overpower Indian thinking, Prime Minister Nehru adumbrated the concept of 'mixed economy'. He was criticised in every quarter, right and left; the mixed economy concept has saved India time and again from political submission and economic dependence''.

''Today, again some seem to think that with the collapse of the communist system and the world having become unipolar there can be no middle way since the world has only one way now. However, from what has happened, it does not seem to follow that there is only one single way for the development of societies for all time to come''. ''Change has to be accepted as a result of deliberate and objective thinking. . . . In the new found enthusiasm for change government should not go overboard and plunge large chunks of their people into mass miseries; they have no right to do that. I am not propounding a theory. I am merely saying that I have no right to throw millions of people out of their jobs overnight because I want a particular change... We have to evolve our own thinking and our own way of mending and re-shaping our path''.

Clarifying India's stand on the new economic policy, at the Symposium organised by the World Economic Forum held at Devos, on February 3, 1992 Narasimha Rao said that ''there is a danger of a new ideological orthodoxy replacing the old, imposing on our minds and prescribing rigid, pre-determined models for vastly different situations. We accept the need for a much wider role for the 'market' principles; there should be a congenial environment for entrepreneurship; and there should be fewer controls on economic activity. Nevertheless, for countries where poverty and destitution are pervasive, the State cannot absolve itself of the responsibility to involve itself in economic decision making. It has to accept the responsibility to ensure a minimal degree of social welfare to its people. There are also cultural differences among nations. In our society, for example, an individual is important, but at the same time there is a strong sense of community interest as well. In India, the cohesion of the family, the community and the village is an important value. This is often regarded as a characteristic of a backward kind of country, but this is not really so. The conditions are so different. It is, therefore, necessary to allow nations and societies to determine their own specific socio-political and economic system even while asserting the universal values of democracy and humanism and acknowledging the greater efficiency of the market principle in most forms of economic activity''. This alone can be the basis for our economic policy.

As we know economic crisis and social tensions do not provide the environment needed for enduring political institution building. Development, therefore, become a pre-condition for sustaining democracy. That is how India has always looked at the Economic Policies followed since the Five Year Plan was launched.

India is a self-confident democracy. The Indian mind is democratically oriented through and through. It has a combination of individualism and collective wisdom in action, which has been demonstrated for thousands of years.

The Indian economy has attained a degree of maturity and sophistication, which naturally makes it ready, willing and even eager to accept the challenge of the international market place. An economically dynamic and politically stable India alone can play a viable role and sustain itself in the contemporary world.

The reforms launched in 1991-1992 have freed the economy from controls and licence raj and also opened for larger participation by the private sector. This policy, however, relates mainly to industry. Other sectors of the economy have not so far benefited by it to a large extent. The new policy has also not improved the lot of the masses. None has it so far taken care to ensure growth with social justice and equity. There has been a need, a long need for a thorough shake up in the direction of redistributive justice in view of the widening gap between poverty and prosperity.

The thrust areas of the economy have been agriculture, infrastructure and social sectors while it is the needs of the industry and private sector which have been taken care of through tax reliefs and concessions. Still the needed investment has not come.

However, the Indian economy is strong enough to sustain a larger growth rate in the coming years. This is mainly because self-sufficiency in the agriculture sector, the production of wage goods and industrial machinery and equipment. The Approach Paper on the Ninth Plan, therefore, envisages an annual growth rate of 7% with an increase of savings of 26.2% and investment at 28%. Thus, the Ninth Plan also points the need to limit the ceiling on current account deficit at 2.4% GDP. The Government, however, is finding it difficult to provide financial resources to the extent of Rs. 8,75,000 crores for implementing the Ninth Plan. The States are having a larger role in the Ninth Plan mainly in rural development and social reforms. However, mobilisation of additional resources by the States has been meagre.

A sustained growth of the economy will necessarily depend on balanced development in all the sectors of the economy as well as of all sections of the society particularly the weaker and poorer sections. The modified methodology of poverty, as suggested by the Lakadawala Committee in 1992 estimated the number of people below the poverty line to be around 45% of the total population. This requires greater effort to take the benefits of economic development to the people while efforts have to be doubled to control he high growth rate of population. Our problem has been mainly distribution of national income. It also means that the liberalisation and reforms have not led to much improvement in the life style of the masses while it has made rich sections of our society richer. Therefore, poverty alleviation programmes have to be implemented vigorously without which neither the people's participation in the development can be ensured nor economic environment will change in the country. It required stronger political will and higher administrative efficiency both at the Central and at the State level to achieve our goals and fulfil the aspirations of the people. The next five ears are going to be crucial for the country. This is the period when people will wait to see change in their living standard, rise in unemployment and all the minimum needs attrained. Failure may make politics unsustainable.

Concern, however, is being expressed about the reforms policy being implemented through a stabilisation and structural adjustment policy, as they do not seem to have led to macro economic balance in the economy. The Government has resorted to cuts in its investment expenditure and infrastructural development. This has, therefore, slowed down the growth and expansion of the economy. The expected private investment still looks farther away. Therefore, State intervention is being suggested in ensuring growth in general and investment in particular. Another point to note is that even after 50 years about two-thirds of the work force is still engaged in agriculture and allied activities. This only stressed urgency for the reappraisal of the direction of the government policies and investment priorities.

India, though a poor country, has made one important achievement. The saving rate though stable today had risen from 10% of the GDP in 1951-1952 to 24% in 1978-79. It is now actually between 20-23% of the GDP.

There is a good deal of talk about foreign (private) direct investment in India. But these investments are directed primarily at consumer goods and service sectors. This does not help the management of balance of payments. Even in technology upgradation not much direct investment is visible.

There is also a great deal of discussion and argument on disinvestment policy of the Government. The new economic policy seems to undermine the public sector while the private sector expansion is yet to begin. The capital raised by selling equity is not being returned to the public sector units for their expansion and development. The Government is taking that money away in meeting its budgetary deficits. The public sector in terms of technology and management has been at the core of balancing globally competitive industry in India. This is being gradually destroyed.

Suresh Kumar, formerly secretary, Department of Public Enterprises suggested in 1991 that for the evaluation of the public enterprises a different methodology should be created for it performs a different role than the sheer profit-oriented private sector. Also, total performance of the two sectors should be the basis for judging their performance. They have developed backward areas, provided large scale employment (about 2.3 million jobs assisted the growth of ancillary and small scale industries and have also provided technology growth and expansion plus highly technical manpower to the Indian industry. The new economic policy, therefore, needs a new direction and new orientation in the context of India's needs and conditions. Only an economically and industrially strong India can enable us to join the world market and to survive competition and grow.

XII

The Indian State - Framework

India, a Union of States, is a sovereign socialist secular democratic Republic with a parliamentary system of government. The Republic is governed in terms of the Constitution, which was adopted by the Constituent Assembly on 26 November 1949 and came into force on 26 January 1950.

The Constitution which envisages parliamentary form of government is federal in structure with unitary features. President of India is constitutional head of executive of the Union. Article 74(1) of the Constitution provides that there shall be a Council of Ministers with the Prime Minister as head to aid and advise. Real executive power thus vests in Council of Ministers with Prime Minister as head, Council of Ministers is collectively responsible to the House of the People (Lok Sabha). Similarly, in States, Governor is head of executive, but it is the Council of Ministers with Chief Minister as head in whom real executive power vests. Council of Ministers of a State is collectively responsible to Legislative Assembly.

The Constitution distributes legislative power between Parliament and State legislatures and provides for vesting of residual powers in Parliament. Power to amend the Constitution also vests in Parliament. The Constitution has provision for independence of judiciary, Comptroller and Auditor General, Public Service Commissions and Chief Election Commissioner.

THE UNION AND ITS TERRITORY

India comprise 26 States and Six Union Territories. States are: Andhra Pradesh, Assam, Arunachal Pradesh, Bihar, Goa, Gujarat, Haryana, Himachal Pradesh, Jammu & Kashmir, Karnataka, Kerala, Madhya Pradesh, Maharashtra, Manipur, Meghalaya, Mizoram, Nagaland, Orissa, Punjab, Rajasthan, Sikkim, Tamilnadu, Tripura, Uttar Pradesh and West Bengal. Union territories are: Andaman and Nicobar Islands, Chandigarh, Dadra and Nagar Haveli, Daman and Diu, Lakshadweep and Pondicherry and Delhi as National Capital Territory of Delhi.

CITIZENSHIP

The Constitution of India provides for a single and uniform citizenship for whole of India. Every person who was at the commencement of the Constitution domiciled in the territory of India and: (a) who was born in the territory of India or (b) either of whose parents was born in the territory of India or (c) who has been ordinarily resident in the territory of India for not less than five years immediately preceding such commencement, shall be a citizen of India. The Citizenship Act, 1955 provides for acquisition and termination of citizenship after the commencement of the Constitution.

DIRECTIVE PRINCIPLES OF STATE POLICY

The Constitution lays down certain Directive Principles of State Policy which though not justiceable, are 'fundamental in governance of the country' and it is 'the duty of the State to apply these principles in making laws'. These lay down that the State shall strive to promote welfare of people by securing and protecting as effectively as it may a social order in which justice— social, economic and political, shall inform all institutions of national life. The State shall direct its policy in such a manner as to secure the right of all men and women to an adequate means of livelihood, equal pay for equal work and within limits of its economic capacity and development, to make effective provision for securing the right to work, education and to public assistance in the event of unemployment, old age, sickness and disablement or other cases of undeserved want. The State shall also endeavour to secure to workers a living wage, humane conditions of work, a decent standard of life and full involvement of workers in management of industries.

In the economic sphere, the State is to direct its policy in such a manner as to secure distribution of ownership and control of material resources of community to observe the common good and to ensure that operation of economic system does not result in concentration of wealth and means of production to common detriment. (In the present context of economic reforms may be, the Constitution has to be amended in this sphere.)

Some of the other important directives relate to provisions of opportunities and facilities for children to develop in a healthy manner, free and compulsory education for all children upto the age of 14; promotion of education and economic interests of scheduled castes, scheduled tribes and other weaker sections; organisation of village panchayats; separation of judiciary from executive, promulgation of a uniform civil code for whole country; protection of national monuments; promotion of justice on a basis of equal opportunity; provision of free legal aid; protection and improvement of environment and safeguarding of forest and wildlife of the country and promotion of international peace and security, just and honourable relations between nations, respect of international law, treaty obligations and settlement of international disputes by arbitration.

The provision of compulsory free education has not yet been fully implemented, though guaranteed under the Constitution.

THE UNION

Exective

The Union executive consists of President, Vice President and Council of Ministers with Prime Minister at the head to aid and advise President.

PRESIDENT

President is elected by members of an electoral college consisting of elected members of both Houses of Parliament and Legislative Assemblies of the States in accordance with system of proportional representation by means of single transferable vote. To secure uniformity among States *inter se* as well as parity between the States, as a whole, and the Union, suitable weightage is given to each vote. President must be a citizen of India, not less than 35 years of age and qualified for election as member of the Lok Sabha. His term of office is five years and he is eligible for re-election. His removal from office is to be in accordance with procedure prescribed in Article 61 of the Constitution. He may, by writing under his hand addressed to Vice President, resign his office.

Executive power of the Union is vested in the President and is exercised by him either directly or through officers subordinate to him in accordance with the Constitution. Supreme Command of Defence Forces of the Union also vests in him. President summons, prorogues, addresses, sends messages to Parliament and dissolves the Lok Sabha; promulgates ordinances at any time, except when both Houses of Parliament are in session; makes recommendations for introducing financial and money bills and gives assent to bills; grants pardons, reprieves, respites or remissions of punishment or suspends, remits or commutes sentences in certain cases. When there is a failure of the constitutional machinery in a State, he can assume to himself all or any of the functions of the government of that State. President can proclaim emergency in the country if he is satisfied that a grave emergency exists whereby security of India or any part of its territory is threatened whether by war or external aggression or armed rebellion.

VICE PRESIDENT

Vice President is elected by members of an electoral college consisting of members of both Houses of Parliament in accordance with the system of proportional representation by means of single transferable vote. He must be a citizen of India, not less than 35 years of age and eligible for election as a member of the Rajya Sabha. His term of office is five years and he is eligible for re-election. His removal from office is to be in accordance with procedure prescribed in Article 67b.

Vice President is ex-officio Chairman of the Rajya Sabha and acts as President when the latter is unable to discharge his functions due to absence, illness or any other cause or till the election of new President (to be held within six months) when a vacancy is caused by death, resignation or removal or otherwise of President. While so acting, he ceases to perform the function of the Chairman of the Rajya Sabha.

COUNCIL OF MINISTERS

There is a Council of Ministers headed by Prime Minister to aid and advise President in exercise of his functions. Prime Minister is appointed by the President who also appoints other ministers on the advice of Prime Minister. The Council is collectively responsible to the Lok Sabha. It is the duty of the Prime Minister to communicate to President all decisions of Council of Ministers relating to administration of affairs of the Union and proposals for legislation and information relating to them.

The Council of Ministers comprises Ministers who are members of Cabinet, Ministers of State (independent charge), Ministers of State and Deputy Ministers.

LEGISLATURE

Legislature of the Union which is called Parliament, consists of President and two Houses, known as Council of States (Rajya Sabha) and House of the People (Lok Sabha). Each House of Parliament has to meet within six months of its previous sitting. A joint sitting of two Houses can be held in certain cases.

RAJYA SABHA

The Constitution provides that the Rajya Sabha shall consist of 250 members, of which 12 members shall be nominated by the President from amongst persons having special knowledge or practical experience in respect of such matters as literature, science, art and social service, and not more than 238 representatives of the States and of the Union territories.

Elections to the Rajya Sabha are indirect members representing States are elected by elected members of legislative assemblies of the States in accordance with the system of proportional representation by means of the single transferable vote, and those representing Union territories are chosen in such manner as Parliament may by law prescribe. The Rajya Sabha is not subject to dissolution; one-third of its members retire on expiry of every second year.

The Rajya Sabha, at present, has 245 seats. Of these, 233 members represent the States and the Union territories and 12 members are nominated by the President.

LOK SABHA

The Lok Sabha is composed of representatives of people chosen by direct election on the basis of adult suffrage. Maximum strength of the House envisaged by the Constitution is now 552 (530 members to represent States. 20 to represent Union territories and not more than two members of Anglo-Indian community to be nominated by President, if, in his opinion, that community is not adequately represented in the House). Total elective membership of the Lok Sabha is distributed among States in such a way that ratio between number of seats allotted to each State and population of the State is, as far as practicable, the same for all States. The Lok Sabha at present consists of 545 members. Of these, 530 members are directly elected from 25 States and 13 from seven Union territories while two are nominated by President to represent Anglo-Indian community. Allocation of seats in the present Lok Sabha is based on 1971 census and under the 42nd Amendment of the Constitution (1976) will continue to be so based until figures of the first census taken after 2000 AD become available.

The term of the Lok Sabha, unless dissolved, is five years from the date appointed for its first meeting. However, while a proclamation of emergency is in operation, this period may be extended by Parliament by law for a period not exceeding one year at a time and not extending in any case, beyond a period of six months after the proclamation has ceased to operate. Ten Lok Sabhas have been constituted so far.

QUALIFICATIONS FOR MEMBERSHIP OF PARLIAMENT

In order to be chosen a Member of Parliament, a person must be a citizen of India and not less than 30 years of age in case of the Rajya Sabha and not less than 25 years of age in case of the Lok Sabha. Additional qualifications may be prescribed by Parliament by law.

FUNCTIONS AND POWERS OF PARLIAMENT

As in other parliamentary democracies, Parliament of India has cardinal functions of legislation, overseeing of administration, passing of budget, ventilation of public grievances, discussing various subjects like development plans, international relations and national policies. Distribution of powers between the Union and States, followed in the Constitution, emphasises in many ways general predominance of Parliament in legislative field. Apart from wide-range of subjects, even in normal times Parliament can, under certain circumstances, assume legislative power and a subject falling within the sphere exclusively reserved for the States. Parliament is Supreme Court and High Courts, Chief Election Commissioner and Comptroller and Auditor General in accordance with procedure laid down in the Constitution.

All legislation requires consent of both Houses of Parliament. In case of money bills, however, the will of the Lok Sabha prevails. Delegated legislation is also subject to review and control by Parliament. Besides power to legislate, the Constitution vests in Parliament power to initiate amendment of the Constitution.

THE STATES

The system of government in States closely resembles that of the Union.

EXECUTIVE

GOVERNOR

State executive consists of Governor and Council of Ministers with Chief Minister as its head, Governor of a State is appointed by the President for a term of five years and holds office during his pleasure. Only Indian citizens above 35 years of age are eligible for appointment to this office. Executive power of the State is vested in Governor.

Council of Ministers with Chief Minister as head, aids and advises Governor in exercise of his functions except in so far as he is by or under the Constitution required to exercise his functions or any of them in his discretion. In respect of Nagaland, Governor has special responsibility under Article 371A of the Constitution with respect to law and order and even though it is necessary for him to consult Council of Ministers in matters relating to law and order, he can exercise his individual judgment as to the action to be taken.

Similarly, in respect of Arunachal Pradesh, Governor has special responsibility under Article 371H of the Constitution with respect to law and order and in discharge of his function in relation thereto Governor shall, after consulting Council of Ministers, exercise his individual judgment as to the action to be taken. These are, however, temporary provisions if President, on receipt of a report from Governor or otherwise is satisfied that it is no longer necessary for Governor to have special responsibility with respect to law and order, he may so direct by an order.

Likewise, in the Sixth Schedule which applies to tribal areas of Assam, Meghalaya, Tripura and Mizoram as specified in Para 20 of that Schedule, discretionary powers are given to Governor in matters relating to sharing of royalties between district council and State government. Sixth Schedule vests additional discretionary powers in Governors of Mizoram and Tripura in almost all their functions (except approving regulations for levy of taxes and money lending by non-tribals by district councils) since December 1988. In Sikkim, Governor has been given special responsibility for peace and social and economic advancement of different sections of population.

As we have continued after Independence, gradually demand for new States were raised in various regions of the country. As a result Pt. Nehru had to agree to the setting up of the States Reorganisation Commission which recommended the formation of States on linguistic basis. Therefore, many new States were created.

Later, the insurgency situation in the Assam State, started growing and it took a violent turn. In addition, there was large influx of refugees from the then East Pakistan (now Bangladesh). This further aggravated the law and order situation and political situation in Assam and the ethnic violence started growing. Ultimately, the Central Government decided to create a new State known as Nagaland. Thereafter, many more States were created by breaking the original Assam State into six new States. As a result, new arrangements for the governace of the North Eastern States had to be made. These States still continue to be very sensitive both ethnically and also from India's security point of view.

COUNCIL OF MINISTERS

Chief Minister is appointed by Governor who also appoints other ministers on advice of Chief Minister. Council of ministers is collectively responsible to legislative assembly of the State.

LEGISLATURE

For every state, there is a legislature which consists of Governor and one House or, as the case many be, two Houses. In Bihar, Jammu and Kashmir, Karnataka, Maharashtra and Uttar Pradesh, there are two Houses known as legislative council and legislative assembly. In remaining States, there is only one House known as legislative assembly. Parliament may, by law, provide for abolition of an existing legislative council or for creation of one where it does not exist, if proposal is supported by a resolution of the legislative assembly concerned.

LEGISLATIVE COUNCIL

Legislative council (Vidhan Parishad) of a State comprises not more than one-third of total number of members in legislative assembly of the state and in no case less than 40 members (Legislative Council of Jammu and Kashmir has 36 members vide Section 50 of the Constitution of Jammu and Kashmir). About one-third of members of the council are elected by members of legislative assembly from amongst persons who are not its members, one-third by electorates consisting of members of municipalities, district boards and other local authorities in the State, one-twelfth by electorate consisting of persons who have been, for at least three years, engaged in teaching in educational institutions within the State not lower in standard than secondary schools and a further one-twelfth by registered graduates of more than three years standing. Remaining members are nominated by Governor from among those who have distinguished themselves in literature, science, art, cooperative movement and social service. Legislative councils are not subject to dissolution but one-third of their members retire every second year.

UNION TERRITORIES

Because of some special circumstances the Government of India created Union territories which will be governed directly by the Centre. Union territories are administered by President acting to such extent as he thinks fit, through an Administrator appointed by him. Administrators of Andaman and Nicobar Islands, Delhi and Pondicherry are designated as Lieutenant Governors, while Administrator of Chandigarh is designated as Chief Commissioner. However, presently, the Governor of Punjab is concurrently the Administrator of Chandigarh. The Administrator of Dadra and Nagar Haveli is concurrently the Administrator of Daman and Diu. Lakshadweep has a separate Administrator.

LOCAL GOVERNMENT

Municipal bodies have a long history in India. The first such Municipal Corporation was set up in the former Presidency Town of Madras in 1688 and was followed by similar corporations in Bombay and Calcutta in the year 1726. The Constitution of India has made detailed provisions for ensuring protection of democracy in Parliament and in the State legislatures. However, Constitution did not make the local self-government in urban areas a clear cut Constitutional obligation. While the Directive Principles of State Policy refer to village Panchayats, there is no specific reference to municipalities except the implicity in Entry-5 of the State List, which places the subject of local self-government as a responsibility of the States.

CONSTITUTIONAL STATUS OF URBAN LOCAL GOVERNMENTS

In order to provide for a common framework for urban local bodies and help to strengthen the functioning of the bodies as effective democratic units of self-government, Parliament enacted the Constitution (7th Amendment) Act, 1992 relating to municipalities in its winter session of 1992. The Act. ... received the assent of the President on 20.4.93. The Govt. of India notified June 1, 1993 as the date from which the Act came into force.

REGISTRATION OF POLITICAL PARTIES

A new part (Part IV A) has been added to the Representation of the People (Amendment) Act, 1951 on registration of political parties. Section 29A now inserted provides for registration with the Commission, of associations and bodies of individual citizens of India as political parties for purposes of this Act. Every application for registration is required to be made (a) if the association or body is in existence at commencement of the Representation of the People (Amendment) Act, 1988 within sixty days following such commencement and (b) if the association or body is formed after such commencement, within thirty days following its formation.

This provision came into force from 15 June 1989. A recognised political party has been classified either as a national party or a State party under paragraph 7 of the Election Symbols (Reservation and Allotment) Order, 1968. If a political party is recognised in four or more States, it is deemed to be a 'national party' and a political party is recognised in four or more States, it is deemed to be a 'national party' and a political party recognised in less than four States, is a 'state party' in state or states in which it is recognised as such. This is a new thing and a major development.

ELECTORAL REFORMS

LOWERING OF VOTING AGE

The Constitution (Sixty-first Amendment) Act, 1988 amends Article 326 by substituting the words 'eighteen years' for 'twenty one years'. This came into force on 28 March 1989. Consequent to this, amendments were also made in the Representation of the People Act, 1950 and the Representation of the People Act, 1951.

The Representation of the People Act, 1951, was amended to facilitate use of electronic voting machines in elections.

Issuing of Photo Identity Cards to the voters throughout the country is in progress. This is likely to be completed soon.

These are the major changes made in the Acts and procedures.

In regard to the reorganisation of the States another major step was taken when Punjab was divided and Haryana became a separate State. The State of Himachal Pradesh was created in 1966.

A problem has arisen about holding simultaneous elections for the Assemblies and the Lok Sabha. But the political uncertainty has created a situation in which the earlier expectation of our Constitution makers to hold elections together did not materialise.

ORDINANCE ON POLL PROCESS

In the wake of an increasing number of independent candidates becoming targets of violence calculated to countermand elections, the Government has issued an Ordinance in January 1922 to amend the Representation of the People Act (RPA), 1951 so that elections are not countermanded in the event of the death of an independent candidate.

GENERAL ELECTIONS

The first general election in India on the basis of adult suffrage was held in 1951-52. This was a simultaneous election both for the

Lok Sabha and all State legislative assemblies (including Part A, B and C States). Second general election held in 1957, shortly after reorganisation of States, was also a simultaneous election. In third general elections in 1962, elections to State assemblies of Kerala and Orissa became out of step with general election with the result that simultaneous elections could not be held in Nagaland and Pondicherry along with fourth general election to the Lok Sabha. After 1967, elections to most of the assemblies had to be held earlier than normally due with the result that Orissa, Tamilnadu and West Bengal had simultaneous elections to the Lok Sabha and State assemblies at fifth general election held in 1971. In 1977, Kerala was the only state where election to legislative assembly was held simultaneously with sixth general election. When seventh general election was held in January 1980, elections to constitute new assemblies were held simultaneously only in Manipur, Arunachal Pradesh, Goa, Daman and Diu and Pondicherry. Polling for Eighth Lok Sabha election was held on 24, 27 and 28 December 1984 in 20 states and nine Union territories except Assam and Punjab. Election for assemblies of Tamilnadu, Manipur, Arunachal Pradesh and Goa, Daman and Diu were also held simultaneously.

In Assam, the Commission in fulfillment of an assurance given to Supreme Court, initiated action to undertake intensive revision of electoral rolls of all assembly constituencies which could not be completed before commencement of the process of general election in the rest of the country.

On the basis of report received from Punjab government and also Chief Electoral Officer regarding prevailing law and order situation, the Commission was satisfied that election in Punjab could not be held along with rest of the country. For this the Representation of the People Act, 1951 was amended and a new Section 73A was inserted by an Ordinance issued on 20 November 1984. The Ordinance was replaced by an Act of Parliament. Except Jammu and Kashmir, Madhya Pradesh, Maharashtra and Uttar Pradesh, all other States and Union territories had one day poll.

India is one of the oldest civilisations with rich cultural heritage. It has achieved multifaceted socio-economic progress during the last 50 years of its Independence. India has become self-sufficient in agricultural production and is now the tenth industrialised country in the world and the sixth nation to have gone into outer space to conquer nature for the benefit of the people. It covers an area of 32,87, 263 sq. km, extending from the snow-covered Himalayan heights to tropical rain forests of the South. As seventh largest country in the world, India is well-marked off from the rest of Asia by mountains and the sea, which give the country a distinct geographical entity. Bounded by the Great Himalayas in the North, it stretches southwards and at the Tropic of Cancer, tapers off into the Indian Ocean between the Bay of Bengal on the East and the Arabian Sea on the West.

Countries having common border with India are Afghanistan and Pakistan to North-west, China, Bhutan and Nepal to North, Myanmar to East and Bangladesh to East of West Bengal. Sri Lanka is separated from India by a narrow channel of sea formed by the Palk Strait and the Gulf of Mannar.

The mainland comprises four regions, namely, the great mountain zone, plains of the Ganga and the Indus, the desert region and the Southern Peninsula.

The plains of the Ganga and the Indus, about 2400 km long and 240 to 320 km broad, are formed by basins of three distinct river systems—the Indus, the Ganga and the Brahmaputra. They are one of the world's greatest stretches of flat alluvium and also one of the most densely populated areas on the earth. Between the Yamuna at Delhi and the Bay of Bengal, nearly 1600 km away, there is a drop of only 200 metres is elevation.

The desert region can be divided into two parts-the great desert and the little desert. The great desert extends from the edge of the Rann of Kutch beyond the Luni river northward. The whole of Rajasthan-Sind Frontier runs through this. The little desert extends from the Luni between Jaisalmer and Jodhpur up to northern wastes. Between the great and the little deserts lies a zone of absolutely sterile country, consisting of rocky land cut-up by limestone ridges.

The Peninsular Plateau is marked off from the plains of the Ganga and the Indus by a mass of mountain and hill ranges varying from 460 to 1220 metres in height. Prominent among these are the Aravalli,

Vindhya, Satpura, Maikàla and Ajanta. The Peninsula is flanked on one side by the Eastern Ghats where average elevation is about 610 metres and on the other by the Western Ghats where it is generally from 915 to 1220 metres, rising in places to over 2440 metres. Between the Western Ghats and the Arabian Sea lies a narrow coastal strip, while between the Eastern Ghats and the Bay of Bengal there is a broader coastal area. The Southern point of plateau is formed by the Nilgiri Hills where the Eastern and the Western Ghats meet. The Cardamom Hills lying beyond may be regarded as a continuation of the Western Ghats.

When we started after Independence, we had very few Ministries and also not very large staff. These were all located in North Block and South Block buildings of the Central Secretariat. But later, as work expanded the Ministries started growing and many new multi-storeyed buildings were constructed South of Raisina Hills on the North and South of Rajpath. Today we have in the Central Government, 35 Ministries, five departments plus Cabinet Secretariat, President's Secretariat, Prime Minister's Office and the Planning Commission which is located at the Yojana Bhavan.

The All India Services have also multiplied. In 1963, the All India Services Act was amended for the constitution of three more Services viz. Indian Service of Engineers (Irrigation, Power, Buildings and Roads), Indian Forest Service and Indian Medical and Health Service and All India Service of Engineers has not yet been constituted. There is also an Indian Foreign Service for which recruitment takes place along with the Indian Administrative Services.

But today, All India Services are facing shortage of high calibre personnel. Large number of our young men and women are lured to technical and management posts in private companies which offer much higher wages and perquisites than government can offer. Not only the All India Services, but also the Armed Forces are not able to recruit the best of men to serve as officers and at technical or command level. This is causing great worry. The Government, therefore, has to advise urgent methods and improve terms of service for the new recruits. The Indian concept of service to the nation, prestige of joining the Armed Forces or the All India Services has gone with the wind. Even patriotism seems to have lost its meaning. This is the net result of scandals that we hear in the Government. Should the youth rot in Government service and be ordered about by corrupt politicians. Today the market has become important in which unaccounted money is the sole criteria of functioning. Values have changed and service before self is no longer the motto. Even the pride of nationhood has become sub-servient to the market philosophy. Political secularism has replaced nationalism. This is a highly lamentable situation which has befallen upon the nation during the past five decades.

India, the world's largest democracy, symbolises the struggle of ancient people to achieve their due place in the new economic order that has overtaken the world. There is a need to repair the damage done to our psyche; Despite our shortcomings we continue to be as a model in the world both in the practice of democracy and in our efforts to achieve economic cmancipation of our people. In science and technology, we are the third largest country in the world. Still we seem to be loosing the game and a new hope generated. Only this situation can be repaired if politicians in general and political leaders in particular change themselves and accept political reforms as a matte of national necessity. The world is watching us. Our own people are looking for a better deal. India is in the threshold of taking off politically and economically. Shall we deny ourselves the benefit of such a take off ?. Our future generations will not forgive us if we fail them again.

LIFE SKETCHES OF NATIONAL LEADERS

Part – I

1. Mahatma Gandhi
2. Vinoba Bhave
3. Jaiprakash Narayan
4. Netaji Subhash Chander Bose
5. Dr. Syama Prasad Mookerjee
6. Dr. Sachchidanand Sinha
7. C. Rajagopalachari

Part – II

1. Dr. Rajendra Prasad
2. Pt. Jawaharlal Nehru
3. Sardar Patel
4. Maulana Azad
5. Lal Bahadur Shastri
6. Govind Ballabh Pant
7. Morarji Desai
8. Indira Gandhi
9. Rajiv Gandhi
10. B. R. Ambedkar
11. Gulzarilal Nanda

Part – I

Mahatma Gandhi

(2 Oct. 1869—30 Jan. 1948)

Mohandas Karamchand Gandhi was born in 1869 in the State of Gujarat in Western India a State which has looked across the waters of the Arabian Sea to West Asia, and to the European world beyond, since time immemorial. The Gandhi family was a family of status; the future Mahatma's father pursued the liberal vocation of civil service in a small principality.

While the epicentres of political and economic activity in colonial India, the port-cities of Bombay, Madras and Calcutta, witnessed to the full the impact of colonial rule, the remote town of Probandar and Rajkot in Gujarat, where the young Gandhi grew up, were largely indigenous in content and texture. The cultural impact of the West was even more marginal. Indeed, the emotional and intellectual consciouness of young Gandhi, the notion of the sacred and the profane in his being, was largely shaped by the saints of devotional Hinduism.

Values of devotional Hinduism were manifest directly in the Gandhi household through the intense religiosity of his mother, Putllibai. This created in the psyche of young Gandhi a sensitivity to matters of the spirit—indeed, a quality of existential immersion in religious concerns—which later blossomed into a powerful force behind the adult Gandhi's intervention in social, political and economic affairs.

Jainism profoundly influenced Gandhi in his career as he led various movements in South Africa and in India. Gandhi's journey as a young student to the great metropolis of London to pursue studies in law, brought him into the very heart of world culture. The initial shock experienced by the young Gujarati in London was formidable. But he was soon at ease in his new surroundings, combining the study of law with a widening of the mind through the exploration of Western culture. The influences of his childhood interacted with the new situation and enriched his intellectual and philosophical experience. Apart from the classics of Hindu and Buddhist literature, he also read some of the seminal Christian texts. Further, the social and economic consequences of industrialization made a tremendous impression on his sensitive mind; and probably played a vital role in shaping his attitude towards industrial societies as a whole. After completing his studies, Gandhiji returned to Gujarat, still committed to the notion of making his mark in life as a lawyer.

Soon after coming to India, legal business took Gandhiji to Pretoria in 1893. The gross inequality to which coloured and black residents were subjected in South Africa touched Gandhiji and apart from attending to legal business, he entered public life to combat racial discrimination.

The racial conflict in South Africa, in the last decade of the 19th century, exercised a profound influence upon Gandhiji. He launched an epic struggle against racial discrimination and political subjugation in Africa and Asia. Gandhiji later observed : "Here it was that the religious force within me became a living force. I had gone to South Africa.... for gaining my own livelihood. But ..... I founded myself in search of God and striving for self-realization."

Gandhiji has said about himself that :

"The politician in me has never dominated a single decision on mine, and if I seem to take part in politics, it is only because politics encircles us today like the coils of a snake from which one cannot get out, no matter how much one tries. I wish therefore to wrestle with the snake... Quite selfishly, as I wish to live in peace in the midst of a bellowing storm howling around, I have been experimenting with myself and my friends by introducing religion into politics. Let me explain what I mean by religion. It is not the Hindu religion... but the religion... which binds on indissolubly to the truth within and which even purifies."

In 1906, the Government of Transval enacted legislation which required Indians to register themselves as residents, thus denying to them their natural rights as citizens of the British empire. To protest against this "Black Act", Gandhiji organized a meeting in Johanesburg. The Mahatma had contemplated the adoption of a resolution encouraging Indians in South Africa to resist discriminatory legislation. However, what was designed as conventional protest against unjust law, acquired a unique significance when a participant declared "in the name of God that he would never submit to that law and advised all present to do likewise."

He developed *satyagraha* as a weapon for fighting untruth and oppression in the world. As spelt out over time Gandhi, there were distinctive features to the moral code of the true *satyagrahi*. He said times without number, "I have no hatred for the British, no hatred for anyone; what we want to change is the system." Most important of all, he believed that no truthful contest ever yielded a victor and a vanquished; instead, the reconciliation which followed *satyagraha* brought the former adversaries together in a firm bond of friendship underpinned by their spiritual upliftment.

The potency of *satygraha*, the novel instrument of political protest devised by Gandhiji, was reflected in the substantial gain which he was able to secure for the Indian community in South Africa before he left for India in 1914. General J. C. Smuts, who negotiated a settlement with Gandhiji was, therefore, delighted when he learnt of the Mahatma's departure for his homeland. When President Nelson Mandela visited Delhi in 1990, he referred to the Gandhian legacy in South Africa. "We have since been influenced by Gandhi's perception and tradition of non-violent struggle," he observed.

Gandhiji returned to India in 1914, after an interval of two decades, he noticed enormous changes in the political scene. By the second decade of the 20th century, the middle classes in the subcontinent were fully drawn into a nationalist stance, ideologically and organisationally. Within few years, he discovered that the peasents, aristans and workers saw the overthrow of British rule as an essential requirement of their material and spiritual welfare. Since it was difficult to reach these classes through the idiom of modern politics, liberal or radical, Gandhiji took recourse to popular religious imagery as a potent means to rally the poor to the cause of nationalism and at the same time to heighten the level of their social consciousness.

When World War - I came to an end, in which the people of India had extended substantial support to Great Britain, Gandhiji embarked upon a movement of *satyagraha* involving India as a whole. Indeed, in a span of three decades, Gandhi initiated a number of nationwide protests with two strategic purposes in view : first, to knit together the different social, linguistic and religious communities within India into modern nationalhood; and secondly, to demonstrate to the British that their empire over South Asia would have to be dismantled at the earliest.

The nationwide *satyagraha* campaigns waged by Gandhiji within India rank among the biggest popular mobilization in the history of mankind. The concept of *satyagraha* caught like fire that engulfed the whole country. The *Dandi March* of 1930 was directed against a tax on salt, which affected adversely even the poorest peasant household in India. To signify his disapproval of the tax on salt, Gandhiji selected a small band of devoted followers, 79 in all, representing different sections of Indian society. The Mahatama and his *satyagrahis* marched from Ahmedabad, in Western India, to a village called Dandi, on the Arabian Sea. By traversing 241 miles in measured marches over the period of a few weeks, Gandhiji and his gallant band of *satyagrahis* united a nation of 400 million against the British empire.

As a student of law in London, Gandhiji explored industrialization in Great Britain intensively and set out his understanding of this phenomenon in a work called "Hind Swaraj". The Mahatma's quarrel was not with industrialisation as such. But with situations which reduce human beings the helpless instruments of technology in the name of development. This de-humanisation was anathema to Gandhiji, whether it emanated in he Capitalist system or the Communist system. He advocated trusteeship principle, namely that those who possess wealth must do so as trustees of the poor. The basic question was about the concentration of wealth.

He advocated middle path as the most desirable of all paths. In the years since 1947, in India the notion of the middle path was one of the central principles behind official policies—particularly policies of economic growth. Very recently, the notion of the 'middle path' has been reiterated in respect of initiatives connected with economic growth.

Mahatma Gandhi made a distinctive innovation of morally oriented political action in the 20th century. He, however, died a death which made him immortal on January 30, 1948.

Vinayak Narahari Bhave

(Pawnar, Wardha - 11 September 1895—15 Nov. 1982)

Vinayak Narahari Bhave, commonly known as Vinoba, was born at Gagoda, Pen taluka, Kolaba district, Maharashtra, on 11 September 1895. The Bhaves had lived there for several decades. His father's name was Narahari Shambhurao and mother's, Rukminibai. Vinoba was very fond of his mother and she of him. Vinoba inherited her austerity, asceticism and altruism. His father, inventive and generous, was a painter, a musician, a textile expert and an ardent advocate of Western learning and science. He wanted his son to go to England to prosecute mathematical and scientific pursuits, but it never materialised. Vinoba was the eldest of five children, four brothers and a sister.

Educated at Baroda in the Government High School, Vinoba was a brilliant student and maintained high rank in his class till the 6th standard. But he soon lost interest in conventional studies. He passed the Matriculation examination in 1913 and was due to appear for the intermediate examination in 1916 for which he had to go to Bombay. Instead of going to Bombay, he detrained at Surat and Proceeded to Banaras, where he studied Sanskrit and became proficient in all Hindu scriptural books. He is a self-taught multilinguist. French was his second language, but he also learnt Arabic, Persian and Urdu as well as most Indian languages.

After Gandhijis return from South Africa early in 1915, Vinoba recognised in him the kindred most of spirits and requested him to adopt himself as his spiritual son in 1916. Before this time, Vinoba had entertained the aspiration of killing at least one Englishman and crowning his career. "But Bapu cured me of that desire. It is he who has extinguished the volcano of anger and passion which was ever alive in me.'' In 1921, Jamnalal Bajaj requested Gandhiji to give him his best and most trusted lieutenant at Sabarmati Ashram to be sent to Wardha to start a similar Ashram there. Gandhiji sent Vinoba. Jamnalal placed his whole family under his charge. Speaking about Vinoba, Gandhiji said : ''He is one of the Ashram's rare pearls – one of those who have come not to be blessed but to bless, not to receive but to give''.

Before Vinoba came into contact with Gandhiji, the perusal of the 'Dasabodh' of Swami Ramdas and Tilak's writings in the *Kesari*, had made him dedicate himself to the service of the country. He began to expound the Gita at Sabarmati and continues to do so till today. In Dhulia Jail, he gave discourses on the Gita which have been recorded originally in Marathi and published in all Indian langauages and English. About the Gita, Vinoba says: ''In all my actions, Gita has been my guide.''

Vinoba lived in accordance with the eleven vows, included in the Gandhian daily prayer, viz. non-violence, truthfulness, absolute honesty, chastity, poverty, manual work, temperance, fearlessness, respect for all religions, independence in the matter of money and non-recognition of caste distinctions. At the Ashram, he took up scavenging work and has ''no trace of untouchability left in his heart''. One day he consigned to the flames his sacred thread, the outward emblem of superiority as a (Chitpavan) Brahmin In his Bhoodan campaign, Harijans have a special consideration. As most of them are landless, he has decided to distribute one-third of his land gains among Harijans His aim is to make universal brotherhood a living reality for the rich and the poor alike. Vinoba was in favour of linguistic provinces, but he does not support religinalism. His entire life's work is a monument to his love of India. He holds that there should bc no violence over the language issue.

He was on the moving spirits of the Nagpur Flag Satyagraha, his companions being Jamnalal Bajaj, Bhagwan Deen and Nilkanthrao Deshmukh. Vinoba was jailed. In 1924, Gandhiji sent Vinoba to Guruvayur (Kerala) to participate in the Harijan Temple Entry Satyagraha, He participated in the famous Dandi march for Salt

Satyagraha in 1930, for which he was again sent to prison. Gandhiji opposed India's committal in the Second World War without his consent. Vinoba was then chosen to be the first satyagrahi. He was imprisoned and released only after the cessation of hostilities. In prison he dedicated his 'Maxims of Independence'.

Vinoba was opposed to Western education. His service in the cause of Gadhian education called basic education, has been lauded by Gandhiji : Vinoba had produced a text-book taking spinning as the handicraft. He made scoffers realise that spinning is a handicraft par excellence which lends itself to being effectively used for basic education. He revolutionalised *takli* spinning and draw out its hitherto unknown possibilities. For perfect spinning he had no rival in India. The Sevagram School was the first experimental base for Gandhiji's educational ideas and Vinoba executed them in practice.

Vinoba wanted each village to be self-sufficient in food and clothing. Under his programme no exports of either of these primary necessities was permissible until local requirements have been met. He did not favour the growing of cash crops, because reliance on them stimulated greed, destroying the farmer's sense of community substituting no social values in their place. After political freedom was attained, he said : "We have to work for the establishment of equality. I have called that Sarvodaya. It is for the establishment of this that I am going from village to village. I call this my five-year plan. If all of you take up this work for the next five years and during that time succeed in transferring five crores of acres of land, then a great non-violent revolution would have taken place in India." He started Bhoodan movement from Kerala and went to Bihar in 1951. Later, he returned to Wardha Ashram where Mrs Indira Gandhi met him. He took to *Maunvrata* and died on 15 November 1982.

Jai Prakash Narain

(11 Oct, 1902—8 Oct., 1979)

Jai Parkash Narain was born on 11 October 1902 in Sitab Diyara in the District of Saran in Bihar. Son of Hansu Dayal, a Government servant in the Revenue Department, and grandson of Devakinandan Lal, a Sub-Inspector of Police who made a name by beating his English Officer, Jai Prakash claimed his descent from a respectable Kayastha middle-class family of Bihar of long-standing. By marriage also he was connected with a respectable family. His father-in-law, Brajkishore Prasad, was an old nationalist leader of Bihar. His mother Phulo Rani was a simple religious-minded woman and she had cast a deep imprint on young Jai Prakash's mind

Having completed his primary education in his native village, Jai Prakash was admitted to Class VII of the Patna Collegiate School. On the results of his Matriculation examination he was awarded a scholarship. But while in the I.Sc. class, the call of no-cooperation movement moved him to give up his studies in the Patna University. He then came to the Bihar Vidyapith and from there he took his I.Sc. He continued his Science studies under the guidance of Professor Phuldeo Sahay Verma of the Banares Hindu University. In May 1922 he obtained a scholarship from an association in Calcutta and went to the United States. There he stayed for eight years and studied at Iowa, Chicago, Wisconsin, California and Ohio Universities. From Ohio he did his M.A. and had a brilliant academic record. While in the States he had to live a hard life and earn his own lifelihood.

On his return from the States in 1929 he worked to join the Banaras Hindu University as a Professor of Sociology. But the Lahore Session of the Indian National Congress and the speeches of

Nehru there influenced him so much that he accepted Nehru's offer to take charge of the Labour portfolio of the Congress.

After his return to India Jai Prakash also came in touch with Gandhiji. The failure of the Gandhi-Irwin talks led to the civil disobedience movement and he was happy to join it. At this time he was surprised to find the Indian Communists denouncing the national movement as bourgeois. He was arrested shortly after and put in the Nasik jail. Here he met Achyut Patwardhan and Minoo Masani, which reinforced his socialist learnings. Later, alongwith Acharya Narendra Deva, he organised the All India Congress Socialist Party, and in support of his cause he wrote in 1936 'Why Socialism'.

Jai Prakash was a vehement critic of the British rule in India. He regarded it as a folly to think that the British had united India. On the contrary he believed that the British had divided the different communities and interests. It was to him 'unity of a dictatorial regime and not a people's or a national unity'. He argued that the British domination could not impart to the Indian people a training in self-government. Had it been the British motto to establish self-government in India right from 1861 why could not the literacy rate be raised beyond ten per cent or why were not the economic resources taped to raise it above that figure ? Even if India had made some progress, it was due to the long and protracted struggle on her part in the teeth of bitter opposition from the British.

Although a great critic of the British rule, Jai Prakash believed in non-violence. However, during the Quit India Movement he supported violent measures against British atrocities. He criticised the War aims of British as imperialistic. He praised Netaji Subash but believed that his venture would not bear fruit.

In the domain of socio-economic reforms Jai Prakash's socialistic zeal prompted him to advocate the abolition of zamindari, nationalisation of natural resources, peasant proprietorship of land, nationalisation of heavy and basic industries and such other measures. He also strongly championed the cause of rural uplift. He believed that a nation, to be united and to remain strong, must bring the remotest village into a common political, economic and cultural life. There mere development of cottage industries to solve the problem of unemployment would not suffice and lead to national prosperity. Jai Prakash was for industrialisation but that industrialisation, he held, should proceed under State control.

He was a great freedom fighter and social reformer though he did not allow his mental powers to be confined merely to these.

He wrote a number of books and booklets which concerned various aspects of Indian life and problems—political as well as economic and social. Chiefly known as among his works are : 'Why Socialism' (Banares, 1936), 'Towards Struggle' (Bombay, 1946), 'In the Lahore Fort' (Patna 1970), 'A Plea for the Reconstruction of Indian Policy' (Varanasi, 1959), 'From Socialism to Sarvodaya' (Wardha, 1959) and 'Swaraj for the People' (Varanasi, 1961).

Jai Prakash later left active Politics and joined the Bhoodan Movement of Sant Vinoba Bhave. The nationalistic career of Jai Prakash is a brilliant record of great deeds and great sacrifices to the cause of Indian freedom. He also fought authoritarian regime of Mrs. Indira Gandhi during Emergency that brought about the Janta Government at the Centre. Vinoba did not like his joining political movement. He later fell ill and was jailed during Emergency. He was kept in Chandigarh and later shifted to Bombay for treatment. He died in Patna on October 8, 1979.

Subhas Chandra Bose

The history India's freedom struggle is replete with selfless sacrifice of many a stalwart. These illustrious sons and daughters fought the mighty British Empire. One such illustrious son of Mother India was Subhas Chandra Bose who was endowed with tremendous revolutionary zeal. He effectively took the Indian freedom movement beyond the frontiers of India that not only shook the foundation of the mighty British Empire but also left an indelible mark on the nation and its people.

His magnificent and inspiring words 'Jai Hind', which echo in every one's ears and the hearing of which indeed ignites patriotic instincts in every citizen's heart, have truly become the national rallying call.

Netaji Subhas Chandra Bose was born on 23 January 1897 at Cuttack in Orissa. His father Jankinath was an advocate, who later became the first non-official Chairman of Cuttack Municipality in 1901 and a Government Pleader and Public Prosecutor. In 1912, he was nominated as a Member of the Bengal Legislative Council and was awarded the title of 'Rai Bahadur'. Later, he gave up the title of Rai Bahadur protesting against the repressive policy of the Government. Subhas's mother Parbhavati belonged to the traditional Dutt family of Hath khola in North Calcutta. Both she and her husband put up with the great fortitude all the sufferings and sacrifices their two sons Sarat and Subhas had to undergo in the cause of country's freedom.

In 1913, he passed the High School examination by standing second in the Calcutta University and thereafter, joined the Presidency college in Calcutta.

At the age of 22 he passed the B.A. examination with first class Honours, securing second rank in the University of Calcutta.

On 15 September 1919, he sailed for England. Though he reached slightly late, he was, however, able to join the Cambridge University and ultimately appeared in the ICS Examination in July 1920. When the results were announced, he was placed in the fourth rank. Bose, however, was not very happy, destined as was to do something 'great' in his life. His success in the Civil Service Examination brought him face to face with the greatest crisis in his life. He carried on a long correspondence with his second elder brother Sarat Chandra poured out his heart to him and sought his counsel. After he had decided to resign from the Service, he wrote to Deshbandhu Chittaranjan Das offering his services for the national cause.

What caused him deep concern was that his decision to resign would, in all probability, hurt his ageing and ailing parents. He depended on his brother Sarat to convince his parents that the interest of the country demanded that their son come forward with this little offering of sacrifice at the alter of India's freedom and that the sacrifice had to be made consciously and deliberately.

On the 22nd April 1921, Subhas Chandra Bose wrote from Cambridge to the Secretary of State for India, E.S. Montague, withdrawing his name from the list of probationers in the Indian Civil Service selected in an open competitive examination in August 1920.

Subhas's resignation from the Indian Civil Service created a sensation among the Indian community in England. The news also travelled fast to India and the subject became one of excited discussion throughout the country. Subhas himself wanted to avoid both sensation and public applause—evidently he wanted it to be a quiet act of self negation. Even to his brother Sarat he wrote: "You have said too many kind words about me in your letter which I know little I deserve.... all that I say is—I am proud of you." However, he added:

He felt greatly comforted when he finally received a letter from his mother in which she said that in spite of what others might think, "she prefers the ideals for which Mahatma Gandhi stands."

In 1921, after passing the Mental and Moral Science Tripes examination from Cambridge, Subhas Chandra Bose hurried back to

India to take plunge into the national struggle. He landed in Bombay on 16th July 1921 and the same afternoon met Mahatma Gandhi. The first thing that Subhas did on meeting Gandhiji was to apologise for his foreign costume. The Mahatma, however, put him at ease and an interesting conversation followed. Subhas's desire was to understand the successive stages of the struggle that the leader had planned which would, step by step, lead the country to capture power from the unwilling hands of the British Government.

Disappointed, however, with his first meeting with the Mahatma, he left for Calcutta with the intention of reporting to Desbandhu Chittranjan Das as early as possible. He offered his personal services to Deshbandhu in three fields; first, teaching at National College started by Deshbandhu; second, journalism—particularly for the English edition of his newspaper 'swaraj'; and third, research for the Congress organisation. Finally, he wrote to Deshbandhu that the Congress must have a determined policy as to the future Constitution of India. He, therefore, emphasised that they must proceed to frame the new Constitution of India on the basis of Swaraj. Deshbandhu welcomed his new youthful lieutenant with open arms, and entrusted him with a number of responsibilities. The country was then convulsing with patriotic fervour.

There was the 'triple boycott'—Congressmen shunned the legislatures, lawyers left the law courts and students came out of educational institutions to take part in the national movement. Deshbandhu put Subhas in charge of publicity for the Bengal Provincial Congress Committee and the National Volunteer Corps.

The British Government sought to prepare the ground for the inauguration of constitutional reforms recommended in 1919 by the Secretary of State for India, Montague and the Viceroy Chelmsford and later embodied them in an Act. A visit to India of the Prince of Wales was announced for November 1921. The Congress called upon the people to observe a total "hartal" on the day the prince's landing was scheduled to take place in Bombay. Like other Indian cities, Calcutta too rose to the occasion and it looked as if Congress volunteers under Subhas Chandra Bose had taken charge of the city. In the second week of December 1921, Subhas Chandra was taken into custody alongwith Deshbandhu and other leaders and later sentenced to six months' imprisonment. Eight months inprison together with Deshbandhu Chittaranjan Das was, for Subhas, one of the most moving and educative experience of his life.

On account of his close association with Deshbandhu, he had the opportunity of coming into contact with some of the outstanding leaders like Motilal Nehru, Lala Lajpat Rai and Maulana Mohmmad Ali.

In 1922, following the Chauri Chaura incident Gandhiji suspended the Civil Disobedience Movement. Subhas at that time was undergoing imprisonment alongwith Deshbandhu. On receipt of the news of termination of the campaign, they were overwhelmed with sorrow and resentment. Congressmen were bewildered at the sudden retreat and the general mood changed from one of the buoyant optimism to depression. Lord Reading, the Viceroy, took advantage of the situation and went on the offensive. Mahatma Gandhi was arrested and sentenced to a long term of imprisonment on charges of sedition. Deshbandhu took the suspension of the mass movement as a *fait accompli* and while in prison, devoted himself to devising a new plan of non-cooperation and struggle inside the legislatures with a view to capturing all points of vantage in a revolutionary struggle. The Congress Working Committee appointed an Enquiry Committee on Civil Disobedience and members were equally divided between those in favour of Deshbandhu's plan and those supporting 'no changers' plan to keep out of legislatures. Subhas obviously stood by his leader.

In September 1922, there were devasting floods in the Northern districts of Bengal. The relief operations directed by Subhas were so successful that they added greatly to the prestige of the Congress while government efforts were niggardly and half-hearted.

In the latter half of 1922, there took place two important political events which were of far-reaching significance for Subhas. The first was the session of the All India Trade Union Congress in Lahore at which Deshbandhu presided. It was at this conference Deshbandhu declared in no uncertain terms, that the Swaraj that they were striving to win, was for the masses who constituted ninety eight per cent of the population. Subhas was thus initiated into the trade union movement of India which resulted in his becoming the President of All India Trade Union Congress in 1931. He also became the President of the Labour Association of the Tata Iron and Steel Company of Jamshedpur. The second event was the holding of the young Men's Conference in Calcutta which became the precursor of the new youth movement in Bengal of which Subhas Chandra Bose emerged soon thereafter as the undisputed and chrismatic leader.

The year 1924 opened with a hopeful outlook for the Swarajists. Elections to the Calcutta Municipal Corporation were held and the Swaraj Party won a comfortable majority both from Hindu and Muslim seats. Deshbandhu was elected the first Mayor of Calcutta and Shaheed Suhrawardy as the Deputy Mayor. Subhas Chandra was appointed the Chief Executive Officer—that is the head of the municipal administration.

The capture of the Calcutta Corporation by the Swarajists, with Deshbandhu as Mayor and Subhas as Chief Executive Officer, marked the beginning of new era in civic progress in India. Deshbandhu's mayoral address was in the nature of a charter of civic right, civic progress and civic freedom. Subhas Chandra's task was to translate the programme into concrete action. For the first time, Khadi became the official uniform of civil employees and many streets and parks named after the Britishers were renamed after India's greatest men. Free primary schools both for boys and girls were started, free dispensaries opened and children's clinics set up in different parts of Calcutta from where free milk was distributed to needy children. Within a few months Subhas was able to give a new orientation and momentum to the administration of the Corporation. The practice of giving civic reception to British dignitaries was given up and instead the same was given to nationalist leaders when they visited the city. To promote civic consciousness among citizens, a weekly journal, the Calcutta Municipal Gazette, was started. A commercial museum was established with purpose of promoting Indian goods. Subhas Chandra accepted only half of his salary as the Chief executive and gave the other half to charity.

In the middle of 1924, the influence and prestige of the Swaraj Party and its leader Deshbandhu reached new heights. The British

Government could no longer wait and watch as the Swaraj Party went on scoring one success after another. In sheer desperation, they, therefore, decided to strike at the root of the organisation. On 25 October 1924, Subhas Chandra Bose was arrested and sent to Rangoon

The Annual Session of Indian National Congress of 1928 was held in Calcutta under the Presidentship of Pandit Motilal Nehru. The attendance at the session was the largest ever since the inception of the Congress and all arrangements had been made on a colossal scale. At this session, Subhas Chandra Bose emerged as the principal spokesman of the younger and leftist forces in the national movement. He was also the General Officer Commanding of the Congress Volunteer Corps which was raised and trained by him on semi/ military lines. He thus introduced a new element in the national movement viz. military discipline among national workers.

At the end of December 1929, the historic session of the Indian National Congress took place under the Presidentship of Jawaharlal Nehru. Mahatma Gandhi himself came forward to move the resolution on the national demand of complete independence. At the stroke of midnight of the 31st December 1921, Jawaharlal Nehru, the youthful Congress President unfurled the flag of independence on the banks of the Ravi in the presence of a mammoth gathering.

Subhas Chandra Bose went a step further from the position he had taken at the Calcutta Congress. He urged that a positive programme of action be adopted to enforce the national demand. He moved a resolution that the Congress should aim at setting up a parallel government in the country and to that end, should, undertake the task of organising workers, peasant and youths.

In the course of his address to the Lahore Congress, Subhas Chandra Bose said: "Mine is a programme of all-round boycott...If you are not prepared to go in for total boycott, it will be of no use your boycotting Council only... I am an extremist and my principle is—all or none."

At the Lahore Congress Subhas Chandra Bose together with Srinivas Iyenger and others were exclude from the Congress Working Committee. Mahatma Gandhi wanted the supreme body in the party to be a homogenous one so that he could proceed with his plans unchallenged from inside the High Command.

In 1930, Subhas formed a Congress Demorcatic Party to promote his militant programme. But before, however, he could proceed with his plans, he was placed under arrest as soon as he returned to Calcutta from Lahore and sentenced to an year's rigorous imprisonment. While in prison, Subhas was elected Mayor of Calcutta, but he could assume office only after his release later in the year.

On January 26, 1931, Subhas Chandra Bose as Calcutta Mayor, accompanied by senior officers and followed by a large procession, advanced from the Municipal headquarters towards the maidan in defiance of a police ban. As they crossed Esplanade, a strong contingent of mounted police made a ruthless attack on them. Subhas was severely injured and taken into custody. He was released in March 1931.

Because of the Civil Disobedience Movement, British Government, in January 1932, launched its offensive against the Congress and National organisations throughout India. Leaders were arrested *en masse*, including Gandhiji, Jawaharlal Nehru and Subhas Chandra Bose. After his arrest Subhas was lodged in a small jail in Seoni in obscure place on Central Provinces. He was joined soon after by his elder brother Sarat Chandra, a leading lawyer of Calcutta and a front ranking Congressman.

In the sub jail in Seoni the health of Subhas Chandra Bose rapidly deteriorated. He was first shifted to Jabalpur Central Jail. In the enforced absence of Sarat Chandra Bose, his wife Bivabati carried on negotiations on behalf of Subhas with the Government in Delhi to send Subhas to Europe for treatment. On 13th February, 1933, Subhas sailed for Europe on board the Italian ship S.S. Ganga on another forced exile.

In March 1933 Subhas reached Vienna. There he received satisfactory medical treatment. As soon as he felt a little better, he began to take active interest in European politics and establish contacts at every level to further the cause of Indian independence. He found a kind spirit in Vithalbhai Patel who shared his interest in securing international support for Indian nationalist aspirations. He visited many countries in Europe.

Towards the end of 1934, Subhas Chandra received news that his father Janakinath was critically ill. The family desired that he should fly to India to be at his father's bedside. He left for India post-haste but arrived late by a day and a half. His father had passed away and his last longing wish was not fulfilled. As soon as he arrived in Calcutta, he was interned in his house on Elgin Road. He lived there for about a month virtually as a prisoner and returned to Europe early in January 1935 to resume his medical treatment and his work for India.

During his exile in Europe, Subhas Chandra wrote the first and major part of his substantive work—'The Indian Struggle'. The book was published in London in January 1935.

In early 1936, Subhas Chandra felt that he had sufficiently recovered his healt and planned to return home. He was particularly keen to attend the Congress session to be held a few months later in Lucknow under the Presidentship of Jawaharlal Nehru.

As soon as he set foot on India soil in Bombay he was taken into custody and lodged in prison. Sometime later he was transferred to Kurseong, near Darjeeling and detained in his brother Sarat's bunglow there. In March 1937, Subhas was released unconditionally for reasons of healt. He was given a mammoth reception in Calcutta on his release. Towards the end of 1937, he decided to undertake a short trip to Europc, firstly as a health measure and secondly to make a quick on-the-spot survey of the European situation.

In January 1938, when he was in London he came to know about his formal election as Congress President. On his arrival at Congress village of Haripura in February 1938, Subhas Chandra was given a classic reception. He was taken to the session site in a chariot pulled by 51 pairs of white bullocks to the accompaniment of brass bands while thousands of rural folk greeted him all along the route. At the flag hoisting ceremony he said: "There is no power on earth that can keep India enslaved any longer."

By the time Subhas Chandra became President, the Congress Party had accepted office in seven out of eleven provinces of British India. In his presidential address Subhas said that the first task of our ministers should be to change the composition and character of the bureaucracy in order that our policies and principles might be put into practice. Secondly, the Congress ministers must put into through schemes of reconstruction in education, health, irrigation, land reform, industry, workers' welfare, prohibition, prison reforms etc. In this context he said that in his judgement, the Congress Working Committee was not merely the directing brain of the national army of freedom fighters but also the shadow cabinet of independent India. Subhas Chandra laid great emphasis on a plan to oppose the inauguration of the federal scheme as envisaged in that Constitution which was designed to dismember India politically and weaken her economically.

To find a solution for the vexed Hindu-Muslim question Subhas Chandra as Congress President held a series of meetings with M.A. Jinnah, the Muslim League leader, in the latter half of 1938 and also had extensive correspondence with him. But the negotiations broke down on Jinnah's insistence that the league must be recognised as the only authoritative and representative organisation of Indian Muslims.

In 1939, Subhas was re-elected as Congress President, defeating Dr. Pattabhi Sitaramayya who had been backed by Mahatmaji and Congress Working Committee. Soon after the election, the members of the Congress Working Committee resigned, and the Congress met at Tripuri under the shadow of a crisis within the Party as well as internationally. Subhas was a sick man at Tripuri. Even so, with almost prophetic foresight, he warned that an imperialist war would break out in Europe within six months, demanded that the Congress should deliver six months' ultimatium to Britain and in the event of its rejection a country-wide struggle for 'Poorna Swaraj' should be launched, taking full advantage of Britain's entanglement in the international imborglio. His warning and advice, however, went unheeded. He, therefore, resigned his Presidentship in April 1939. In May 1939, he announced the formation of the forward Block within the Congress. In August, Subhas was removed from Presidentship of the Bengal Provincial Congress Committee, and further debarred from holding any elective office in the Congress for a period of three years.

In 1939-40, Subhas Bose felt dissatisfied with the political ideology of the Indian National Congress. He decided to carve out a separate path wherein he could show his talents for the achievement of Swaraj for India. The great hindrance was the repressive policy of the British Raj which had lodged Bose in jail. After his conditional release, he was not allowed to move out of his home and could not meet anybody. A few dozens of CID personnel were posted round about his home at Elgin road, Calcutta. Day by day, his anxiety increased and he wished to leave the country so that he could have a broader base for his political scheme in a foreign land. He sought the secret support from the Kirti Kisan Party and several other devoted patriots like Comrade Ram Kishan and Aachar Singh Cheema. This involved in serious risks but helped Subhas Bose's exist from India.

On January 16-17, 1941, Subhas Bose slipped out of his Elgin Road home in disguise and with an assumed name of Maulvi Ziauddin and reached Delhi in the evening of 18 January, 1941 and boarded the Frontier Mail for Peshawar. At Peshawar, he was pursued by the CID but they could not spot out Bose. He moved from place to place in disguise and had to face unbearable problems before he could cross the Afghan border and entered Kabul. Thereafter, he was in touch with German and other European leaders in order to seek their support for the cause of Swaraj. Ultimately, Subhas Bose landed in Japan and was welcomed by the local government as well as by Rash Behari Bose. The Prime Minister, Hikedi Tojo welcomed him and promised him support in his mission. The main plan was to organise and mobilise the Indian National Army which could generate the spirit of Swaraj and ultimately win complete independence.

July 5, 1943, which Netaji called "produest day of my life", on that day he reviewed for the first time as its Supreme Commander of the Azad Hind Fauj drawn up in battle formation on the spacious grounds facing the Town Hall in Singapore. Addressing his army he said: "...With the force of arms and at the cost of your blood you have to win liberty. Then, when India is free, you will have to organise a permanent army to free India whose task will be to preserve our liberty for all times. We must build up our national defence on such unshakable foundations that never again in our history shall we lose our freedom..."

During the three months that followed, Netaji laboured ceaselessly and toured extensively to rouse the Indain community scattered all over East Asia to a new sense of national identity and patriotism and set up a disciplined organisation with its headquarters in Singapore to take charge of the movement. On 21 October, 1943, he proclaimed the Provisional Government of Azad Hind at a historic assembly in Singapore. The Provisional Government was recognised by nine States including three world powers—Japan, Germany and Italy.

On the 22nd October 1943, Netaji formally inaugurated the Rani of Jhansi Regiment of the Azad Hind Fauj. The fighting unit of India's women warriors was a concrete expression of Netaji's belief in the equality of men and women.

On February 4, 1944, on the Arkan front and on 18 March 1944, the INA crossed the Burma border and for the first time, stood on the soil of India. The liberation forces were unfortunately halted within three miles of Imphal as they lacked air cover. They were unable to go further into Assamese territory and the British forces, under Lord Mountbatten, reinforced by air, were able successfully to stop their march. The torrential rains of Burma, which started just at that time, submerged the INA supply lines. Netaji ordered the retreat of forces. Germany surrendered in 1945 to Allied Forces.

At about this time, the news came through in June 1945 that the British Viceroy of India, Lord Wavell was trying to convince Mahatma Gandhi and the Congress leaders that they should cooperate with British in carrying on the war. In return for the inclusion of more Indians in the Viceroy's Executive Council. On hearing about the offer, Netaji flew from Bangkok to Singapore and spoke on the radio and asked the Congress leaders not to accept the offer made by the Viceroy. He argued that the British offer was meant to divert the attention of the world from the Indian problem and make it merely a domestic issue of the British Empire. He also said that the purpose of the Conservative Government to make this offer was that it hoped by settling the Indian problem, it would be able to win the next general election. His appeal had the effect and the Congress finally rejected the offer made by Lord Wavell.

In the meantime, the United States had dropped atomic bombs on

Hiroshima and Japan surrendered on 11 August. On 17 August 1945 encouraging the morale of INA soldiers Netaji Subhas Chandra Bose said: "Comrades, I feel that in this critical hour, thirty-eight crores of our countrymen at home are looking at us, the members of India's Army of Liberation. Therefore, remain true to India and do not for a moment waver in your faith in India's destiny. The roads to Delhi are many and Delhi still remains our goal. The sacrifices of your immortal comrades and of yourselves will certainly achieve their fulfilment. There is no power on earth that can keep India enslaved. India shall be free and before long."

After the suspension of INA activities, Subhas Chandra Bose went back to Singapore and issued instructions to the civilians and army wings of the Government as to what they should do. The Cabinet Ministers agreed to leave Singapore and move further East. In the meantime, the surrender of Japan was officially announced on 15 August and on 17 August 1945 Netaji took a plane from Saigon. Five days later, on 22 August, Tokyo Radio announced that Subhas Chandra Bose had died in an air crash in Formosa on 18 August, 1945 on his way to Japan.

Syama Prasad Mookerjee

(6 July 1901—23 June 1953)

One of the founding fathers of independent India Dr. Syama Prasad Mookerjee was a great patriot, educationist, Parliamentarian, statesman, humanitarian and above all, a campaigner for national unity and integrity. Born on 6 July 1901 in Calcutta, Syama Prasad inherited a rich tradition of erudite scholarship, fervent nationalism and fearlessness from his father, Sir Ashutosh Mookerjee, who as the Vice Chancellor of the Calcutta University and a Judge of the Calcutta High Court occupied a unique position in the life of Bengal. His mother, Smt. Jogamaya Devi was a dovout Hindu lady, devoted entirely to her husband, family and Dharma. Being an upper class Brahmin family with a high social status, the Mookerjee house in Bhowanipur, Calcutta, was known as much for its 'Poojas' as for its being an abode of Saraswati.

Young Syama Prasad grew in an atmosphere where he could watch poojas, religious ceremonies and rituals and also listen to discussions on the most modern and scientific subjects between his father and great scholars coming from all parts of India and abroad. This, crated in him deep respect for India's age-old culture and close attachment to Western thought and learning. A happy blending of Hindu spirituality, tolerance and humanity with scientific outlook and broad understanding, characterised the life of Syama Prasad throughout, both as an academician and as a Parliamentarian.

At the age of sixteen he passed his matriculation examination from Mitter Institute. He stood first in the University in Inter Arts examination in 1919 and passed BA. examination with honours in English in 1921, securing first class first. In April 1922, when he was doing his M.A. he was married to Sudha Devi, who became mother of his four children before she died in 1934. Syama Prasad at that time a young man of only 33, however, decided not to remarry.

In 1924, he passed his B.L., once again standing first in the University. He also had to his credit the degrees of D.Litt. and LL.D. In 1927, he was called to the English Bar from the Lincolon's Inn (England), which he had joined in 1926. He did not, however, practise law.

The death of his father in 1923, whom he had been assisting in running the Calcutta University from his student days, brought him into the educational field even while he was still a student. He was known to have closest insight into the educational plans and policies of his Vice Chancellor father. He was elected to the University Senate and Syndicate in 1924 and represented the Calcutta University as a Congress candidate in the Bengal Legislative Council.

In 1934, Syama Prasad became the youngest Vice Chancellor of Calcutta University. It was under his Vice Chancellorship that Rabindra Nath Tagore delivered the Convocation address in Bengali which marked the beginning of the end of the era of superiority of English over Bengali and other Indian languages.

The introduction in 1937 of the Provincial part of the Government of India Act, 1935 and the elections to the Provincial Legislatures gave a new twist to the situation in the country. In a House of 250 Members Hindus had been given only 80 seats for which mostly Congressmen were elected. The rest were divided between the Muslims & the British interests. Had the Congress Party formed a coalition with Krishak Praja Party, Bengal could have got a non-Muslim League stable Government.

After the formation of its Ministry in Province the Muslim League decided to strike at the educational structure which his father and he himself had so assidously built. Having failed to persuade the Congress leadership to change its policy of allowing the Muslim League a safe spell of power, he decided to go ahead all alone to topple the Muslim League Ministry. He mustered together all the non-Congress Hindu forces in the Legislature and formed the Progressive Coalition with Krishak Praja Party under the leadership of Fazal-ul-haq with himself as the Finance Minister in the coalition ministry.

During the same period under the influence of Veer Savarkar, he joined the Hindu Mahasabha and made it an instrument for checkmating the anti-national forces. Soom after in 1939 he became its acting President and declared complete independence of India as the political goal of Hindu Mahasabha. His joining the Hindu Mahasabha was welcomed by Mahatma Gandhi who accepted that "somebody was needed to lead the Hindus after Malviyaji." Gandhiji was greatly impressed by the broad and thoroughly nationalistic outlook of Syama Prasad and is understood to have told him that "Patel is a Congressman with a Hindu mind, you be a Hindu Sabhaite with a Congress mind."

In 1943, Syama Prasad resigned from the Bengal Cabinet protesting against the interference of the Governor and the bureaucracy in the ministerial discharge of the affairs of the police and the general administration and characterising the much advertised provincial autonomy as a mere farce.

The Bengal famine of 1943 brought the humanitarian in Syama Prasad to the forefront which the people of Bengal can never forget. It was mainly because of him that the whole country rose like one man in providing relief, thereby saving lakhs of lives from the clutches of sure death.

Later, he was shocked to find when the British Cabinet Mission before which he was arguing against partion, confronted him with the Poona Resolution of the Congress Working Committee which said that the Congress would not coerce any unwilling party to remain in India.

When the demand for Pakistan was conceded it was due to his efforts that half of Punjab and half of Bengal was saved for India. That explains his famous retort: "Congress partitioned India and I partitioned Pakistan."

In August 1947, Syama Prasad was invited by Gandhiji to join the first National Government. He accepted the invitation in the hope that he would be able to influence the policies of free India in its formative period and safeguard the interests of crores of Hindus who had been left back in Pakistan much against their will.

As a Minister for Industry and Supply in the Union Cabinet, he laid the firm foundation of the industrial development of the country by setting up the three most successful and gigantic industrial undertakings, viz. the Chittaranjan Locomotive Factory, the Sindhri Fertiliser Corporation and the Hindustan Aircrafts Factory, Bangalore.

The Nehru-Liaqat pact of 1950 brought the differences between Syama Prasad and Nehru to climax. The original draft of the Nehru-Liaqat Agreement, which committed the Government of India to reservation of seats to Muslims in legislatures and services, was modified to eliminate these provisions on his insistence.

The statement Syama Prasad made in Parliament about his resignation on 19 April, 1950 is a dignified but pathetic document of Indo-Pak relations. The reasons he enumerated as to why the Nehru-Liaqat Pact would not solve any problem, are as valid to day as they were in 1950.

Syama Prasad decided to give shape to a new national leadership in opposition. As a result of his efforts, the All India Bharatiya Jana Sangh was formally launched in October 1950. He was elected to lead the new organisation as its first All India President. He visualised Jana Sangh as the spearhead of the nationalist forces in the country and wanted it to be so broad-based as to be able to comprehend and consolidate all of them into an effective political organisation. It was to be open to all citizens who owned unflinching allegiance to India and her great culture and heritage.

Syama Prasad spent the rest of his life in building up this organisation as an alternative to the party then in power. His dream has materialised in the shape of the Bharatiya Janta Party.

Syama Prasad was returned to the first Lok Sabha in the general elections held in 1952. However, the Jana Sangh, the party that he launched, could return only two more members. But his pre-eminence was recognised by all.

He brought together a number of small parties including the Ganatantra Parishad of Orissa, the Akali Dal of Punjab, the Hindu Mahasabha and a number of independents to form the National Democratic Party in Parliament, of which he was the elected leader.

His constructive and nationalistic attitude together with his enlightened but determined resistance to all anti-national and totalitarian policies and trends, made him the bulwark of freedom and democracy in the country. His role in Parliament as leader of the Opposition earned him the title. "The Lion of Parliament."

The final act in the parliamentary life of this great statesman and Parliamentarian took place in 1953. By this time, his mind was fully engrossed with the problem of Jammu & Kashmir with a view to curbing the then prevalent successionist activities. He decided to take up the cause of Jammu & Kashmir Praja Parishad which had been demanding that the State be fully integrated with the rest of India and should have the same Constitution. During his visit to Jammu in August 1952, he once told a mammoth meeting : "I will get you the Indian Constitution or lay down my life for it." His words proved prophetic. He decided to visit Jammu again in May 1953 to study, on the spot, the situation prevailing there. He was not in good health. His love of Hindus was so great and his passion for keeping the State of Jammu & Kashmir within the Indian Union was so irresistible that he rushed to Jammu where he was arrested. He fell seriously ill in prison and died a martyr's death on 23 June, 1953 to the cause of Indian unity.

The Parliament, the State Legislatures, the Press and the leaders of public opinion irrespective of party affiliations, as also the leaders and rulers of the Buddhist countries of South-East Asia mourned his death as a great loss and paid glowing tributes and homage to his dedicated life devoted entirely to the service of his motherland.

Sachchidananda Sinha

Dr. Sachchidananda Sinha was elected to be the temporary Chairman of the Constituent Assembly. He was the oldest among all the members of the Constituent Assembly and also the oldest Parliamentarian in India, having served, a member of the Imperial Legislative Council from 1910 to 1920. He entered the Central Legislative Assembly in 1921 not only as one of its members but its Deputy President also. He was entrusted with the portfolio of an Executive Councillor and Finance Member of the Government of Bihar and Orissa. So Dr. Sinha was the first Indian who was even appointed as a Finance Member of a Province. He has a particular taste for education having been Vice Chancellor of the Patna University for eight years. Up till 1920 he was a member of the Congress, being at one time its Secretary.

C. Rajagopalachari

(10th Dec. 1879—25 Dec. 1972)

A combination of multi-faceted personality—a patriot, statesman, scholar, thinker and humanist—Chakravarti Rajagopalachari, endearingly called 'Rajaji' was born on 10 December 1879 in Thorappalli village in Salem district of Madras. His father, Chakravarti Iyengar also known as Venkata Arya, was the munsif of Hosur Taluka.

Rajagopalachari had his early education at his village school and later he joined an English school at Hosur Taluka. In 1897, he graduated from the Central Hindu College, Bangalore and joined the Law College at Madras. In 1899, having passed the Bachelor of Law Examination, he started practice at Salem.

In 1905, Lord Curzon gave a blow to nationalism by deciding to partition Bengal which seethed with discontent and to Rajagopalchari and his elite group, the decision to partition Bengal on communal lines came as a bolt from the blue. It was difficult to see the motive behind the move. It became evident that Britain was launching a new drive aimed at dividing the population on communal lines, make the Hindus fight with their Muslim brethren and thus weaken the will of the two communities to fight the aliens. Rajagopalachari was able to see through this move. He kept himself abreast of the developments in Bengal.

Rajagopalachari was influenced by the call of Lokmanya Bal Gangadhar Tilak which exhorted every Indian to fight for complete freedom from British Rule as it was his birth-right. He accepted Tilak as his mentor and kept himself in touch with him.

The opinion in the Congress about the right course of action to be adopted to accelerate the pace of India's liberation was divided. There were moderates in the party, led by Dadabhai Naoroji and Pherozshah Mehta who exhorted the Congresmen to fight, through constitutional means. Tilak on the other hand, advocated a more aggressive policy and a more militant stance. Rajagopalachari found reason in Tilak's plea, determination in his moves. Tilak symbolised the man of action. This facet of Tilak won Rajagopalachari over to the Lokmanya's side. As a delegate from Madras to the Indian National Congress Session at Calcutta in 1906, Rajagopalachari had the opportunity to watch the leaders at work. He heard the perorations of Dadabhai Naoroji. Pherozshah Mehta delivered a fiery speech, pressing for quick reforms which would give a better share in the administration to Indian. Tilak presented a plan, which did not limit the moves of the Congress to purely constitutional methods.

Rajagopalachari remained true to the tenets set down by Tilak. He got an opportunity to take up the cudgels against the Moderates. In 1908, the Congress session was held at Madras. The organisers instructed that only those Congressmen who agreed to give an undertaking in writing that they fully endorsed the policy of the Moderates should be allowed to attend the session. The situation seemed intolerable to Rajagopalachari. After careful deliberation, he drafted the pamphlet, detailing the inconsistency in the stand of the Moderates. He condemned the denial of admission to the session to those nationalists who, due to their convictions, could not give the undertaking. Thousands of copies of the pamphlet were circulated all around the country.

In December 1916, the congress met at Lucknow. The delegates discussed the state of the nation. The concept of Home Rule found wider acceptance. The Congress and the Muslim League agreed on the *modus operandi* for Home Rule. They declared that the Hindus and the Muslims desired freedom for India. Tilak, Besant and Jinnah carved out this agreement.

The Governor of Madras declared that sterm measures would be taken against those who pleaded for Home Rule. Rajagopalachari wrote extensively in the national newspapers condemning the Governor's stand. In June 1917, Rajagopalachari was nominated as the Chairman of Salem Municipality. He saw it as an opportunity to serve the people.

The call for Civil Disobedience movement by Gandhiji was responded to by Rajagopalachari. The government moved in, arrested Rajagopalachari and kept him in prison. He sensed that freedom was round the corner. The signs were there. What was needed was a push forward with vigour.

Shri Ratnasabhapati Gaunder, a Zamindar of Tiruchengode, near district Salem gifted four acres of land to Shri Rajagopalachari for the Ashram which was formally inaugurated in February 1925. Rajagopalachari conceived the idea of having, in the Ashram, a hospital with qualified doctor. Ratnasabhapati Gaunder donated additional land for the construction of this hospital which was inaugurated by Dr. Prafulla Chandra Ray, the then top scientist of Bengal. Rajagopalachari explained to the villagers about the evils of drinking by citing the example of many families which had been ruined by this bad habit. Accompanied by his close associates such as K. Santhanam, P.S. Ramadurai, Kalki Krishnamurti and N.S. Vardachari, he moved into the neighbouring villages carrying the message of rural reconstruction. Rajaji and his followers won the confidence of the people.

Rajagopalachari lived in a small cottage. He enlarged the activities of the Ashram. Bee-keeping became a paying hobby. Manufacturing soaps, using nonedible oils provided work for many. Stress on production of good quality seeds, better manuring and organised cultivation proved beneficial to the farmers.

A Commission under Sir John Simon came to India in 1928 to investigate and to suggest changes, if any, needed in the Indian political system. Such a survey once every ten years, was provided for in the Government of India Act of 1919. The Viceroy Lord Irwin hoped that the political leaders would testify before the Commission. All political parties in India, including the Liberals and Muslim League found the terms and composition of the Commission obnoxious. On 3 February 1928, the Commission arrived at Bombay. Black flags greeted the members of the Commission. Out of thousands of throats emerged the cry, "Go Back, Simon." Wherever it went, the boycott was complete.

On 12 March, 1930 Gandhiji planned to set out on his historic Dandi March. He left Sabarmati for Dandi. Rajagopalachari in Madras Province led the long march to the sea coast to break the Salt Law. He planned the march from Tiruchi to Vedaranyam. On 13 April, 1930, the party, led by Rajagopalachari started from Tiruchi. Rajagopalachari learnt that then District Collector, one Mr Thorne declared that any person who gave help or aid to the marchers would make himself liable to penal action. At this Rajagopalachari commented, "Thorns and thistles cannot stem this tide of freedom".

The party received warm welcome all along the route at Tanjore, Kumbakonam, Thiruthiraipoondi etc. For 16 days, the party headed by Rajagopalachari marched to reach Vedaranam. He and sixteen other volunteers reached the venue. They burnt down and picked up a handful of salt; and were immediately arrested. Rajagopalachari was sentenced to six months imprisonment.

Waves of *Satyagrahis* moved to Vedaranyam. Thousands broke the Salt Law. Thousands were beaten on the fists and palms on which they sported the precious salt. Hundreds were arrested and taken away to prisons. Rajagopalachari was detained at Vellore jail. Rajaji emerged from the Vedaranyam *Satyagraha* as a national hero, taking his place along with the Sardar.

The Government of India Act of 1935 offered more rights to the elected representatives. It proposed a federal government with a large measure of autonomy to the Province. The elections to the provincial legislatures were to be held forthwith. Both Sardar Patel and Rajagopalachari pressed for acceptance of the new provisions. They viewed the entry into the arena of power as a means to work from within for liberations. However, Pandit Madan Mohan Malaviya opposed the plea for acceptance of office by the Congress.

On 14 July 1937, Rajagopalachari assumed the office as the Prime Minister of Madras. The civil service, at the higher level, were manned mostly by Englishmen, who, for the first time, had to take orders from Indians. Rajagopalachari brought about the resurrection of confidence between the permanent service and the elected representatives by his enlightened policy. Rajagopalachari enjoyed the support of the Governor, Lord Erkshine. The Governor was keen to make the experiment a success. He sympathised with the nuetral aspirations of the people and subscribed to the theory that Indians should be prepared for freedom. Rajagopalachari included a Harijan in Cabinet.

The Temple Entry Reforms further brought the Harijans into the mainstream of life. No longer could they be denied access to the temples. Rajagopalachari joined the Harijans when they entered a temple.

The arrival of the Cripps Mission in March 1942 indicated that the efforts to find a compromise between the British stand and the Indian demands would be worked out. The negotiations began. Cripps hinted on his arrival in India of a National Government with a Cabinet and with the Viceroy as titular head. The talks bogged down. The main difference hinged around the induction of an Indian as a War Member with the authority to issue orders to the Commander in Chief. This became the bone of contention. Finally the talks failed.

The Cabinet Mission led by Lord Pethwick Lawrence Secretary of State for India reached Delhi on 23 March 1946. After preliminary talks with the leaders of various groups the Mission called a Conference at Shimla. The Congress and the Muslim League sent four delegates each to the Conference. But nothing could bridge the gap to bring the two parties to a common plan for liberation of India.

In the wake of the Mission's proposal, Lord Wavell, the Viceroy, readied himself for the induction of an interim Cabinet. Rajagopalachari advised the Congress to accept the recommendations of the Mission. He came to Delhi, met the members of the Congress Working Committee, argued that there could perhaps be no better solution to problem than the one now suggested by the Mission. Ultimately, an interim Government was formed in 1946 by Jawaharlal Nehur and Rajagopalachari who joined it.

After Independence, Rajagopalachari was appointed Governor of Bengal. His simplicity, utter absence of pose and ostentation, perfect harmony with the politicians in charge of affairs and love for the people made him an ideal head of State.

In 1947, when the term of Lord Mountbatten, the first Governor General of independent India ended, Chakravarty Rajagopalachari was chosen to take his place. He accepted the higher office because Pandit Nehru had so wished and thus became the first Indian Governor-General. He moved round the country, met people, heard their problems and tried to resolve them through the normal channels of administration. Jawaharlal Nehru invariably consulted him on all important matters.

After the death of Sardar Patel in December 1950, Rajagopalachari was appointed the Home Minister. The major problem which faced him was the guerilla movement in Andhra Pradesh areas of Madras Province. Razakars were still running missions of destruction and distruption. Rajagopalachari deputed the Intelligence Agency Chief to make a detailed study of the situation. He piloted the Preventive Detention Act in Parliament, which invited critical comments from the Opposition. Even many Congressmen felt that the Act smacked of authoritarianism. But Rajagopalachari defended the move stating that the minimum powers necessary to secure the security of the nation, had to be assumed by the Government.

His advice was sought with regard to the preparation of the First Five Year Plan, handling of delicate Kashmir question and in making preparations for the first national elections under the new Constitution. In December 1951, he resigned from the Central Cabinet.

In the general elections held in 1952 Congress suffered a reverse in the Madras Province when it was able to secure only 152 seats in a House of 375. There were 62 independent Members and an equal number of MLAs belonged to the Communist Block. There were another solid group of 38 MLAs of the Krishikar Lok Party. On 29th March 1952, the Madras Congress passed a resolution moved by Shri C. Subramanian calling upon Shri Rajagopalachari to take over the leadership of the Congress Party in the State legislature. On 31 March Karmaraj presented the resolution proposing of Rajaji as the leader of the Congress Legislature Party. Kamaraj revealed that Rajagopalachari was reluctant to accept the responsibility as his health was fragile but added that Rajagopalachari by accepting to the request of the Party, had put the country before self.

Rajagopalachari discouraged the tendency on the part of legislators to interfere in day-to-day administration. He directed the MLAs to work in their constituencies, to keep in touch with the people, and not to unnecessarily pressurise the local administration to get things done.

The mounting demand for a separate State of Andhra comprising the Telugu speaking populace of the Madras Province, gained momentum. There were riots in many areas. Students abstained from classes and politicians resorted to *Satyagrahas*. The law and order situation was causing concern. Rajagopalachari stood firmly against the demand. He considered linguistic reorganisation of the country unrealistic and dangerous. The Central leadership yielded to the pressure and the Andhra State was carved out of the Madras Province. Finally, he relinquished the office of the Chief Minister.

In 1962, Rajagopalachari led the delegation of Gandhi Peace Foundation to the USA to plead for a ban on nuclear tests. The other members of the delegation were R. R. Diwakar and B. Shiva Rao. Nehru instructed the Indian Embassy at Washington to extend all courtesies to Rajagopalachari. Indian envoy B.K. Nehru received the delegation and arranged for Rajagopalachari's visit to the White House. Rajagopalachari came back hopeful of the result of his personal contact with President Kennedy.

Rajagopalachari also visited the United Nations. The then Secretary General, U Thant welcomed Rajagopalachari and listened to his suggestion that the General Assembly should pass a resolution calling upon both the USA and the USSR to stop all nuclear tests.

On 25 December, 1972 this eminent statesman and a great son of Mother India joined the galaxy of immortals. As a legacy he left behind him a great treasure of his political, philosophical and literary works which will remain an asset to this nation for all times to come.

While paying glowing tributes to the departed soul the then Prime Minister Smt. Indira Gandhi said: 'He was the last Governor General and the first and only Indian to hold that office marking the triumph of our struggle for independence.

Mourning the demise of the elder statesman, Lok Nayak Jayaprakash Narayan described Rajaji as "Timeless Teacher of Man."

Part – II

Rajendra Prasad

(Dec., 3, 1884 – Feb. 28, 1963)

Rajendra Basu was one leader who was admired, respected and loved at the same time. Sarojini Naidu once said that she needed a golden pen dipped in honey to write about Rajendra Babu. Nehru always admired and praised him. Dr. Radhakrishnan called him Ajeya Saujanya - embodiment of the spirit of invincible gentleness.

Rajendra Prasad was a brilliant student. In 1902 he startled the Bengalis by securing the first position in Matriculation. Dr. Sachchidanand Sinha had prophesied that the highest position which could be available to an Indian would be open to him. He was a rural boy but performed better that than the most sophisticated. In 1921 Mazaharul Hazaque told a journalist that "India has proved her fitness to Home Rule because she has produced a gem like Rajendra Babu. In 1922, after the split at the Gaya Session of the Indian National Congress, Deshbandhu C.R. Das, as President of the Congress remarked, "at the moment Rajendra Prasad appears to be sole excuse for further honest trial of Gandhism to solve a political problem and with this statement Pandit Motilal Nehru agreed fully.

Bengal specially Calcutta had become the Centre of Independence Movement and therefore, he has greatly attracted towards the freedom movement. The British Government decided to divide with the hope that it will weaken the national movement for freedom. But soon they proved to be wrong.

He became members of the Congress at its Calcutta Session in 1911. He also started his practice in Calcutta the same year. After five years he shifted to Patna again in 1916.

Rajendra Babu met Mahatma Gandhi for the first time at Calcutta in 1915 when the Congress decided to protect the interests of the farmers of Champaran in North Bihar. He came closer to Gandhiji who visited Champaran in 1917.

In 1920, when the Congress at its Session at Nagpur adopted the resolution to launch the Non-cooperation Movement, Rajendra Babu left his practice and joined the Non-Cooperation Movement actively. The Independence Movement became very strong after 1920. But at that time Rajendra Babu was not well yet he joined Jhanda Satyagraha in 1923 and wrote article in the 'Searchlight' published from Patna. He also participated in the protest against the Simon Commission and he was arrested in 1930 for promoting the cause of Satyagraha launched by Gandhiji. He was released in 1934 when North Bihar was struck by the severe earthquake. Rajendra Babu accompanied Gandhiji during his tour of the rural areas in Bihar during 1925-37. In 1924, he had been elected Chairman of the Patna Municipality and became a member of the Parliamentary Board when the Congress formed government in 1937.

Rajendra Babu was simple in his habits and in his living. He led a simple life and had once said that his meeting with Gandhiji gave a new turn in his life.

He practised as a lawyer for sometime and built up a flourishing practice with a brief period. Mahatma Gandhi and Rajendra Babu lived almost the same way and often travelled in the same dress. Only at the pursuasion of his nephew Janardhan Prasad and Pandit Nehru that he put on a properly tailored *Sheriwani* and *chooridar* on the occasion of the First Republic Day. Later on, his sons and his relatives made him to continue with the new dress which a Rashtrapati of India had to wear. However, he always felt comfortable only in *Dhoti* and *Kurta*. Rajendra Babu used a new twig daily to clean his teeth. Once a nurse attending on him asked : "false teeth, sir," Rajendra Basu replied: "There is nothing false about me." Some people had said that he was too much of a traditionalist and that he was greatly attached to religion and had high respect for Brahmins. But he never thought it as 'anti-progress'. A vastly learned man, a distinguished lawyer, a persuasive speaker and a clear-headed leader Rajendra Babu excelled in every field even as a social reformer. His famous book 'India Divided' earned him great regard and respect. In his book he placed facts and figures before Jinnah that Pakistan would not be and could not be a practical proposition.

Rajendra Babu accepted the invitation to open new Somnath temple in Saurashtra which became controversial. The question asked was : 'How would the Muslims react?' Dr. Rajendra Babu ignored all objections and went to Somnath in his individual capacity and not as the President. There was a great happiness all over the country over the resuscitation of the Somnath temple which had been destroyed by the invaders. Once he said : "Much has become possible in the age of science but the past, with its polity, its society and its thinking could not just be resuscitated. When a modern man, therefore, looks towards the past of his country it is not to take the country to bygone ages which in any case would be an impossible feat. But to draw upon these views and inspirations which had given the people their strange quality, there resilience, their distinctive features as a national and cultural group and the essence of the past of India was tolerance and a growth in alround prosperity and alround betterment."

Rajendra Babu believed in human dignity and supported programmes of rural development. That is why he chose Food & Agriculture when he became a Minister in the interim government at the Centre. He was offered chairmanship of the Planning Commission which he declined to accept. He did not support large-scale industrialisation. Later on his chairmanship of the Constituent Assembly was exemplary. He guided and regulated the debates with skill and consciousness and gave opportunity to members who wanted to speak and participate in the proceedings of the Constitutent Assembly.

As a President of the Indian Union he exercised a moderating influence and even influenced policies as they were developed and adopted. There have been occasions when he differed with the Prime Minister. His wife Smt. Raj Banshi Devi died early September 1962 within months of his retirement. He passed his last days at Sadaqat Asharm at Patna which had been the headquarters of the Congress. The Chinese aggression in 1962 had shaken him completely.

Memorable Dates

December 3, 1884 : Birth

March 1902; Matriculated from Calcutta University

1915 : M.L. from Calcutta University

1917-18 : In Champaran with Mahatma Gandhi

October, 1934: President of the All India Congress Session at Bombay.

December 11, 1946 to 1949 : President of the Indian Constitutent Assembly

He joined the Government headed by Jawaharlal Nehru and was sworn in as Deputy Prime Minister on August 15, 1947 and later became also the Home Minister, till 15 December, 1950.

January 26, 1950 to May 13, 1952: Interim President of the Indian Republic

May 13, 1952 to May 12, 1957: First President of the Indian Republic

May 13, 1962: Retired from the Presidentship of Indian Republic

May 13, 1962: Honoured with the title of 'Bharat Ratna'

February 28, 1963: Left for his heavenly abode while in Sadaqat Ashram, Patna.

Pandit Jawaharlal Nehru

(14 Nov., 1889 – 27th May 1964)

Pandit Jawaharlal Nehru, the architect of modern India, was born on 14 November, 1889 in Anand Bhawan of Allahabad. Regarding the backdrop in which the family surname (Nehru) was coined, he wrote in his Autobiography :

"A Jagir with a house situated on the banks of a canal had been granted to Raj Kaul and, from the back of this residence, 'Nehru' (from nahar a canal) came to be attached to his name. Kaul had been the family name, this changed to Kaul Nehru and in later years, became simply Nehrus".

His father Motilal Nehru had earlier moved from Kanpur to Allahabad where he carved out a niche for himself. A lawyer by profession, Motilal by dint of perseverance, had established himself as a leading lawyer of the town. Enlightened and educated, Motilal followed a westernized life style. Jawaharlal's mother Swarup Rani, schooled in Indian ethos and values, extended to him, in his own words, "excessive and undiscriminating love". As the male child of prosperous parents, born after 11 year of their marriage, Jawaharlal grew up in opulence.

In 1905, Motilal Nehru decided to admit young Nehru, in a public school in England. Therefore, he took his family to England when Jawaharlal was fifteen and got him admitted at Harrow. Jawaharlal left Harrow after two years with his father's permission and joined Trinity College, Cambridge in the beginning of October, 1907 at the age of seventeen.

On his return from England in 1912, Jawaharlal started practising law at the Allahabad High Court as his father's junior. After having been abroad for seven years, he enjoyed the early months renewing old contacts. However, the dry and drab demands of the profession gradually made him feel uneasy. It was against this backdrop that he decided to join Congress to take part in its activities.

On 8 February, 1916, on Vasanta Panchami day, which is the precursor of spring in India, Jawaharlal got married to Kamla Kaul. It was an arranged marriage, the bride being chosen by Motilal himself.

He was introduced to Mahatma Gandhi at the Lucknow Session of the Congress held during the Christmas of 1916. He had, however, seen Gandhi earlier at the Bombay Session of the Indian National Congress in 1915. Gandhiji's fight against the obnoxious practice of apartheid in South Africa appealed to him a great deal. Though somewhat bewildered by Gandhi's political philosophy and earthly political common sense, was particularly impressed by the agrarian agitation which Gandhiji led in Bihar in 1917. What appealed to the young Nehru was Gandhi's strength, his rock-like commitment to India's freedom, the way in which he had perfected his character and personality so as to make himself an effective instrument of political change in India.

After World War I, there was greater political expectation towards self government in India. The rising expectations, however, met with disappointment when the British Government passed the repressive and draconian Rowlatt Bills. This evoked mass protest and demonstrations all over India in the form of Satyagraha at the call of Mahtama Gandhi. The bizarre incidence of Jallianwala Bagh massacre took place at Amritsar in Punjab. These unfortunate developments agitated Jawaharlal so much that he gave up the profession of law. There was a metamorphic change in his life style. He became more of a Congress activist. Sacrificing the comforts of life, he became a lieutenant of Gandhiji.

On his last leg of the Europen tour, Jawaharlal landed in Moscow in November 1927. His four-day visit to the Soviet Union left a lasting imprint on his mind. His travels abroad, particularly participation in the Brussels Congress and subsequent visit to Moscow, had convinced him of the need for a socialistic pattern of society for India.

With such disposition, Jawaharlal sailed for India, accompanied by his family, in December 1927. The militancy of the freedom struggle which had mellowed down when he left for Europe, had again picked up momentum since the visit of Simon Commission in November 1927. Jawaharlal reached Madras in December 1927 at the most opportune time when the Congress was meeting there.

The controversy over complete independence or dominion status for India was given a definite direction by Jawaharlal when he moved on 27 December 1927 at the Madras Congress – the famous resolution that the 'Congress declares the goal of the Indian people to be complete National Independence.' The Resolution was indeed revolutionary. At a time when most of the Congress leaders were reconciled to gradualism as a mode of freedom struggle, the clarion call for complete National Independence came like a bolt.

At the historic Lahore Congress held in late December 1929, the son succeeded the father at the podium. The socialist credo of Jawaharlal was given a public expression at this Congress. Later, he participated in Dandi March in 1930. He spent four years in Jail (1930-1935). His wife Kamla Nehru died in Switzerland in Feb. 1931.

Jawaharlal was elected President of the Indian National Congress at its Lucknow session for the year 1936. The challenging task of steering the Congress, reconciling the Left and the Right now fell on his shoulders. He performed this duty with dexterity.

During this period, he also took keen interest in world affairs. He laid down the goal and objective of foreign policy of Congress Party. As the President of the Indian National Congress in 1936-37, he organised a 'Foreign Department' in the party Secretariat to maintain contacts with individuals and parties abroad who were sympathetic to the Indian cause. In 1937, he paid goodwill visits to Burma and Malaya. And in the summer of 1939, he visited Ceylon (Sri Lanka) in an effort to reduce the friction between Indian settlers and the Sinhalese.

The British Cabinet despatched the Crips Mission to India in 1942. The 'Draft Declaration' recognised India's right to convene a Constitutent Assembly for framing the Constitution. But the seeds of the 'divide and rule' germane in it agitated the Congress and Jawaharlal Nehru. Ultimately, the Congress rejected the offer. This precipitated in launching the 'Quit India Movement' on August 8, 1942.

The British Government tried to quell the mass uprising with an iron hand putting the front ranking leaders like Jawaharlal Nehru, behind the bars. This was also Jawaharlal's longest spell in the Jail. He was released in June 1945 just when the Viceroy, Lord Wavell, convened a Conference in Shimla to break the deadlock. Nehru's pivotal role in these negotiations and later with Lord Mountbatten in 1947 was a feat of great statesmanship.

The freedom struggle cultiminated in India's independence from the clutches of colonialism. On 15 August, 1947 at the stroke of the midnight, Lord Mountbatten, the last British Governor General and Viceroy of India, entered the Assembly chamber to address the Legislature and give a message of greeting and goodwill from the King, who ceased from that moment to be the Emperor of India. Pandit Nehru, the first Prime Minister of Independent India, rose to move the adoption of the pledge of dedication to the new Dominion of India in an atmosphere surcharged with emotion.

On 27 May 1964, India's great son, the nation's first Prime Minister, eminent writer and historian, Jawaharlal reached his journey's end. However, he bequeathed to us a right legacy which sustains us even today.

Sardar Vallabh Bhai Patel

His parents were Jhaverbhai Patel and Ladbai. He was born at Nadiad in Gujarat. There is no record on his date of birth. The generally accepted date, 31st October, 1875 of which the source is his Matriculation Certificate, was chosen by Vallabhbhai himself while filling in a form. The family was agricultural one, of the Lewa Patidar Community and could in terms of economic status be described as lower middle class. It was poor and had no tradition of education. Vallabhabhai's childhood was spent away from books in the ancestral fields of Karamsad. He was in his late teens when he passed out from the Middle School at Karamsad and went to the High School at Nadiad from where he matriculated in 1897.

Vallabhbhai must have inherited attributes of leadership from his father who, it is said, had fought the Mutiny under the Rani of Jhansi and was subsequently taken prisoner by Malharrao Holkar.

Vallabhbhai was a young man of twenty-two when he matriculated. Owing to the impecunious circumstances of the family higher education was not within his reach. The next best thing was to take a course in law. This he did and established a small practice at Godhra. But an attack of plague, which he contracted while nursing a friend, made him leave the town and after spending some time in Nadiad he moved on to Borsad in 1902, a town in the Kheda district where at times the largest number of criminal cases in Gujarat were recorded. Vallabhbhai became quite popular here as a defence lawyer. Vallabhbhai wanted to go to England and qualify as a Barrister.

His wife, Zaverbai, died early in 1909 after an operation for some abdominal malady. When news of the bereavement reached Vallabhbhai, he was cross-examining a witness in a murder case at Anand. With an impregnable composure for which he became known later, he did not show his grief but went on with the cross-examination in hand.

He sailed for England in 1910 and joined the Middle Temple. Here he worked so hard and conscientiously that he topped in Roman Law, securing a prize, and was called to the Bar at the end of two years instead of the usual period of three years.

On his return to India in 1913, he set up practice in Ahmedabad and made a great success of it. He came to enjoy a position in public life that surpassed his eminence as a Barrister. He accepted Mahtama Gandhi's leadership, having been tremendously impressed by the fearless lead that Mahatma Gandhi gave to right public wrongs. In 1917 he was for the first time elected as a Municipal Councillor in Ahmedabad. From 1924 to 1928 he was Chairman of the Municipal Committee. The association of Patel with the Municipal administration were marked by much meaningful work for the improvement of civic life. There were also calamities like plague in 1917 and famine in 1918 and on both occasions Vallabhbhai did important work to relieve distress.

In 1917 he was elected Secretary of the Gujarat Sabha, a political body which was of great assistance to Gandhiji. His association with Gandhi became closer during the Kheda Satyagraha in 1918 aimed at securing exemption from payment of land revenue since the crops had failed. Gandhiji one said : "If it were not for Vallabhbhai's assistance this campaign would not have been carried through so successfully.

The five years from 1917 to 1922 were years of popular agitations in India. The end of the war followed by the Rowlatt Act and still further curtailment of individual freedoms. And then followed the Khailafat Movement with massacres and terror in the Punjab. Gandhiji and the Congress decided on non-cooperation. Vallabhbhai left his practice for good and gave himself up wholly to political and constructive work, touring the villages, addressing meetings, organizing picketing of foreign cloth shops and liquor shops.

Then came Bardoli Satyagraha which was organised against the Government's decision to increase the assessment of land revenue from Bardoli taluka by 22 per cent and in some villages by as much as 50 to 60 per cent. The agriculturalists of the area failed to secure redress by other means, and they held a Conference on 12 February 1928 to withhold payment of land revenue under the leadership of Valabhbhai. The Government had ultimately to low before popular resolve and the realization of the increased revenue was postponed. It was a triumph not only of the 89,000 peasants of Bardoli but more particularly of Vallabhbhai personally who was given the little of 'Sardar' by the nation.

About this time, the Congress had accepted its goal of Purna Swaraj for the country, while the British Government through their policy of pitting one interest against another and trying to stifle the voice of freedom. The boycott of the Simon Commission was followed by the launching of the famous Salt Satyagraha by Gandhiji. Vallabhbhai Patel though he had not committed any breach of the Salt Law, was the first of the national leaders to be arrested, on March 7, 1930 – some days before Gandhiji set out on the march to Dandi. He was released in June and by then Gandhiji, Jawaharlal Nehru and other leaders were in jail and the tempo of the struggle in the country was rising. In a few months Vallabhbhai was back in prison.

In March 1931 Vallabhbhai presided over the 46th Session of the Indian National Congress which was called upon to ratify the Gandhi-Irwin Pact, which had just been concluded. The task was not an easy one, for, Bhagat Singh and a few others had been executed on the very day of the Congress Session opened and delegates, particularly the younger sections were in an angry mood, while Jawaharlal Nehru and Subas Bose were not happy with the terms of the Pact. But the Congress finally put its seal on the Pact with one voice. Civil Disobedience was suspended, political prisoners were released and the Congress agreed to participate in the Round Table Conference which, however, failed. Gandhiji as also the other top leaders were arrested and a policy of repression followed. Vallabhbhai was lodged with Gandhiji in Yeravada Jail and they were together there for sixteen months from January 1932 to May 1933. Vallabhbhai spent another one year in the Nasik Jail.

When the Government of India Act, 1935 came, the Congress though generally critical of the Act, decided to try out those of its constitutional provisions that seemed to grant to India a measure of self-government and to take part in elections for Provincial Legislatures that were envisaged under it.

The British Government tried to perpetuate the existence of princely States both under the Government of India Act 1935 and the Indian Independence Act. The interim national Government at the Centre, however, opposed it and said that there could be only one paramountcy and that was the paramountcy of the people. However, rulers were assured of dignified place in the new political and social set up. Sardar did join the interim government and later the Government of the Independent India of which Pandit Jawaharlal Nehru was the Prime Minister. He worked all through for building up an united India. Later his efforts towards smooth integration of armed forces of the States and the Indian Union were brought about in 1948. This was another notable chapter in the history of the process of consolidation of free and united India. Sardar was also emphatic on the implementation of land reforms everywhere. There were talks of difference of opinion between him and Pandit Jawaharlal Nehru. Speaking at Indore after Gandhiji's death Sardar said that there was a talk or rivalry between him and Panditji and made it clear that Pandit Nehru was the undisputed national leader.

He joined the Government headed by Jawaharlal Nehru and was sworn in as Deputy Prime Minister on August 15, 1947 and later became also the Home Minister, till 15th December, 1950.

Maulana Abul Kalam Azad

Maulana Abul Kalam Azad was born in Mecca in 1888. His father Maulana Khairuddin had married an Arab lady of noble lineage. Azad was the youngest child. M. Khairuddin was influenced by a distinguished scholar which gave his son great inspiration. In Mecca, Azad and his brother Abu Nasar studied together and before they left in 1898, they had completed their study of the Quran and also had learn the fundamentals of Arabic. Maulana returned to India and settled in Calcutta. He was given training in all fields of Islamic knowledge by tutor followed by his father himself.

In 1905, when he had become a trained theologean and came under the influence of Maulana Shibli Nomani. He was an eminent poet and journalist. He also imbibed some of the rationalist positions of Sir Syed Ahmad Khan. The first major turning point in Azad's life came after the Partition of Bengal in 1905. He rejected the views of Muslim middle class which wanted Partition and supported close relationship with the colonial government. Thereafter, he even joined some of the secret revolutionary society. It was during this period that he came into contact with Aurobindo Ghosh and Shyam Sunder Chakraborty. Both of them were leaders of the militant anti-colonial movement in Bengal.

In 1908, Maulana Azad went on tour of Hejaz, Iraq, Syria and Egypt where he met various groups including the Young Turks and Arab nationalists. He soon realised that without the liberation of India from British the colonial power could not be compelled to leave the Near and Middle East. Later he founded his well known journal Al Hilal in 1912 which became very popular among the Muslim intelligentia. In 1914 the British Government confiscated the Al Hilal Press. Between 1912 to 1920 Maulana was put in Jail at Ranchi. His association with the intellectuals of Arab nationalists many of whom were Christians and the Young Turks gave him new vision of multi-religious and anti-colonial politics. He worked for the strengthening of ties between the Khilafat Movement and the Congress.

Four years after the First World War (1919-1923) became very important in shaping his views and basic positions for Azad which he served and practised till his death in 1958. Azad met Gandhiji and Tilak on his release from Ranchi Jail in 1919.

Maulana Azad was a member both of the Congress and the Muslim League for sometime. But when the Muslim League at its Session in 1921 denounced the Civil Disobedience Movement, Maulana Azad alongwith many others left the Muslim League. He continued to work devotedly for the Congress and for the liberation of India from British colonial rulers. Maulana Azad made his life-long mission and commitment to serve India's secular and multi-religious nationalism. He became very close to Mahatma Gandhi and Jawaharlal Nehru and was a pillar of strength in the Union Government after Independence and till his death. He was elected President of the Indian National Congress in 1923 at the age of 35. At the Ramgarh Session of the Congress in 1940 he was again elected President and continued in that position till 1946. In 1947 he joined the interim Government as the Member of Education & Arts. In the First Cabinet of Independent India Maulana was appointed Minister of Education, Natural Resources and Scientific Research. He died while in office on February 22, 1958. He was protagonist of United India. Maulana had said at the Special Session of the Congress in 1923 that he shall be willing to forego Swaraj but would not discard Hindu-Muslim unity.

Lal Bahadur Shastri

A son was born to Shri Sharda Prasad Srivastava and Ram Dulari Devi in Mughal Sarai (Uttar Pradesh) on 2nd October, name was "Nahne". He was born in a middle class Kayastha family. Incidentally, Lal Bahadur's birthday falls on the same date as that of Mahatma Gandhi. His father was a school teacher and subsequently became a Clerk in the Revenue Department at Allahabad. His father died when he was only one and a half year old.

At the age of ten he came to Banaras for his studies and stayed with his maternal uncle. He studied at Harish Chandra High School, Banaras & Kashi Vidyapeeth. In 1926 he secured a first class degree of Shastri in Philosophy. Dr. Bhagwan Das, the Principal of the Vidyapeeth was greatly responsible in moulding the personality of Lal Bahadur through his own example that moral and spiritual greatness could be achieved by simple living and high thinking. Acharya Narendra Dev, Acharya J. B. Kripalani, Sri Prakasa and Dr. Sampurnanand were the teachers in Kashi Vidyapeeth. He was brought up in holy cities of Banaras and Allahabad which shaped his mind and personality into an orthodox, moral purity and humility. Gandhiji was a model for him. In 1921 he responded to Gandhiji's call for joining the Independence Struggle and gave up his studies to take part in the Non-Cooperation Movement and courted imprisonment. He was greatly influenced by the speeches of Lala Lajpat Rai, Gokhale, Tilak, Pal and others which he read as a school boy.

On completing his studies in 1926, he became a member of the Servants of the People Society which was founded by Lala Lajpat Rai in 1921 and was inaugurated by Mahatma Gandhi the same year. Later, he was made its life member. He worked among the Harijans in Allahabad.

Lal Bahadur was married in 1927 to Lalmani now Lalita Devi of Mirzapur. He refused to accept anything except a "Charkha" and little yarn in dowry.

Jawaharlal Nehru was one of his early associates and he had watched him unfurling the flag of Independence on the banks of Ravi in 1929. In the thirties he served on the Allahabad Municipal Board for seven years. In 1930, he was arrested and sentenced to two and a half year imprisonment for participating in the Salt-Satyagraha. While in jail, he read biographies of great leaders and also the political philosophies of Kant, Hegel, Laski, Marxs and Lenin. He translated into Hindi the autobiography of Madam Curie.

He became General Secretary of the Allahabad District Congress Committee from 1935-37. In 1937 Lal Bahadur was elected as a member of the UP Legislative Assembly. He was jailed seven times in 1930, 1932, 1934, 1941 and 1942 and in all he spent nine glorious years of his life in prison. His ability was recognised and in 1946 he was re-elected to the UP Legislative Assembly and the then Chief Minister, Pandit Pant made him his Parliamentary Secretary. In 1947, he was appointed Minister of Police and Transport. He always considered himself as the servant of the people. His small size, simple dress and meek manners often made the officials of his concerned departments feel very small as he did not believe in pomp and show but showed utter modesty with a great sense of humour.

In 1951, he resigned from the UP Ministry and was made General Secretary of the A.I.C.C. when Jawaharlal Nehru was the President. In 1952 he was elected as Member of Rajya Sabha from U.P. and he joined the Union Cabinet as Minister of Railways & Transport, which he resigned in November 1956 taking the constitutional responsibility for Aliyalur Railway Accident. He again joined the Central Cabinet in 1957 after the second general elections and held several important portfolios such as Transport and Communications, Commerce & Industry and Home Affairs. In 1952, 1957 and 1962 Parliamentary elections, Lal Bahadur Shastri organised the Party Campaigns and was instrumental in the selection of Congress candidates. In all these elections, Congress achieved brilliant victories.

In 1963, he voluntarily resigned from the Cabinet under Kamraj

Plan. In March 1963, he made a trip to Nepal. He was a tactful negotiator and never let the talks deadlocked. He was once again inducted into Union Cabinet on 24th January 1964 as Minister without Portfolio to assist the Prime Minister.

He had a spotless reputation. Behind his soft and silky words were hidden his iron will and firmness. On June 9, 1964 after Pandit Nehru's death on 27th May he was elected as leader of the Congress Party in Parliament. He participated in the Non-Alignment Conference at Cairo in October, 1964. He successfully led the nation during the 22 Days Indo-Pak War of 1965.

During 1965 he visited Russia, Yugoslavia, England, Canada and Burma. On January 10, 1966 he signed the historic Joint Communique with President Ayub Khan of Pakistan at Tashkent. Within a few hours after signing the Declaration, the hero of Tashkent passed away at Tashkent. The end came at 1.32 a.m. on 11.1.1966. The great little man died at the height of his career. He was man of the masses.

Lal Bahadur Shastri served as Prime Minister for 19 (Nineteen) months and 2 (two) days at a very difficult time in the history of the country. He was quiet and determined nationalist. Lal Bahadur Shastri left behind, besides his widow,, the old mother, four sons and two daughters who are married. He honoured the man behind the plough and raised the slogan "Jai Jawan Jai Kisan". He was simple, kind and a thorough gentleman. He was a vegetarian and did not smoke or drink. He rarely lost his temper. He was awarded "Bharat Ratna" posthumously.

Pandit Govind Ballabh Pant

Pt. Govind Ballab Pant was born on Anant Chaturdashi day, 16 Bhadrapada, Vikram Samvat 1944. As the Anant Chaturdashi fell on 10 September in the year 1946 when his birthday was first officially celebrated in Lucknow, this date since been recognised as the date of his birth. His father Pt. Manorath Pant was serving in the Revenue Department in Garhwal. His Mother Smt. Govindi was the daughter of Rai Bahadur Pt. Badri Dat Joshi of Dania.

He joined the Allahabad University in 1905 and passed the LLB examination in 1909 standing first, for which he was awarded a gold medal. While he was at Allahabad, India was passing through a period of awakening and Lal, Bal and Pal were the heroes of students. Pant attended the Banaras Session of the Congress in 1905 and it was here that he had the first 'darshan' of his political guru Gokhale. The logic of Gokhale and the temperament of Malaviya impressed him most. He also became an ardent admirer of bankim Chandra Chatterji, the great inspiring novelist. Besides, he got actively involved in political activity for which he was debarred from appearing for the B.A. examination. His Mathematics teacher Prof. Cox, however, had to intervene to secure for him the permission to appear for this examination.

At Allahabad, he spent some time learning classical Hindustani music, but could not make much headway except developing a good ear for music. He was extremely fond of the Kumaoni style of Holi singing and musical sittings were organised at his residence both in Lucknow and New Delhi.

Soon after passing the LLB. examination, Pant started legal practice at Almora. He soon migrated to Ranikhet, Kashipur and ultimately settled in Nainital. He was the most sought-after lawyer of

Kumaon and he earned name, fame and wealth. As a lawyer he was at his zenith in the famous Kakori case.

His wife Smt. Kaladevi bore him three children-two daughters Laxmi and Pushpa and one son Krishna Chandra, who was a Minister in the Central Cabinet.

He was elected to the UP Legislative Council in 1923 and soon became the leader of the Swaraj Party. His speeches in the Council were demonstrative of the fact that he was an extraordinary debater. He was elected President of the UPCC in 1927 and at its session at Aligarh, he highlighted the communal problem, gnawing at the entrails of the Indian society. In 1928, along with Nehru, he led a demonstration against Simon Commission and received severe lathi blows which rendered him partially invalid throughout the rest of his life. This was followed by his arrest in 1930 for six months in connection with the Salt Satyagraha. In 1932, he again landed in Bareilly and Dehradun Jails. Jawaharlal Nehru was with him in the prison and Pt. Pant used to read through the manuscript of the Autobiography which Nehru was then busy writing.

In 1934, Pt. Pant was elected a member of the Central Legislative Assembly where he crossed swords with official members and came to be known as a great Parliamentarian and financial expert.

He was imprisoned for individual satyagraha in 1940 and also in 1942 during the 'Quit India' Movement launched by Mahatma Gandhi. He was lodged in Ahmednagar prison along with Nehru, Patel and other leaders. He was released in 1945 to be elected again to the UP Assembly in 1946 and was the Chief Minister for eight years. Earlier he was premier of U.P. as a congress leader, and continued on the post till 1939.

He joined the Central Cabinet in December 1954 and became Home Minister in February 1955. His Home Ministership was conspicuous for various achievements including the task of redrawing the map of India in the light of the recommendations of the States Reorganisation Commission.

For his outstanding services to the Nation he was awarded the Bharat Ratna in 1957.

On the fateful day of 20 February 1961, Pt. Pant was busy working on official files when he abruptly sent for Shri Asoke Sen, the Law Minister and asked him to reply to a debate in the Rajya Sabha next day. As he was explained some points to Shri Sen, he suffered a stroke and lost consciousness never to regain it. He passed away on 7th of March 1961.

Morarji Desai

Morarji Desai was born on February 29, 1896, at village Bhadeli, near Bulsar in Surat district of Gujarat, in a middle-class Anavil Brahmin family. His father, Ranchhodiji, was a school teacher at Bhavnagar. His mother, Vajiaben was not educated. Morarji was married to Gajaraben. When he was only 15, his father died and the responsibility of supporting his mother and a family of seven children fell of his shoulders. There was no money. Morarji got a scholarship of Rs. 10/- per month from the erstwhile Bhavnagar State and entered the Goculdas Tejpal boarding house in Bombay. Boarding and lodging was free and he sent the scholarship money to his mother. The only time he needed money was for the rail fare for going home during the holidays. Years later, he calculated the money that the boarding house had spent on him and sent a cheque for the amount.

In response to the call of Mahatma Gandhi to government servants to give up their jobs, Morarji resigned his post of Deputy Collector in 1930 and joined the Civil Disobedience Movement. During the next four years he was imprisoned thrice for participating in the freedom movement. Morarji was elected a member of the Gujarat Pradesh Congress Committee and was also made its Secretary, in which capacity he continued for six years from 1931 to 1937 and again from 1939 to 1946. He had joined Provincial Civil Service in 1918 and severed for 12 years.

In 1937, he has elected to the Bombay Legislative Assembly and was Minister for Revenue and Forests in the first Congress Government (1937-39). His Ministry decided to grant pensions to all Government servants who had resigned or had been removed from service for taking part in the freedom struggle. A day before he signed the order granting pension, Morarji Desai renounced his own claim so that there might be no adverse criticism. After relinquishing office in 1939, he participated in the Individual Civil Disobedience Movement and was later detained for about three years in connection with the 'Quit India' Movement.

In 1946, Morarji was again elected to the Bombay Legislative Assembly and served as Home and Revenue Minister from 1946 to 1952. After the first General Elections in 1952, he became the Chief Minister of Bombay and continued in that capacity till the reorganisation of States in 1956. He was instrumental in introducing far-reaching reforms in the land revenue administration and also in police and jail reorganisation. He thought of the peasant and tenant both and enacted progressive legislation for them, much before any State of India did anything in this direction. His administration in Bombay State was known for its efficiency, strength and integrity.

He joined the Union Cabinet as Minister of Commerce and Industry on November 1, 1956. On March 22, 1958 he took over the portfolio of Finance.

Morarji Desai led the Indian Delegation to the annual meetings of the Boards of Governors of the International Monetary Fund (IMF) and the International Bank for Reconstruction and Development (IBRD). He also attained the Commonwealth Trade and Economic Conference in Montreal in 1958 and the Commonwealth Finance Ministers Conference in London in 1960 and 1961.

He was elected to Lok Sabha in 1962 and 1967 General Elections from Surat constituency. He again became the Union Minister of Finance in 1962, but he volunteered to retire under the Kamraj Plan in August 1963. He became the Chairman of the Administrative Reforms Commission during 1966-67.

Morarji Desai joined Indira Gandhi's Cabinet in March 1967 as Deputy Prime Minister and held Finance portfolio. He made a goodwill visit to Japan in August 1967 and a long foreign tour to London, Montreal, Washington, Rio-de-Janeiro, Port of Spain, Paris and Bonn in September - October 1967. He resigned from the post of Deputy Prime Minister in July 1969.

In the formation of the Janta Party, Morarji Desai played a leading role. When the Janta Party won the 1977 General Elections, he became the Prime Minister in the first non-Congress Government at the Centre. Following a split in the Janta Party he resigned in 1979 and later retired from active politics.

A veteran Gandhian, Morarji Desai always wore Khadi. Vegetarian, Naturopath, non-smoker and teetolaller, Morarji was a Spartan and a person with strong convictions. Compromising on truth and morality was against the grain of his character.

The nation had started celebrating his 100th year, it was not to be. He died on April 10, 1995.

Indira Gandhi (Priyadarshini)

Indira Nehru, only child of Jawaharlal and Kamala Nehru, was born in Allahabad, in Ananda Bhavan, on 19 November, 1917. Her grandfather, Motilal Nehru, named her Indira after his own mother. The Nehru family had been actively involved in the Indian Freedom Movement and Indira was brought up in that environment. While Motilal and Jawaharlal were in prison little Indira with other women members of the family went to see Gandhiji at Sabarmati Ashram. This was her meeting with the Mahatma and for the rest of her life the latter had a profound influence on her. In 1923 she was admitted to St. Cicilias, a private school in Allhabad. In March 1926 she accompanied her parents to Switzerland and studied there at L'Ecole Nauvelle. In December 1927 she returned to India and joined St. Mary' Convent in Allahabad. As a teenager she herself began to take active part in the freedom struggle. In April 1930 she formed 'Vanar Sena' (Monkey Brigade) with other children to work for the Congress. In May 1931 she took admission into Jahangir Vakil's Pupil's Own School at Pune and passed the Matriculation Examination in April 1934. From July 1934 to April 1935 she studied in Visva-Bharati, Santiniketan and came to be deeply influenced by the magnetic personality, philosophy, educational ideas and universalism of Rabindranath Tagore.

After her mother's death (28 February, 1936) Jawaharlal took Indira to England and got her admitted into Badminton School, Bristol. The same year, on 21 December, Rabindranath wrote to Jawaharlal about Indira, "She has your strength of character as well as your ideas and I am not surprised she finds herself rather alien to the complacent English society ...". In February 1938, Indira went to study at Somerville College, Oxford. The same year she joined the India League, came in touch with Harold Laski and became a member of the Indian National Congress. In March 1941 she came back to India. She married Feroze Gandhi (26 March, 1942) who hailed from a well-known Parsi family settled in Allahabad. She participated in the Quit India Movement and was imprisoned for about eight months in Naini Jail. Her first child Rajiv was born in Bombay on 20 August, 1944. Second child, Sanjay, was born in Delhi on 14 December, 1946. She participated in relief work in riot-striken areas of Delhi in August 1947 under the inspiration of Gandhiji. After her father Jawaharlal became first Prime Minister of Independent India, Indira mostly stayed with him and from 1950 became the official hostess at her father's official residence at Teen Murti Bhawan. She accompanied Jawaharlal to numerous countries in the world in the succeeding years and personally came to be known to world leaders, acquired first hand knowledge of the Non-Aligned Movement and problems and aspirations of the peoples of the Third World countries.

In February 1955 Indira was elected to the Congress Working Committee and a few months later became a member of the Congress Central Election Committee. In February, 1958, she was elected member of the Congress Central Parliamentary Board. Indira was elected President of the Congress on 2 February, 1959. Feroze Gandhi died on 8 September, 1960. After the death of Jawaharlal (27 May, 1964) Indira joined the Cabinet of lal Bahadur Shastri as Minister of Information and Broadcasting (2 July, 1964). She was elected unopposed to the Rajya Sabha (20 August, 1964).

On 24 January, 1966, after the sudden death of lal Bahadur Shastri in Tashkent (10 January) Indira was sworn in as Prime Minister of India having been earlier elected leader of the Congress Parliamentary Party (19 January) defeating Morarji Desai. Among the major events in the following years of her Prime Ministership were visits to foreign countries such as France, U.S.A.., Great Britain, USSR, RAR, Yugoslavia, Nepal, devaluation of the rupee (6 June, 1966), and formation of the New States of Punjab and Haryana (1 November, 1966). She was elected to the Lok Sabha from Rai Bareilly, U.P. (23 February, 1967), and on 13 March was sworn in as Prime Minister of India for the second time. Differences between her and old Congress leadership on socio-economic issues began to widen which was accentuated by nationalization of major Indian Banks (19 July, 1969) and resignation of Finance Minister Morarji Desai. On 29 August, V.V. Giri was elected President of the Republic of India, with the support of Indira defeating the official Congress candidate Sanjeeva Reddy. This led to her expulsion from the Congress Party and the 'First Split' in the Indian National Congress (12 November). Indira continued as Prime Minister with the support of a majority of the Congress M.Ps. who had joined her, and the support of some opposition parties in the Parliament.

Her party won a massive victory in the Parliamentary elections and Indira was sworn in as Prime Minister for the third time (18 March, 1971). Most important events during this term of her Prime Ministership were beginning of the liberation struggle in East Pakistan (26 March, 1971), war with Pakistan and emergence of the independent State of Bangladesh (December, 1971), signing of the Indo-Soviet Treaty of Peace, Friendship and Cooperation (9 August, 1971), conferment of Bharatratna on Indira (26 January, 1972), abolition of Privy Purse (11 February, 1972), signing of the Simla Pact with Pakistani President Z.A. Bhutto (2 July, 1972), underground nuclear blast at Pokhran in Rajasthan (18 May, 1974), setting aside of Indira's election to Lok Sabha by Allahabad High Court (12 June, 1975) and partial stay order by the Supreme Court (24 June). The Lok Sangharsh Samity threatened country-wide agitation for Indira's removal (25 June and the next day 26 June 1975) Emergency was declared to meet internal threat to the nations's security. On 1 July, Indira announced 20 point economic programme. On 7 November the Supreme Court upheld Indira's election to the Lok Sabha.

She continued in office till March 24, 1977 when her Council of Ministers was dissolved. In the meantime elections were held for the Lok Sabha and on March 24, 1977 Morarji Desai was sworn in as Prime Minister of the Janata Government. Mrs. Gandhi came into power again and continued on the post from January 1980 to October 31, 1984. She died in the hands of assassins while in office on October 31, 1984.

During her tenure as Prime Minister she had held temporary charge of Defence, External Affairs, Industry, Atomic Energy, Home and Finance.

Rajiv Gandhi

Rajiv Gandhi's passion for machines and their technical aspects led to a keen interest in him for aviation. He had learnt some flying during the holidays in England and India. On returning home, Rajiv Gandhi joined the Indian Airlines training course at Hyderabad in December 1967, and started learning to fly Dakotas. His amazing sense of inquisitiveness about how things worked impressed many people. Rajiv Gandhi officially joined the Indian Airlines as an apprentice on 5 May, 1968 and captained HS-748 type aircrafts before finally securing the much cherished Being Commander's License in 1980.

Unassuming and simple, Rajiv Gandhi, after his marriage with Sonia, settled down to a happy life. Even though he was staying at 1, Safdarjung Road, the official residence of the Prime Minister and his mother Shrimati Indira Gandhi, he kept a distance from politics immensely enjoying the pleasures of flying and the charm of a happy family life. The sudden death in June 1980 of his politically active brother Sanjay changed the whole political atmosphere. Considerable psychological and political pressure were exerted on him to join active politics. He was torn between his duty to family and country and his love for flying.

Finally, Rajiv Gandhi relinquished a bright prospect in his chosen career and plunged into politics and contested for the Lok Sabha election from Amethi constituency in June 1981 which he won by a thumping majority. He was sworn in as a Member of Lok Sabha on 17 August, 1981. For long he quietly observed the proceedings of the House before making his maiden speech on 11 March, 1982 which was well-received by all sections of the House.

Rajiv Gandhi was appointed General Secretary of the All India Congress Committe AICC (I) on 3 February, 1983 and was entrusted the task of looking after the party affairs in four States viz. Arunachal Pradesh, Bihar, Himachal Pradesh and Nagaland. Simultaneously, he was given the charge of managing the affairs of the Congress Seva Dal, the Youth Congress (I), the National Students' Union of India (NSUI).

The brutal assassination of Prime Minister Indira Gandhi on 31 October, 1984 sent shock waves all over the country. On that fateful day, Rajiv was away in the interior of West Bengal addressing political meetings. A grief-stricken Rajiv rushed back to Delhi and even before he could recover from the trauma of the tragedy, he was sworn in as the Prime Minister of India the same evening.

Soon after taking the reins of administration, Rajiv Gandhi stoically faced the challenges that confronted the nation and set out to rejuvenate the country and further reinforce it as a strong, secular, socialist and modern state. To Rajiv Gandhi nothing was above India's unity and integrity.

Within days of becoming the Prime Minister, Rajiv Gandhi announced that elections for the Lok Sabha would be held in December 1984. It demonstrated his firm mandate of the people. This was his way of renewing the country's commitment to democracy. In the Eighth general elections he led the Congress Party to a landslide victory, winning 401 seats out of 508 contested and a higher percentage of the popular vote than ever before, a feat not achieved even by Pandit Jawaharlal Nehru and Shrimati Indira Gandhi. He faithfully initiated serious and earnest negotiations to tackle the seemingly intractable problems confronting this country whether in Punjab or in the North-Eastern part of India. All these efforts yielded good dividends in the form of the Punjab, Assam and Mizo Accords, thus brightening the prospects of moving the nation forward unitedly. He gave major thrust to agriculture in the Seventh Five Year Plan. During his tenure as Prime Minister, the production of foodgrains touched an all-time record.

Rajiv Gandhi gave new orientation to the Industrial Policy so as to achieve a higher growth rate. Long Term Fiscal Policy (LTFP) was declared along with and was incorporated in the Seventh Five Year Plan document.

Rajiv Gandhi's much cherished dream was to take India into the 21st Century as a country free from poverty, exploitation and the legacy of its colonial past. The five-day week system was introduced in India to promote efficiency and agility of the employees. He wanted to devolve financial power to the people through the Panchayati Raj and Nagar Palika Bills. Amply realising the fact that the key to economic and social transformation lies in administrative reforms, he brought the Department of Personnel and Administrative Reforms under his direct control and made constant review of the administrative organisation, policies and procedures. He provided a new channel to the people in government service with the establishment of the Administrative Tribunals. Besides, he also raised the strength of the judges in the Supreme Court and High courts as also enhancing their salary. He also took steps to fill but the vacancies in these Courts within a reasonable time limit so that cases could be disposed of quickly.

Rajiv Gandhi masterminded the 52nd Constitution (Amendment) Act, popularly known as Anti-Defection Law to get rid of corruption and venality in politics. To give the youth of India a feeling of active participation in the democratic process, the voting age was lowered from 21 to 18 years through an amendment to the Constitution.

During his tenure as Prime Minister, Rajiv Gandhi gave new directions and prompted several programmes in the areas of space, atomic energy, electronics, ocean development, environment and biotechnology. Hc exhorted the people to make the fight against terrorism and communalism a people's war.

As far as India's foreign policy was concerned Rajiv Gandhi gave utmost importance to improving India's relations with the neighboring countries while not making any kind of compromise with the country's unity, integrity and the principles she stood for. With all good intentions he signed the Indo-Sri Lanka Accord on 29 July 1987 which provided for the safety of life and property of the Tamils and ensuring the national sovereignty and territorial integrity of Sri Lanka.

Rajiv Gandhi was determined to promote close relations with

China and, thus, visited Beijing in 1988 for heralding a new phase in Indo-China relations. The visit was a tremendous success as it provided a forum for understanding the bilateral problems at the higher level. Rajiv Gandhi faithfully worked also for reviving the stalled North-South dialogue while bringing vitality to the South-South cooperation.

He played a prominent role at the Commonwealth heads of Government meeting at Nassau in bringing about a consensus on the measures to be taken against the racist regime in South Africa. He was instrumental in establishing the AFRICA was thus one of his major objectives.

Rajiv Gandhi's eventful public life came to an abrupt end on 21 May 1991. He was brutally assassinated at Sriperumbudur, a small town 41 kms. west of Madras, where he had gone to address a political meeting while campaigning for his party in the general elections to Tenth Lok Sabha. Both the houses of Parliament passed resolutions to mourn the sad demise of the countries youthful leader, a Crusador of peace and devoted to the service of the country and its people.

Bhimrao Ramji Ambedkar

Among the galaxy of stalwarts born in the 19th century, who played a pivotal role in shaping the destiny of free India and left an indelible imprint on our national life and polity, the name of Dr. Bhimrao Ramji Ambedkar shines like a star. An architect of our Constitution and champion of the down-trodden, a rebel against all forms of social and economic inequalities.

Dr. Bhimrao Ramji Ambedkar, was born on 14 April 1891 to Ramji Maloji Sankpal and Bhimbai of Mhow, Madhya Pradesh. Being the youngest child in the family, he was obviously the favourite of all. His father Ramji was a very industrious, religious and generous person and mother Bhimbai, was a self-reliant and deeply devoted lady. Though economically poor, the family earned respect and regard from neighbours. Ramji a Subedar-Major in the military services moved from one military camp to another. After his wife's death, Ramji who was a Kabir panthi brought up the children with care and affection and used to recite to them devotional lyrics and epics like the Ramayana and the Mahabharata. Religious atmosphere at home had a profound impact on young Bhimrao's mind.

Bhimrao, who was sent to a primary school at the age of five, completed his primary education from Satara and pursued higher education. Being a boy belonging to an untouchable community, he had to face all the miseries, humiliations and difficulties. He was not allowed to drink water from the common source. He was forced to study Persian as the Sanskrit teacher refused to teach this language to him. He, however, learnt Sanskrit at a later stage.

In 1907, Bhimrao passed his Matriculation examination. Considering this to be splendid achievement, his community organised a function and a copy of the "The Life of Gautama Buddha" was presented to him by one of its members. The book tremendously influenced the life of Bhimrao.

Considering Bhimrao's interest in education, and his sincerity and a zeal for hard work, the Maharaja of Baroda, Sayyajirao Gaekwad, not only granted a monthly scholarship of Rs. 25 during his graduate level studies but also invited him to serve in his State after completing graduation. Though he joined the service, he was not happy and social challenges remained unchanged. The Maharaja then agreed to sent him to Columbia University as a Gaekwad scholar on the condition that Bhimrao, on return, would serve the State.

Prof. Seligman – the famous economist – was his teacher at the University. The academic atmosphere, the free environment and his passion for books enlarged Bhimrao's mental horizon. During this time he came into contact with the staunch nationalist, Lala Lajpat Rai, who at that time was living in exile in America. The two used to discuss the freedom struggle in India. Thus, still as a student, Bhimrao imbedded the patriotic ideas and ideals and western liberal democratic thought which made him a strong nationalist and an ardent defender of human rights and study.

In 1915, he obtained his M.A. (Economics) degree for his thesis "Ancient Indian Commerce". In 1916, he was awarded Ph.D. for his thesis "National Dividend for India : Historic and Analytical Study."

The same year, Dr. Ambedkar joined the London School of Economics and Political Science. He also got admission to the famous Gray's Inn for Law. However, he could not pursue his studies as the Maharaja called him back and appointed him as his Secretary with the intention of grooming him for the post of the State Finance Minister.

After a years struggle, Dr. Ambedkar joined as Professor of Political Science in a College in Bombay. After teaching for only five months, he left for London, to pursue his further studies. He was helped in his objective by the enlightened Maharaja of Kolhapur. He rejoined both the London School of Economic and Political Science and the Gray's Inn to qualify as a barrister.

To launch his struggle against untouchability, Dr. Ambedkar founded in 1924 an organisation in Bombay called "Bahishkrit Hitkrini Samba" for the moral and material progress of untouchables.

Dr. Ambedkar's dream of a separate electorate for the depressed classes partially came true with the announcement of the Communal Award by the British Prime Minister.

Shocked by the decision of the British Government, Mahatma Gandhi declared a fast unto death in the Aga Khan Palace at Pune. In order to save the life ofMahatma, Dr. Ambedkar had to yield and settle down for reserved constituencies instead of a separate electrorate.

In 1942, Dr. Ambedkar formed the All India Scheduled Castes Federation as an all India political party to fight for the interests of the depressed classes. The Party, however, did not achieve much in the general elections held in February 1946.

The Governor of Bombay had nominated him to the Bombay Legislative Council in 1926, the membership of which he held till 1934.

In 1936, Dr. Ambedkar founded the independent Labour Party of India. In pursuance of the provisions of the Government of India Act 1935 the country went to the polls in 1937 to elect India's first popular legislatures. The Independent Labour Party won 15 of the 17 seats in contest in Bombay.

In 1946, when the interim Government was formed, Prime Minister Jawaharlal Nehru's choice of Law Minister fell on Ambedkar. He painstakingly drafted the Hindu Code Bill and introduced it in the Parliament on 4 February 1951. The purpose of the Bill, Ambedkar explained, was to bring about reforms in the Hindu Society and codify certain branches of the Hindu Law.

Another landmark legislation introduced in the Provisional Parliament on 9 May 1951 by Dr. Ambedkar as Law Minister was the representation of the People's Bill, 1950 providing inter-alia for the conduct offree elections to Parliament and State Assemblies, stipulating qualifications and disqualifications of membership and to deal with corrupt and illegal practices during elections.

On 25 September, 1951, Dr. Ambedkar resigned from the Government as he had differences of opinion with Prime Minister Nehru and other colleagues on various issues.

He was elected to the Constituent Assembly first from Bengal and then from Bombay. He was appointed on the Drafting Committee on 29 August 1947 and was subsequently elected as its Chairman.

The Draft Constitution as prepared by the Drafing Committee was introduced in the Constituent Assembly by Dr. Ambedkar on 4 November, 1948. Speaking on the vitality and the endurability of the Constitution during the time of crisis and of peace, he had remarked: "The Constitution as settled by the Drafing Committee is workable, it is flexible and it is strong enough to hold the country both in peace time and war time indeed, if I may say so, if things go wrong under the new Constitution, the reason will not be that we have a bad Constitution.

On the day before the adoption of the Constitution by the Constituent Assembly, Members placed on record their appreciation and paid glowing tributes to Dr. Ambedkar for his outstanding contribution towards the making of the Constitution.

Earlier the then Viceroy had appointed him in 1942 as on the Members of Defence Council. Later, he was given the portfolio of Labour which he held till June 1946.

As Labour Member, Ambedkar succeeded in reserving 5 to 6 per cent posts for untouchables in the Central Government. The most important labour legislation that was introduced in the Assembly towards the end of his tenure was the Minimum Wages Bill.

With a view to encouraging students belonging to untouchables communities, Dr. Ambedkar had set up hostels and provided them with free books and clothing.

In 1945-46, Dr. Ambedkar founded his own educational institution, the People's Education Society. As he was then a Member of the Viceroy's Executive Council he managed to get a generous grant of Rs. 3 lakh and an equal amount of loan without interest from the then Government of India.

The social inequalities his experiences as an untouchable boy, lawyer and Professors made Dr. Ambedkar a relentless critic of Hindu society and its orthodoxy. He embraced Buddhism in 1956.

He attained Mahanirvana on 6 December 1956. Government of India honoured him by confering the nation's highest award, Bharat Ratna, posthumously.

Gulzari Lal Nanda

The son of a school teacher, Nanda was born on July 4, 1898 in Badoki Gosai village in Gujranwalla, now in Pakistan.

In 1921, he joined the National College, Mumbai, as professor of economics. It was here that he came in contact with Mahatma Gandhi and decided to join the freedom movement.

Gandhiji decided to put the young professor's interest in labour economics to practical use and asked him to work in the trade unions of various textile mills of Ahmedabad. And so Nanda arrived in Ahmedabad in 1921 to help organise and strengthen the textile labour association.

In 1922, Nanda became secretary of the Mazdoor Mahajan Sangh, founded by Mahatma Gandhi, and served the textile labour of Gujarat for 23 years.

The comparative Industrial peace that Gujarat has enjoyed all these years is due in no small measure to the silent constructive work done by this Gandhian in the early formative years.

In 1937, Nanda was elected to the Bombay provincial assembly and became parliamentary secretary (Labour and excise) to the chief minister of Bombay state. He also worked as labour and housing minister in the Bombay state during 1946-50.

During his tenure there, he was responsible for framing the Bombay Industrial Relations Act, a piece of legislation which has had far-reaching impact on the all-important textile industry of Bombay and Ahmedabad region.

In May 1947, on the eve of independence, he became one of the pioneers of the Indian National Trade Union Congress. (INTUC).

After independence, Gulzari Lal Nanda played a crucial role in framing development plans for the country.

In 1950, he was appointed the first deputy chairman of the Planning Commission. In the first general election in 1952 after India became a republic, Nanda was elected from Sabarkantha in north Gujarat.

He was appointed as the Union Minister for planning, irrigation and power in 1952. From 1957 to 1963 he worked as Union Minister for planning, labour and employment.

Though Mr. Nanda had the drive, dedication and commitment, he never hankered after power. In 1964, when Nehru died, he became the interim Prime Minister. Sixteen days later, he stepped down in favour of Lal Bahadur Shastri.

However, two years later after the death of Shastriji, he was once again made the interim Prime Minister for fourteen days before the mantle was handed over to Indira Gandhi. In between, he worked as the Union Home Minister.

While Nanda represented Sabarkantha constituency in north Gujarat in the Lok Sabha for most of his Parliamentary career, in his later years, he shifted to Kaithal in Kurukshetra, Haryana.

During his two terms of Prime Ministership, Nanda performed his duties commendably. His political carrier ended tragically when a group of sadhus demostrating outside the Parliament on the issue of cow slaughter were lathi charged by the police. The uproar in the Parliament over the incident resulted in Nanda tendering his resignation as home ministers in 1966.

Though he did come back for a brief tenure as railway minister, he never contested, elections again.

Despite a hectic political career, Nanda could take out time for recreation work. He has some note-worthy publications to his credit. These include ; *Some Aspects of Khadi, History of Wage Adjustment in the Ahmedabad Textile Industry, Approach to Second Five Year Plan – Some Basic Consideration.*

From 1972 onwards, Nanda devoted his time and energy on religion and building up the town of Kurukshetra. He continued to work on his Kuruskshetra. He continued to work on his Kurukshetra project till the rip age of 91. In 1989, he suffered a fall whilst staying at the Haryana Bhavan in Delhi and fractured his hip. That finally put an end to the die-hard Gandhian's public life.

FAMOUS TREATIES

Path - Breaking Historical Documents of the early years of Post Independence Era These led to the Foundation of India's Foreign Policy

Path - Breaking Historical Documents of the early years of Post Independence Era These led to the Foundation of India's Foreign Policy

The text of The Famous Indo-Nepalese Treaty of Peace and Friendship Issued in Khatmandu on July 31, 1950

The Government of India and the Government of Nepal, recognising the ancient ties which have happily existed between the two countries for centuries;

Desiring still further to strengthen and develop these ties and to perpetuate peace between the two countries;

Have resolved therefore to enter into a treaty of Peace and Friendship with each other, and have, for this purpose, appointed as their Plenipotentiaries the following persons, namely,

The Government of India :

His excellency Shri Chandreshwar Prasad Narain Singh, Ambassador of India in Nepal.

The Government of Nepal :

Mohun Shamsher Jung Bahadur Rana, Maharaja, Prime Minister and Supreme Commander-in-Chief of Nepal,

who having, examined each other's credentials and found them good and in due form have agreed as follows :

Article I

These shall be everlasting peace and friendship between the Government of India and the Government of Nepal. The two Governments agree mutually to acknowledge and respect the complete sovereignty, territorial integrity and independence of each other.

Article II

The two Governments hereby undertake to inform each other of any serious friction or misunderstanding with any neighbouring State likely to cause any breach in the friendly relations subsisting between the two Governments.

Article III

In order to establish and maintain the relations referred to in Article I the two governments agree to continue diplomatic relations with each other by means of representatives with such staff as is necessary for the due performance of their functions.

The representatives and such of their staff as may be agreed upon shall enjoy such diplomatic privileges and immunities as are customarily granted by international law on a reciprocal basis .

Provided that in no case shall these be less than those granted to persons of a similar status of any other State having diplomatic relations with either Government.

Article IV

The two Governments agree to appoint Consuls-General, Consuls, Vice-Consuls and other consular agents, who shall reside in towns, ports and other places in each other's territory as may be agreed to.

Consuls-General, Consuls, Vice-Consuls and consular agents shall be provided with exequaturs or other valid authorization of their appointment. Such exequatur or authorization is liable to be withdrawn by the country which issued it, if considered necessary. The reasons for the withdrawal shall be indicated wherever possible.

The persons mentioned above shall enjoy on a reciprocal basis all the rights, privileges, exemptions and immunities that are accorded to persons of corresponding status of any other State.

Article V

The Government of Nepal shall be free to import, from or through the territory of India, arms, ammunition or warlike material and equipment necessary for the security of Nepal. The procedure for giving effect to this arrangement shall be worked out by the Two Governments acting in Consultation.

Article VI

Each Government undertakes, in token of the neighbourly friendship between India and Nepal, to give to the nationals of the other, in its territory, national treatment with regard to participation in industrial and economic development of such territory and to the grant of concessions and contracts relating to such development.

Article VII

The Governments of India and Nepal agree to grant, on a reciprocal basis, to the nationals of one country in the territories of the other the same privileges in the matter of residence, ownership of property, participation in trade and commerce, movement and other privileges of a similar nature.

Article VIII

So far as matters dealt with herein are concerned, this Treaty cancels all previous treaties, agreements and arrangements entered into on behalf of India between the British Government and the Government of Nepal.

Article IX

This Treaty shall come into force from the date of signature by both Governments.

Article X

This Treaty shall remain in force until it is terminated by either party by giving one year's notice.

India ends State of War With Japan

The text of The Indo-Japanese Treaty of Peace Issued in Tokyo on June 9, 1952

WHEREAS the Government of India have by public notification issued on the ninth day of June, 1952, terminated the state of war between India and Japan;

AND WHEREAS the Government of India and the Government of Japan are desirous of cooperating in friendly association for the promotion of the common welfare of their peoples and the maintenance of international peace and security in conformity with the principles of the Charter of the United Nations;

The Government of India and the Government of Japan have, therefore, determined to conclude this Treaty of Peace, and to this end have appointed as their Plenipotentiaries:

THE GOVERNMENT OF INDIA

AND

THE GOVERNMENT OF JAPAN

who, having indicated to each other their respective Full Powers, and found them good and in due form, have agreed on the following Articles:–

Article I

There shall be firm and perpetual peace and amity between India and Japan and their respective peoples.

Article II

(a) The Contracting Parties agree to enter into negotiations for the conclusion of treaties or agreements to place their trading, maritime, aviation and other commercial relations on a stable and friendly basis.

(b) Pending the conclusion of the relevant treaty or agreement, during a period of four years from the date of the issue of the notification by the Government of India terminating the state of war between India and Japan–

(1) the Contracting Parties shall accord to each other most-favoured-nation treatment also with respect to air traffic rights and privileges;

(2) the Contracting Parties shall accord to each other most-favoured-nation treatment also with respect to customs duties and charges of any kind and restrictions and other regulations in connection with the importation and exportation of goods or imposed on the international transfer of payments for imports or exports and with respect to the method of levying such duties and charges and with respect to all rules and formalities in connection with importation and exportation and charges to which customs clearing may be subject; and any advantage, favour, privilege or immunity granted by either of the parties to any product originating in or destined for any other country shall be accorded immediately and unconditionally to the like products originating in or destined for the territory of the other Party;

(3) Japan will accord to India national treatment, to the extent that India accords Japan the same, with respect to shipping, navigation and imported goods, and with respect to natural and juridical persons and their interests– such treatment to include all matters pertaining to the levying and collection of taxes, access to the courts, the making and performance of contracts, rights to property (tangible and intangible), participation in juridical entities constituted under Japanese law, and generally the conduct of all kinds of business and professional activities :

Provided that in the application of this Article, a discriminatory measure shall not be considered to derogate for the grant of national or most favoured-nation treatment, if such measure is based on an exception customarily provided for in the commercial treaties of the party applying it, or on the necessity of safeguarding that party's external financial position or balance of payments, or on the need to maintain its essential security interests, and provided such measure is proportionate to the circumstances and is not applied in an arbitrary or unreasonable manner :

Provided further that nothing contained in sub-paragraph (2) above shall apply to the preferences or advantages which have existed since before the 15th August, 1947, or which are accorded by India to contiguous countries.

(c) No provision of this Article shall be deemed to limit the undertakings assumed by Japan under Article V of this Treaty.

Article III

Japan agrees to enter into negotiations with India, when India so desires, for the conclusion of an agreement providing for the regulation or limitation of fishing and the conservation and development of fisheries on the high seas.

Article IV

India will return to restore in their present form all property, tangible and intangible, and rights or interests of Japan or its national which were within India at the time of the commencement of the war and are under the control of the Government of India at the time of the coming into force of this Treaty; provided that the expenses which may have been incurred for the preservation and administration of such property shall be paid by Japan or its nationals concerned. If any such property has been liquidated, the proceeds thereof shall be returned, deducting the above-mentioned expense.

Article V

Upon application made within 9 months of the coming into force of this Treaty Japan will, within 6 months of the date of such application, return the property, tangible and intangible, and all rights or interests of any kind in Japan of India and her nationals which was within Japan at any time between the 7th December 1941 and the 2nd September 1945 unless the owner has freely disposed thereof without duress or fraud.

Such property will be returned free of all encumbrances and charges to which it may have become subject because of the war, and without any charges of its return.

Property the return of which is not applied for by or on behalf of its owner or by the Government of India within the prescribed period may be disposed of by the Japanese Government in its discretion.

If any such property was with Japan on the 7th December, 1941 and cannot be returned or has suffered injury or damage as a result of the war, compensation will be made on terms not less favourable than the terms provided in the Allied Powers Property Compensation Law of Japan (Law number 164, 1951).

Article VI

(a) India waives all reparations claims against Japan

(b) Except as otherwise provided in this Treaty, India waives all claims of India and Indian nationals arising out of action taken by Japan and its nationals in the course of the prosecution of the war as also claims of India arising from the fact that it participated in the occupation of Japan.

Article VII

Japan agrees to take the necessary measures to enable nationals of India to apply within one year of the coming into force of this Treaty to the appropriate Japanese authorities for review of any judgment given by a Japanese Court between December 7, 1941, and such coming into force, if in the proceedings in which the judgment was given any Indian national was not able to present his case adequately either as plaintiff or as defendant, Japan further agrees that where an Indian national has suffered injury by reason of any such judgement, he shall be restored to the position in which he was before the judgement was given or shall be afforded such relief as may be just and equitable in the circumstances of the case.

Article VIII

(a) The Contracting Parties recognize that the intervention of the state of war has not affected the obligation to pay pecuniary debts arising out of obligations and contracts (including those in respect of bonds) which existed and rights which were acquired before the existence of the state of war, and which are due by the Government or nationals of Japan to the Government or nationals of India, or are due by the Government or nationals of India to the Government or nationals of Japan; nor has the intervention of the state of war affected the obligation to consider on their merits claims for loss or damage to property or for personal injury or death which arose between the existence of a state of war, and which may be presented or re-presented by the Government of India to the Government of Japan or by the Government of Japan to the Government of India.

(b) Japan affirms its liability for the pre-war external debt of the Japanese State and for debts of corporate bodies subsequently declared to be liabilities of the Japanese State, and expresses its intention to enter into negotiations at an early date with its creditors with respect to the resumption of payments on these debts.

(c) The Contracting Parties will encourage negotiations in respect to other pre-war claims and obligations and facilitate the transfer of sums accordingly.

Article IX

(a) Japan waives all claims of Japan and her nationals against India and her nationals arising out of the war or out of actions taken because of the existence of a state of war, and waives all claims arising from the presence, operations or actions of forces or authorities of India in Japanese territory prior to the coming into force of this Treaty.

(b) The foregoing waiver includes any claims arising out of actions taken by India with respect to Japanese ships between September 1, 1939, and the coming into force of this Treaty, as well as any claims and debts arising in respect to Japanese prisoners of war and civilian internees in the hands of India; but does not include Japanese claims specifically recognised in the laws of India enacted since September 2, 1945.

(c) Japan recognises the validity of all acts and omissions done during the period of occupation under or in consequence of directives of the occupation authorities or authorised by Japanese law at that time, and will take no action subjecting Indian nationals to civil or criminal liability arising out of such acts or omissions.

Article X

Any dispute arising out of the interpretation or application of this Treaty or one or more of its Articles shall be settled in the first instance by negotiations, and, if no settlement is reached within a period of six months from the commencement of negotiations by arbitration in such manner as may hereafter be determined by a general or special agreement between the Contracting Parties.

Article XI

This Treaty shall be ratified and shall come into force on the date of exchange of ratifications which shall take place as soon as possible at New Delhi (or Tokyo).

IN WITNESS WHEREOF, the undersigned Plenipotentiaries have signed this Treaty;

DONE in duplicate at Tokyo this Ninth day of June, 1952 in the English language. Hindi and Japanese texts of this Treaty will be exchanged by the two Governments within a month of this date.

FOR JAPAN
(*Katsuo Okazaki*)

FOR INDIA
(*K. K. Chattur*)

First Visit of a Chinese Prime Minister

The text of The Joint Statement by the Prime Ministers of India and China Issued in New Delhi on June 28, 1954

His Excellency Chou En-lai, Prime Minister and Foreign Minister of the People's Republic of China, came to Delhi at the invitation of His Excellency Jawaharlal Nehru, Prime Minister and Foreign Minister of the Republic of India. He stayed here for three days. During this period the two Prime Ministers discussed many matters of common concern to India and China. In particular they discussed the prospects of peace in South Asia and the developments that had taken place in the Geneva Conference in regard to Indo-China. The situation in Indo-China was of vital importance to the peace of Asia and the world and the Prime Ministers were anxious that the efforts that were being made at Geneva should succeed. They noted with satisfaction that some progress had been made in the talks at Geneva in regard to an armistice. They earnestly hoped that these efforts will meet with success in the near future and that they would result in a political settlement of the problems of that area.

2. The talks between the Prime Ministers aimed at helping in such way as were possible, the efforts at peaceful settlement that were being made in Geneva and elsewhere. Their main purpose was to arrive at a clearer understanding of each other's point of view in order to help the maintenance of peace, both in co-operation with each other and with other countries.

3. Recently India and China have come to an agreement in which they laid down certain principles which should guide the relations between the two countries. These principles are :

(1) Mutual respect for each other's territorial integrity and sovereignty;

(2) Non-aggression;

(3) Non-interference in each other's internal affairs ;

(4) Equality and mutual benefit; and

(5) Peaceful co-existence. (first time initiated)

The Prime Ministers reaffirmed these principles and felt that they should be applied in their relations with other countries in Asia as well as in other parts of the world. If these principles are applied not only between various countries but also in international relations generally, they would form a solid foundation for peace and security and the fears and apprehensions that exist today would give place to a feeling of confidence.

4. The Prime Ministers recognised that different social and political systems exist in various parts of Asia and the world. If, however, the above-mentioned principles are accepted and acted upon and their is non interference by any one country with another, these differences should not come in the way of peace or create conflicts. With the assurance of territorial integrity and sovereignty of each country and of non-aggression, there would be peaceful co-existence and friendly relations between the countries concerned. This would lessen the tension that exists in the world today and help in creating a climate of peace.

5. In particular, the Prime Ministers hoped that these principles would be applied to the solution of the problems in Indo-China where the political settlement should aim at the creation of free, democratic, unified and independent States, which should not be used for aggressive purposes or be subjected to foreign intervention. This will lead to a growth of self-confidence in these countries as well as to friendly relations between them and their neighbours. The adoption of the principles referred to above will also help in creating an area of peace which, as circumstances permit, can be enlarged, thus lessening the chances of war and strengthening the cause of peace all over the world.

6. The Prime Minister expressed their confidence in the friendship between India and China which would help the cause of world peace and the peaceful development of their respective countries as well as the other countries of Asia.

7. These conversations were held with a view to help in bringing about a greater understanding of the problems of Asia and to further a peaceful and co-operative effort, in common with the other countries of the world, in solving these and like problems.

The Prime Ministers agreed that their respective countries should maintain close contacts so that there should continue to be full understanding between them. They appreciated greatly the present opportunity of meeting together and having a full enhance of ideas leading to a clearer understanding and co-operation in the cause of peace.

This led to the Policy of Non-alignment

The text of The Final Communique of Asian-African Conference issued in bandung on April 24, 1955

The Asian-African Conference, convened upon the invitation of the Prime Ministers of Burma, Ceylon, India, Indonesia, and Pakistan. met in Bandung from the 18th to the 24th April, 1955. In addition to the sponsoring countries the following 24 countries participated in the Conference :

1. Afghanistan
2. Cambodia
3. People's Republic of China
4. Egypt
5. Ethiopia
6. Gold Coast
7. Iran
8. Iraq
9. Japan
10. Jordan
11. Laos
12. Lebanon
13. Liberia
14. Libya
15. Nepal
16. Philippines
17. Saudi Arabia
18. Sudan
19. Syria
20. Thailand
21. Turkey
22. Democratic Republic of Viet-Nam
23. State of Viet-Nam
24. Yemen.

The Asian-African Conference considered problems of common interest and concern to countries of Asia and Africa and discussed ways and means by which their people could achieve fuller economic, cultural and political co-operation.

A. Economic Co-operation

1. The Asian-African Conference recognised the urgency of promoting economic development in the Asian-African region. These was general desire for economic co-operation among the participating countries on the basis of mutual interest and respect for national sovereignty. The proposals with regard to economic co-operation within the participating countries do not preclude either the desirability or the need for co-operation with countries outside the region including the investment of foreign capital. It was further recognised that the assistance being received by certain participating countries from outside the region, through international or under bilateral arrangements, had made a valuable contribution to the implementation of their development programmes.

2. The participating countries agreed to provide technical assistance to one another, to the maximum extent practicable, in the form of experts, trainees, pilot projects and equipment for demonstration purposes; exchange of know-how and establishment of national, and where possible, regional training and research institutes for imparting technical knowledge and skills in co-operation with the existing international agencies.

3. The Asian-African Conference recommended the early establishment of the Special United Nations Fund for Economic Development; the allocation by the International Bank for Reconstruction and Development of a greater part of its resources to Asian-African countries; the early establishment of the International Finance Corporation which should include in its activities the undertaking of equity investment; and encouragement to the promotion of joint ventures among Asian-African countries in so far as this will promote their common interest.

4. The Asian-African Conference recognised the vital need for establishing commodity trade in the region. The principle of enlarging the scope of multilateral trade and payments was accepted. However,

it was recognised that some countries would have to take resourse to bilateral trade agreements in view of their prevailing economic conditions.

5. The Asian-African Conference recommended that collective action be taken by participating countries for stablising the international prices of and demand for primary commodities through bilateral and multilateral arrangements, and that as far as practicable and desirable, they should adopt a unified approach on the subject in the United Nations Permanent Advisory Commission on International Commodity Trade and other international forums.

6. The Asian-African Conference further recommended that Asian-African countries should diversify their export trade by processing their raw materials, wherever economically feasible, before export; that intra-regional trade fairs should be promoted and encouragement given to the exchange of trade delegations and groups of businessmen; that exchange of information and of samples should be encouraged with a view to promoting intra-regional trade, and that normal facilities should be provided for transit trade of land-locked countries.

7. The Asian-African Conference attached considerable importance to shipping and expressed concern that shipping lines reviewed from time to time their freight rates, often to the detriment of participating countries. It recommended a study of this problem, and collective action thereafter, to induce the shipping lines to adopt a more reasonable attitude. It was suggested that a study of railway freight of transit trade might be made.

8. The Asian-African Conference agreed that encouragement should be given to the establishment of national and regional banks and insurance companies.

9. The Asian-African Conference felt that exchange of information of matters relating to oil, such as remittance of profits and taxation, might eventually lead to the formulation of common policies.

10. The Asian-African Conference emphasised the particular significance of the development of nuclear energy for peaceful purposes for the Asian-African countries. The Conference welcomed the initiative of the Power principally concerned in offering to make available information regarding the use of atomic energy for peaceful

purposes; urged the speedy establishment of the International Atomic Energy Agency which should provide for adequate representation of the Asian-African countries on the executive authority of the Agency ; and recommended to the Asian and African Governments to take full advantage of the training and other facilities in the peaceful uses of atomic energy offered by the countries sponsoring such programmes.

11. The Asian-African Conference agreed to the appointment of Liaison Officers in participating countries, to be nominated by their respective national Governments, for the exchange of information and ideas on matters of mutual interest. It recommended that fuller use should be made of the existing international organisations, and participating countries who were not members of such international organisations but were eligible, should secure membership.

12. The Asian-African Conference recommended that there should be prior consultation of participating countries in international forums with a view, as far as possible, to furthering their mutual economic interest. It, is, however, not intended to form a regional bloc.

B. Cultural Co-operation

1. The Asian-African Conference was convinced that among the most powerful means of promoting understanding among nationals is the development of cultural co-operation. Asia and Africa have been the cradle of great religions and civilisations, which influenced other civilizations and cultures while themselves being enriched in the process. Thus the cultures of Asia and Africa are based on spiritual and universal foundations. Unfortunately, contacts among Asian and African countries were interrupted during the past centuries. The peoples of Asia and Africa are now animated by a keen and sincere desire to renew their old cultural contacts and develop new ones in the context of the modern world. All participating Governments at the Conference reiterated their determination to work for closer cultural co-operation.

2. The Asian-African Conference took note of the fact that the existence of colonialism in many parts of Asia and Africa, in whatever form it may be, not only prevents cultural co-operation but also suppresses the national cultures of the people. Some colonial powers

have denied to their dependent peoples basic rights in the sphere of education and culture which hampers the development of their personality and also prevents cultural intercourse with other Asian and African peoples. This is particularly true in the case of Tunisia, Algeria and Morocco, where the basic right of the people to study their own language and culture has been suppressed. Similar discrimination has been practised against African and coloured peoples in some parts of the Continent of Africa. The Conference felt that these policies amount to a denial of the fundamental rights of man and impede cultural advancement in this region and also hamper cultural co-operation on the wider international plane. The Conference condemned such a denial of fundamental rights in the sphere of education and culture in some parts of Asia and Africa by this and other forms of cultural suppression.

In particular, the Conference condemned racialism as a means of cultural suppression.

3. It was not from any sense of exclusiveness or rivalry with other groups of nations and other civilisations and cultures that the Conference viewed the development of cultural co-operation among Asian and African countries. True to the age-old tradition of tolerance and universality, the Conference believed that Asian and African cultural co-operation should be developed in the larger context of world co-operation.

Side by side with the development of Asian-African cultural co-operation, the countries of Asia and Africa desire to develop cultural contacts with others. This would enrich their own culture and would also help in the promotion of world peace and understanding.

4. There are many countries in Asia and Africa which have not yet been able to develop their educational, scientific and technical institutions. The Conference recommended that countries in Asia and Africa which are more fortunately placed in this respect should give facilities for the admission of students and trainees from such countries to their institutions. Such facilities should also be made available to the Asian and African people in Africa to whom opportunity for acquiring education are at present denied.

5. The Asian-African Conference felt that the promotion of

cultural co-operation among countries of Asia and Africa should be directed towards :

(i) the acquisition of knowledge of each other's country;
(ii) mutual cultural exchange; and
(iii) exchange of information.

6. The Asian-African Conference was of opinion that at this stage the best results in cultural co-operation would be achieved by pursuing bilateral arrangements to implement its recommendations and by each country taking action on its own, wherever possible and feasible.

C. Human Rights and Self-Determination

1. The Asian-African Conference declared its full support of the fundamental principles of Human Rights as set forth in the Charter of the United Nations and took note of the Universal Declaration of Human Rights as a common standard of achievement for all peoples and all nations.

The Conference declared its full support of the principle of self-determination of peoples and nations as set forth in the Charter of the United Nations and took note of the United Nations resolutions on the rights of peoples and nations to self-determination which is a pre-requisite of the full enjoyment of all fundamental Human Rights.

2. The Asian-African Conference deplored the policies and practices of racial segregation find discrimination which from the basis of government and human relations in large regions of Africa and in other parts of the world. Such conduct is not only a gross violation of human rights, but also a denial of the fundamental values of civilisation and dignity of man.

The Conference extended its warm sympathy and support for the courageous stand taken by the victims of racial discrimination, especially by the peoples of African and Indian and Pakistani origin in South Africa; applauded all those who sustain their cause; re-affirmed the determination of Asian-African peoples to eradicate every trace of racialism that might exist in their own countries; and pledged to use its full moral influence to guard against the danger of falling victims to the same evil in their struggle to eradicate it.

D. Problems of Dependent Peoples

1. The Asian-African Conference discussed the problems of dependent peoples and colonialism and the evils arising from the subjection of peoples to alien subjugation, domination and exploitation.

The Conference is agreed :

(a) In declaring that colonialism in all its manifestations is an evil which should speedily be brought to an end;

(b) in affirming that the subjection of peoples to alien subjugation, domination and exploitation constitutes a denial of fundamental human rights, is contrary to the Charter of the United Nations and is an impediment to the promotion of world peace and co-operation.

(c) in declaring its support of the cause of freedom and independence for all such peoples; and

(d) in calling upon the support of the cause of freedom and independence to such peoples.

2. In view of the unsettled situation in North Africa and of the persisting denial to the peoples of North Africa of their right to self-determination, the Asian-African Conference declared its support of the rights of the people of Algeria, Morocco and Tunisia to self-determination and independence and urged the French Government to bring about a peaceful settlement of the issue without delay.

E. Other Problems

1. In view of the existing tension in the Middle East, caused by the situation in Palestine and of the danger of that tension to world peace, the Asian-African Conference declared its support of the rights of the Arab people of Palestine and called for the implementation of the United Nations resolutions of Palestine and the achievement of the peaceful settlement of the Palestine question.

2. The Asian-African Conference, in the context of its expressed attitude on the abolition of colonialism, supported the position of Indonesia in the case of West Irian based on the relevant agreements between Indonesia and the Netherlands.

The Asian-African Conference urged the Netherlands Government to reopen negotiations as soon as possible to implement their obligations under the above-mentioned agreements and expressed the earnest hope that the United Nations would assist the parties concerned in finding a peaceful solution to the dispute.

F. Promotions of World Peace and Co-operation

The Asian-African Conference, taking note of the fact that several States have still not been admitted to the United Nations, considered that for effective co-operation for world peace, membership in the United Nations should be universal, called on the Security Council to support the admission of all those States which are qualified for membership in terms of the Charter. In the opinion of the Asian-African Conference, the following among the participating countries viz., Cambodia, Ceylon, Japan, Jordan, Libya, Nepal, a unified Viet-Nam, were so qualified.

The Conference considered that the representation of the countries of the Asian-African region on the Security Council, in relation to the principle of equitable geographical distribution, was inadequate. It expressed the view that as regards the distribution of the non-permanent seats, the Asian-African countries which, under the arrangement arrived at in London in 1946, are precluded from being elected, should be enabled to serve on the Security Council, so that they might make a more effective contribution to the maintenance of international peace and security.

2. The Asian-African Conference having considered the dangerous situation of international tension existing and the risks confronting the whole human race from the outbreak of global war in which the destructive power of all types of armaments, including nuclear and thermo-nuclear weapons, would be employed, invited the attention of all nations to the terrible consequences that would follow if such a war were to break out.

The Conference considered that disarmament and the prohibition of the production, experimentation and use of nuclear and thermo-nuclear weapons and imperative to save mankind and civilisation from the fear and prospect of wholesale destruction. It considered that the nations of Asia and Africa assembled here have a duty towards humanity and civilisation to proclaim their support for disarmament and for the prohibition of these weapons and to appeal to nations principally concerned and to world opinion, to bring about such disarmament and prohibition.

The Conference considered that effective international control should be established and maintained to implement such disarmament and prohibition and that speedy and determined efforts should be made to this end.

Pending the total prohibition of the manufacture of nuclear and thermo-nuclear weapons, this Conference appealed to all the Powers concerned to reach an agreement to suspend experiments with such weapons.

The Conference declared the universal disarmament is an absolute necessity for the preservation of peace and requested the United Nations to continue its efforts and appealed to all concerned speedily to bring about the regulation, limitation, control and reduction of all armed forces and armaments, including the prohibition of the production, experimentation and use of all weapons of mass destruction, and to establish effective international control to this end.

G. Declaration on the Promotion of World Peace and Co-operation

The Asian-African Conference gave anxious thought to the question of world peace and co-operation. It viewed with deep concern the present state of international tension with its danger of an atomic world war. The problem of peace is correlative with the problem of international security. In this connection, all States should co-operate, especially through the United Nations, in bringing about the reduction of armaments and the elimination of nuclear weapons under effective international control. In this way, international peace can be promoted and nuclear energy may be used exclusively for peaceful purposes. This would help answer the needs, particularly of Asia and Africa, for what they urgently require are social progress and better standards of life in larger freedom. Freedom and peace are interdependent. The right of self-determination must be enjoyed by all peoples, and freedom and independence must be granted, with the least possible delay, to those who are still dependent peoples. Indeed all nations should have the right freely to choose their own political and economic systems and their own way of life in conformity with the purposes and principles of the Charter of the United Nations.

Free from mistrust and fear, and with confidence and goodwill towards each other, the nationals should practise tolerance and live together in peace with one another as good neighbours and develop friendly co-operation on the basis of the following principles :

1. Respect for fundamental human rights and for the purposes and principles of the Charter of the United Nations.
2. Respect for the sovereignty and territorial integrity of all nations.
3. Recognition of the equality of all races and of the equality of all nations, large and small.
4. Abstention from intervention or interference in the internal affairs of another country.
5. Respect for the right of each nation to defend itself, singly or collectively, in conformity with the Charter of the United Nations.
6. (a) Abstention from the use of arrangements of collective defence to serve the particular interests of any of the big Powers.

   (b) Abstention by any country from exerting pressures on other countries.
7. Refraining from acts or threats of aggression or the use of force against the territorial integrity or political independence of any country.
8. Settlement of all international disputes by peaceful means, such as negotiation, conciliation, arbitration or judicial settlement as well as other peaceful means of the parties' own choice, in conformity with the Charter of the United Nations.
9. Promotion of mutual interests and co-operation.
10. Respect for justice and international obligations.

The Asian-African Conference declares its conviction that friendly co-operation in accordance with these principles would effectively contribute to the maintenance and promotion of international peace and security, while co-operation in the economic, social and cultural fields would help bring about the common prosperity and well-being of all.

The Asian-African Conference recommended that the five sponsoring countries consider the convening of the next meeting of the Conference in consultation with the participating countries.

First Visit of Soviet leaders outside the iron-curtains

The text of The Joint Statement by the Prime Ministers of India and the Soviet Union and Mr. Khrushchev Issued in New Delhi on December 13, 1955

The Prime Minister of India visited the Soviet Union in June 1955 at the invitation of the Government of the Soviet Union. He received a warm welcome their and this visit strengthened the friendship and understanding between the peoples of the two countries. At the conclusion of the visit, a joint statement was issued by the Prime Minister of India and the Chairman of the Council of Ministers of the U.S.S.R. on June 22, 1955.

In response to an invitation extended by the Government of India, Mr. N.A. Bulganin, Chairman of the Council of Ministers of the U.S.S.R., and Mr. N.S. Khrushchev, Member of the Presidium of the Supreme Soviet of the U.S.S.R., accompanied by other official representatives of the Soviet Union, visited India in November-December 1955. Wherever they have travelled in India they have received an enthusiastic welcome from the people of this country. Their visit has strengthened ties of friendship that bind the two countries and their peoples. Mr. Bulganin and Mr. Khrushchev have visited various agricultural, industrial and river valley projects as well as community schemes, State farms and other centres of developmental activity in India.

The visits to the Soviet Union by Shri Jawaharlal Nehru, Prime Minister of India, and to India by Mr. N.A. Bulganin, Chairman of the Council of Ministers of the U.S.S.R., and Mr. N.S. Khurshchev, Member of Presidium of the Supreme Soviet of the U.S.S.R., have enabled them to gain some personal knowledge of the peoples and their ways of life, of the problems, achievements and aspirations of each country and have resulted in an understanding between them and their peoples which is based on mutual respect, goodwill and tolerance.

In the joint statement issued on June 22, 1955, firm adherence to the Five Principles, sometimes known as the *Panchsheel,* was expressed. These principles have laid down that countries different from each other in their political, social and economic systems, can and should co-operate with each other on the basis of mutual respect and non-interference in internal matters and follow a policy of active and peaceful co-existence in the common pursuit of the ideals of peace and the betterment of the conditions of human life.

Ever since these Five Principles were enunciated, an increasing number of countries have associated themselves with them or expressed their agreement with them. At the Bandung Conference the nations represented unanimously accepted a declaration which affirmed these principles which are now widely recognized to be the firm basis for co-operation among nations.

During the present visit of Mr. Bulganin and Mr Khrushchev to India, free and frank discussions have taken place with Shri Jawaharlal Nehru, Prime Minister of India, in regard to the international situation. These discussions have resulted in a reiteration of their firm conviction that international relations should be governed by the Five Principles and that every effort should be made to lessen international tensions and promote the cause of peace and co-operation between nations. The meting of the Heads of Governments at Geneva in July 1955 led to the recognition by the Great Powers represented there of the futility of war which, owing to the development of nuclear and thermo-nuclear weapons, could only bring disaster to mankind. This basic recognition to rule out was as a method of settling international disputes was received with acclamation by the peoples of the world and led to a considerable lessening of tensions. While the major problems in Europe and Asia still awaited solution, the natural consequences of ruling out war led to a change of approach and to attempts at negotiations. Diplomatic relations were established between the Soviet Union and the German Federal Republic. Talks were initiated and are still continuing between the United States of America and the People's Republic of China at ambassadorial level. The Conference on the peaceful uses of atomic energy successfully concluded its deliberations in August last and the General Assembly has adopted a resolution concerning the establishment of the International Atomic Energy Agency.

In order to further this process of negotiation, the meeting of the Heads of Governments held at Geneva in July last directed that the meeting of the Foreign Ministers of the countries concerned be convened. This meeting of Foreign Ministers has recently been held in Geneva. It has not led to agreements on the problems discussed and the high expectations which resulted from the meeting of Heads of Government have not yet been realised. The meeting has, however, led to a clearer understanding of the problems which face the world, and the basic fact remains that these problems can only be solved by peaceful methods and by the process of peaceful negotiations if war is to be ruled out, as is well recognized that it must be. The disappointment at the result of the Foreign Ministers' Conference in Geneva need, therefore, only be temporary, and every effort should continue to be made for the relaxation of international tension and for sole reliance on the approach of settlement of differences by negotiation. The leaders of both countries express the hope that the talks that are continuing to take place between the United States of America and the People's Republic of China at ambassadorial level will not only lead to a solution of the problems that are being discussed by them but also to a wider understanding through meetings at higher levels. They are convinced that there can be no lasting peace in Asia so long as the People's Republic of China is not given its rightful place in the United Nations. They deplore the delay in recognizing this patent fact. It is earnestly hoped that the other problems of the Far East of Asia will also be settled at an early date by agreement, that is to say, the legitimate rights of the Chinese People's Republic in regard to the coastal island and Taiwan should be satisfied and the Korean problem should be settled on the basis of the recognition of the national rights of the Korean people and in accordance with the interests of peace in the Far East.

The Prime Minister of India and the leaders of the U.S.S.R. had welcomed the Conference on Indo-China held in Geneva last year. This conference had ended the disastrous war in Indo-China and laid down the procedure for the settlement of the problems of the States of Indo-China. They note with regret that impediments have been placed in the way of carrying out the Geneva Agreement in Viet-Nam and that difficulties have also arisen in regard to the implementation of the Geneva Agreement in Laos. A breakdown of these Agreements would produce consequences of the utmost gravity, both to Indo-

China and to the world at large. The Leaders of both countries, therefore, desire to appeal to all parties and interests concerned to remove the obstacles now standing in the way of the effective implementation of the Geneva Agreement and to co-operate fully in carrying out in letter and in spirit the provisions of these agreements.

They are strongly of the opinion that the principles of universality should be applied to membership of the United Nations. Unless this is done, the United Nations will not be fully representative of the world community. They welcome, therefore, the recommendation of the General Assembly of the United Nations for the simultaneous admission of 18 nations and sincerely hope that this recommendation will be accepted by the Security Council and acted upon soon.

In order to establish world peace and to eliminate conditions leading to the inconceivable disaster of another world war there is no course open but that of disarmament is a constant invitation to war and leads to fear and a competition in the production of the latest type of weapons for mass destruction. The urgency of disarmament grows in proportion to the invention and accumulation of weapons of ever-increasing destructive potential. The widespread desire that war should be totally ruled out necessitates that positive, adequate and early steps should be taken towards disarmament. There has already been a large measure of agreement on this subject and there appears to be no reason why the remaining obstacles should not be overcome soon if enduring peace is the aim. In particular, the leaders of both countries wish to emphasize again their strong conviction that there should be an unconditional prohibition of the production, use and experimentation of nuclear and thermo-nuclear weapons. Together with this, there must inevitably be a substantial reduction of conventional armaments coupled with arrangements for effective international control designed to ensure the strict implementation of such prohibition and disarmament. So long as this is no achieved, the fear of war will shadow and oppress the world and people will doubt that peace is being really sought for.

The Prime Minister of India and the leaders of the U.S.S.R. agreed that the method of ensuring peace and security was not by the formation of military alliances or regional military blocks. Such alliances widened the frontiers of the cold war and introduced an element of instability in the areas concerned and increased fear and tension in addition to coming in the way of the peaceful development of the countries concerned. Peace and real security can be ensured only by the collective efforts of States.

One of the most effective ways of lessening international fears and tension is to remove the barriers to mutual co-operation and understanding. For this purpose, cultural and economic contacts between countries should be encouraged. The leaders of both countries have noted with satisfaction the increasing opportunities afforded to the peoples of the two countries to get to know each other by the regular exchange of visits by scientists, technicians, economists, parliamentarians, writers and others engaged in cultural pursuits. They hope that there will be a steady expansion of such opportunities for mutual contacts on a basis which will promote understanding and respect for the differing ways of life in the two countries.

The Prime Minister of India, the Chairman of the Council of Ministers of the U.S.S.R. and the Member of the Presidium of the Supreme Soviet of the U.S.S.R. welcome, therefore, the development of co-operation between the two countries in the establishment of the Bhilai Steel Works in India and the talks that are now proceeding in regard to a number of other projects. The Second Five-Year Plan of India, with its emphasis on the development of heavy industry, may reveal further such opportunities of co-operation. They consider it desirable that when the requisite preparatory work has been completed, competent representatives of the two countries should meet together for the purpose of considering further mutually advantageous forms of economic and technical co-operation and to arrive at agreements on specific matters wherever considered necessary.

The visit of Mr. Bulganin and Mr. Khrushchev to India is a significant event not only in bringing the two countries nearer to one another but also in the advancement of the cause of world peace. Shri Jawaharlal Nehru, Prime Minister of India, N.A. Bulganin, Chairman of the Council of Ministers of the U.S.S.R., and N.S. Khrushchev, member of the Presidium of the Supreme Soviet of the U.S.S.R., declare anew their faith in the future and their firm resolve to devote their energies to the promotion of peace for the benefit not only of the people of their two countries but of the world as a whole.

First-ever Visit of an American President to India

The text of The Joint Communique by the President of the United States of America and the Prime Minister of India issued in New Delhi on December 13, 1959

At the invitation of the Government of India, the President of the United States of America paid a visit to India, lasting from December 9 to 14. President Eisenhower received on his arrival in New Delhi a warm and cordial welcome, marked by popular enthusiasm and goodwill. Throughout his stay and wherever he went, these friendly manifestations of goodwill were repeated by millions of Delhi citizens and others who had come to Delhi to join in this welcome.

During his strenuous four-day visit, President Eisenhower fulfilled a number of public engagements. He addressed Members of the Indian Parliament, received an Honorary Doctorate of Law from the University of Delhi, participated in the inauguration of the World Agriculture Fair, attended a Civic Reception on behalf of the City of Delhi and visited rural areas near Agra.

In thus fulfilling a desire of many years, the President was deeply touched by the warmth of the welcome extended to him by the people of India, by the generous hospitality of the Government and the excellence of the arrangements made for him.

The President was impressed by the vitality of India's democratic institutions, of Parliament, Press and University, and by India's strength of spirit combined with practical idealism. He saw how India, like the United States, has created national strength out of diversity, neither country boasting that theirs is the only way. He confirmed the bond of shared ideals between India and the United States, their identity of objectives, and their common quest for just and lasting pcacc.

President Eisenhower met the President of India, the Prime Minister and other members of the Government of India. He and the Prime Minister had intimate talks in which they reviewed the world situation and exchanged views on matters of mutual interest.

Among other things, the President told the Prime Minister that he was happy to report to him that all the leaders of the countries he had visited during his recent journey had expressed to him the hope that problems involving one form or another of conflict of interest or views could be solved by peaceful methods of conciliation. He said that this was true in Italy. Turkey, Pakistan and Afghanistan. The President found this heartening and in harmony with his own thinking. He did not wish in any way to minimize the importance of or the inherent difficulties involved in some of the problems. The spirit he found was good and forward-looking.

The Prime Minister expressed gratification and pleasure at President Eisenhower's visit to India, and thanked him for the warmth and generosity of the sentiments he had expressed. He assured the President of the wholehearted support of India in his unremitting errors in the cause of world peace. India herself is dedicated to a policy of peace and has been steadfast in her conviction that differences between nations should be resolved peacefully by the method of negotiation and settlement and not by resort to force. She has consistently pursued this policy in relation to problems of this nature affecting her and other countries.

The Prime Minister gave President Eisenhower a review of the major aspects of some of these problems and of recent developments in regard to them.

The Prime Minister also referred to the great effort that India was making, through her Five-Year Plans, to develop the country, both in regard to agriculture and industry, so as to raise the living standards of the people as rapidly as possible. To this great task, involving the future of 400 million people, India was devoting herself with all her strength and will.

The President and the Prime Minister expressed their deep satisfaction at the friendly and cordial relations existing between their two countries, and their firm belief that their common ideals and objectives and their quest for peace will ensure the maintenance and development of the strong ties of friendship between the two countries.

President Eisenhower's visit to India has afforded the welcome opportunity of a meeting between the Presidents of the two countries, and for the renewal of the friendship between him and the Prime

Minister of India. He was happy to meet other members of the Government, as well as men and women young and old, in city and village, Parliament and University, and to bring to them, personally, assurance of the genuine friendship of the people of the United States for the people of India and their sincere and continuing interest in India's welfare.

To the people of India, this visit, which had been long hoped for, has been the opportunity for the demonstration of the sincere friendship, goodwill and sympathy which they feel for the people of the United States.

PARLIAMENTARY DEVELOPMENT

Parties and Symbols

Parties are at the centre of Indian politics, as they are in all major democracies. The choices facing the voters are simplified by the fact that politicians find it necessary to ally with each other under party labels. Opinion polls in India have repeatedly shown that people generally vote more for the party than for the candidate. But parties vary greatly in their support base and in their permanence. They may be rooted in religion, or region, or caste, or in specific issues, or in general ideologies or based on leadership of a charismatic individual. Parties may also be solid, lasting associations, creating deep loyalties that continue from generation to generation, or they may be ephemeral groupings that endure only for a year or two before they split or amalgamate or simply disappear. India has experience of every type of party.

In India, as in most but not all democracies, parties have to be formally registered with a central body. The Election Commission allots symbols to parties so that illiterate voters can identify them in the secrecy of the booth. Before Independence, different types of voting methods were used in different parts of the country for the limited elections that took place. These included the marking system (with polling staff assisting voters to mark the ballot paper—which involved an obvious loss of secrecy) and the 'colour box system' (where a distinctive coloured box was allotted to each candidate and the voter had to cast his vote in the box belonging to his candidate). After surveying all the different voting procedures, the Indian Franchise Committee of 1931 advocated the use of either the colour box system or the symbol system.

For the first general elections in 1952, the Election Commission chose the balloting system, a compromise between the colour box and the symbol system. Each candidate was allotted one symbol from a list approved and published by the Commission after taking into account the preferences of the candidate. Each polling station had as many ballot boxes as the number of candidates in the constituency with the symbols of the candidates pasted outside the ballot boxes. As symbols were granted constituency-wise, a possible confusion was that the same symbol could be allotted to candidates of different parties in different constituencies. Different ballot boxes also endangered the secrecy of the ballot. It was only in the third general election in 1962 that multiple ballot boxes were replaced with just one box and the more secret 'marking system' now used was introduced. Each ballot paper has both the name and the symbol of each candidate. Voters express their choice by marking the ballot paper in the appropriate space.

In 1982, the first experiment was made with electronic voting machines at some polling stations in the Parur assembly constituency in Kerala. These ingenious battery-operated devices were designed in India and were the first in the world to be used in such simple first-past-the-post elections. They merely required the voter to press a button on the voting machine marked with a candidate's name and the allotted symbol. The design looked very similar to a ballot paper with buttons where crosses are normally marked. These machines were used successfully in ten further contests. But in the meantime the Parur election had been challenged because of the use of voting machines. On 5 March, 1984 the Supreme Court disallowed the voting machines on the grounds that the expression 'votes shall be given by ballots', used in Section 59 of the Representation of the People Act (1951), does not cover the recording of votes by voting machines. The Election Commission recommended that the Act should be amended and subsequently the Law Minister said that this would be done in time for the ninth general election. However, this did not happen. In 1990 a government committee, charged with looking at the ethical and practical problems involved, reported favourably on the proposal. The Act has now been amended enabling the Election Commission to use the machines. But the batteries have gone dead and will have to be manufactured again. Therefore it is unlikely that electronic voting machines will be used for the 1996 Lok Sabha elections.

For the first general election, the Commission recognised 14 'national parties' on the basis of the claims presented by various political groups. No objective criterion such as performance in the

SPLITS IN THE CONGRESS PARTY SINCE 1952

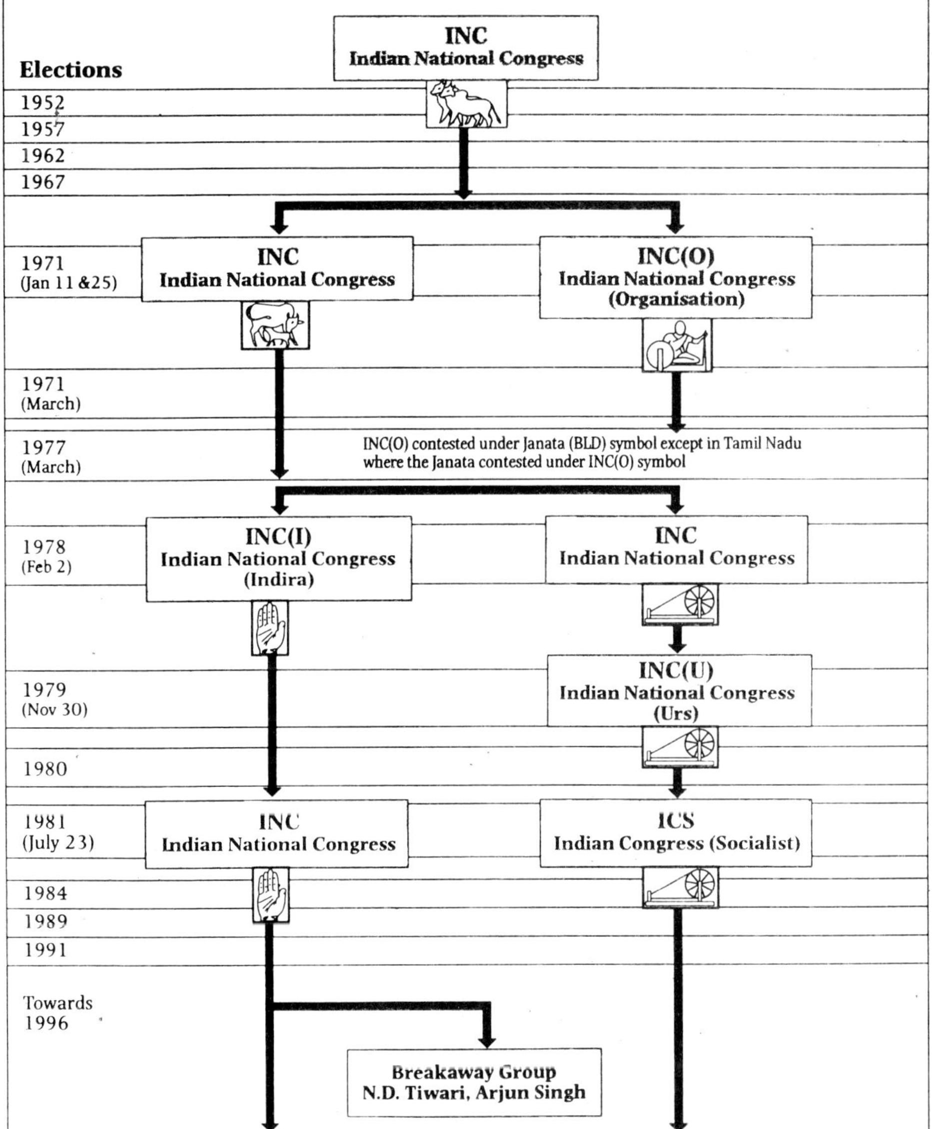

Dates refer to formal Election Commission recognition

last election was available to be used. Each national party had a symbol reserved for its candidates in the State. All other candidates were supposed to choose a symbol from the list of 'free' symbols. After the first general election the four parties that received more than three per cent of the Nationwide Lok Sabha vote were recognised as 'national parties'; 12 parties won over three per cent of the vote in the State Vidhan Sabha elections and these were recognised as 'State parties'.

After the second general election in 1957, the concept of a 'national party' was abandoned (it was later reintroduced at the time of the 1971 election). Recognition of a party was granted on a state-by-state basis to parties which has polled three per cent of the vote both in the Lok Sabha contests in the State as well as in the Vidhan Sabha election. However, for the fourth general election in 1967, the Election Commission, while continuing with the procedure of granting recognition on a state-by-state basis, discarded the practice of making it necessary to win three percent of the vote in both the Lok Sabha and Vidhan Sabha elections. The new criteria was the percentage of votes either in the preceding Lok Sabha or in the preceding Vidhan Sabha elections. The cut-off point for recognition was raised from three per cent to four percent of the votes. Moreover, in order to discourage the tendency of parties to field candidates who forfeited their deposits were to be disregarded in the calculation.

Shortly after the fourth general election in 1967, the Election Commission issued the Election Symbol (Reservation and Allotment) Order, 1968, which introduced the present system under which associations and bodies must register with the Commission as political parties. A registered political party is not automatically 'recognised'. Recognition is granted to a party (again on a state-by-state basis) on the basis of one of two criteria: either (i) its existence and participation in political activity for a period of five years or (ii) its securing at least four percent of the votes cast in the State for Lok Sabha or Vidhan Sabha elections (after excluding the votes polled by the Party's candidates who forfeited their deposits).

The votes polled by a member of the Lok Sabha or Vidhan Sabha who joined a party after the election is not counted for the purpose of calculating the threshold required for recognition. From the second general election onwards, the procedure for judging whether a candidate belonged to a political party involved a declaration by the candidate as well as endorsement by party functionaries. The 'Symbols Order' also contained procedures for resolving disputes when recognised parties split into rival sections or when two or more political parties amalgamated.

Any candidate belonging to a party that is not 'recognised' is officially recorded as an Independent. For example, candidates of the Telugu Desam, which emerged from nowhere to full power in Andhra Pradesh at its first election in 1983, were initially classified as Independents. This kind of problem often makes it difficult to compare the performance of a party over time. With painstaking research, many of the Independent candidates in earlier elections could be reclassified as nominees of unrecognised parties so that this anomaly in election records could be completely removed.

No party in India has survived the last forty years without splits or amalgamations. In the early 50s, for example, the Provincial Zamindara League (Punjab) merged with the Kirshikar Lok Party. The Republican Party of India and the Akali Dal each split. The Socialist Party, first divided into the Praja Socialist Party and the All India Socialist Party and the All India Socialist Party and then came together in 1964 to form the Samyukta Socialist Party only to break up once again within a year into the Samyukta Socialist Party and Praja Socialist Party. It was not until after the fifth general election in 1971 that the two parties merged once again to form the Socialist Party of India.

From the mid-sixties onwards, party splits and amalgamations became more frequent. In 1964 a substantial section broke away from the Communist Party of India to give birth to a new party called the Communist Party of India (Marxist) which has now emerged as the dominant faction. The Swatantra Party, which was formed in 1961, took into its fold the Janata Party of Bihar, the Indian Democratic Congress of Madras and the United Independent Front of Madhya Pradesh.

The Indian National Congress faced its first serious split (in the post-Independence period) in 1969. The party divided into two groups, one led by Najalingappa and the other led by C. Subramaniam (later by Jagjivan Ram); these constituted the anti-Mrs. Gandhi and pro-Mrs. Gandhi groups respectively. The Election Commission recognised both as national parties and allotted them separate symbols (charkha-being-plied-by-a-woman and calf-and-cow). The original Congress symbol was frozen. The name was allotted to the pro- Mrs. Gandhi, Jagjivan Ram group. The Commission's decision that the party presided over by Jagjivan Ram should be recognised as the Indian National Congress was challenged, but the Supreme Court upheld the Commission's ruling and the other Congress faction came to be known as the Indian National Congress (Organisation).

In an unprecedented step just before the 1977 election, four national parties (the Indian National Congress (Organisation), Bharatiya Lok Dal, Bharatiya Jan Sangh and the Socialist Party) merged informally to form the Janata Party. These parties also had an electoral understanding with the Communist Party of India (Marxist). This meant that for the first time the opposition to the Congress Party was almost wholly united except to the Communist Party of India, which supported the Congress. Since the Janata Party was not formed by a *de jure* merger, the Election Commission could not grant legal recognition to the new party. Consequently, it fought throughout India (except for Tamil Nadu and Pondicherry) under the symbol ploughman-within-wheel (chakra-haldhar) which was actually the symbol of one of its constituent parties, the Bharatiya Lok Dal. In Tamil Nadu and Pondicherry, where the Bharatiya Lok Dal did not have any organisation, the Janata Party contested under the symbol of a charkha-being-plied-by-a-woman of the Indian National Congress (Organisation). For this reason the tables - both in the official Election Commission Reports and in this book-refer to the Janata Party in 1977 as the BLD, the official name under which it contested the election. The Janata Party was only recognised as a national party after the 1977 election and the symbol of the chakra-haldar was then reserved for it.

Indian democracy was never so close to a two-party system as it was during the 1977 election. However, the next few years saw a complete change. Soon after its defeat, the Indian National Congress split into two groups - one led by Indira Gandhi and the other by

K. Brahamananda Reddy (and later by Devraj Urs). After a protracted struggle between the two groups, the Commission decided to freeze the earlier Congress symbol of the calf-and-cow, and allot two different symbols to the two groups. Both were declared national parties. The symbol of the 'hand' was given to the Indian National Congress(I) and the 'charkha' to the Indian National Congress(U). (The 'I' and 'U' stood for the names of the leaders of each of the parties: Indira Gandhi and Devraj Urs). Figure 3.1 records the splits and other changes in the Congress party since 1952.

Number of Recognised Parties In the General Elections

Election Year	Total	National Parties	State Parties
1952	74	14	60
1957	16	4	12
1962*	16	—	16
1967*	21	—	21
1971	25	8	17
1977	23	5	18
1980	25	6	19
1984	26	7	19
1989	28	8	20
1991	36	9	27

* There were no national parties in 1962 and 1967 as parties were given recognition only on a state by state basis.

The Janta Party also went through major convulsions. By July 1979, it split into two groups, one led by Chandrashekhar and the other by Charan Singh and Raj Narain. The Election Commission continued to recognise the Chandrashekhar group as the Janata Party with the chakra-haldhar symbol. The other faction was recognised as a national party with the name Janata Party (S), (the 'S' in this case stood for "secular") and the symbol of a farmer-ploughing-the-field was allotted to it. This party, however, soon became popularly

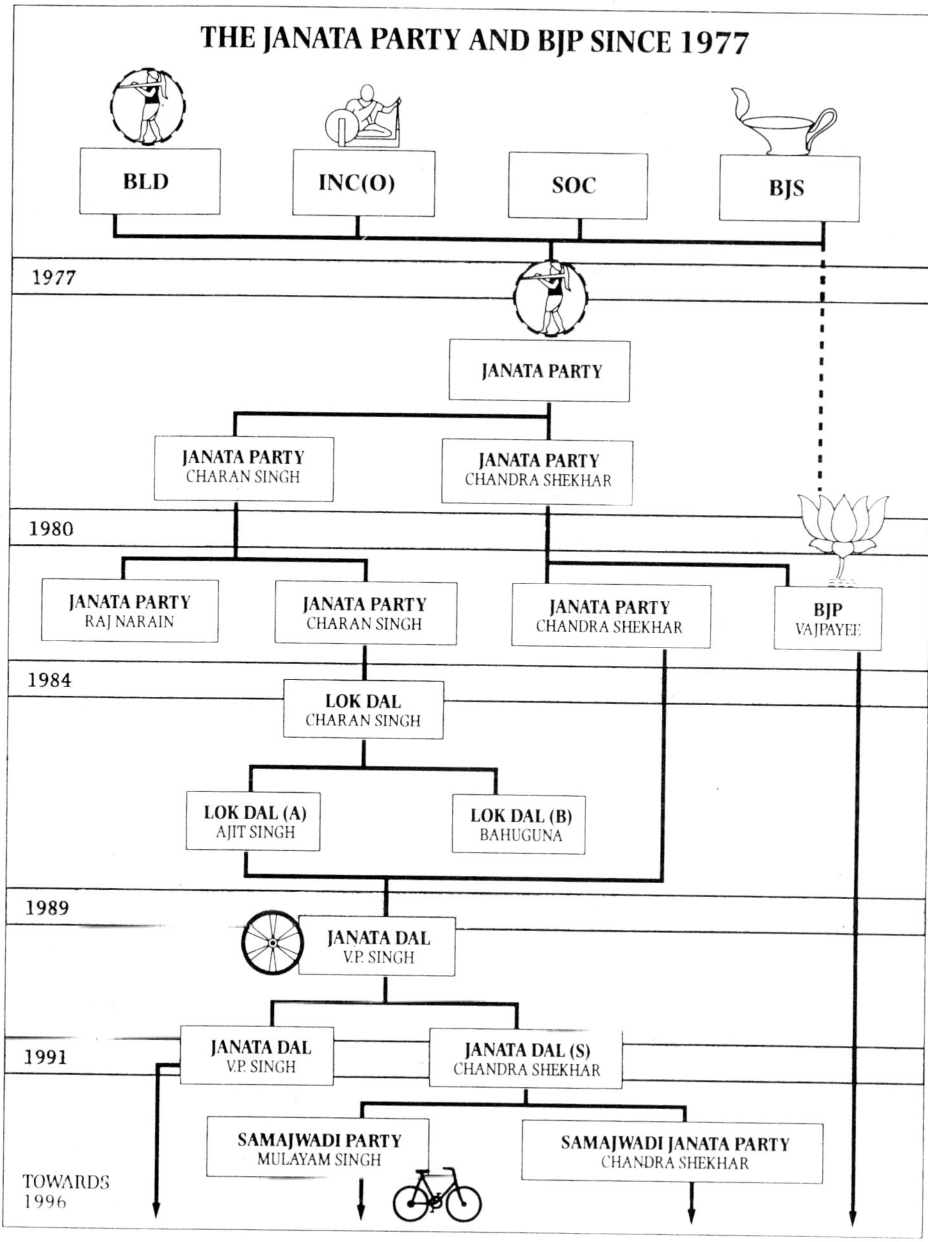
THE JANATA PARTY AND BJP SINCE 1977
BLD
INC(O)
SOC
BJS
1977
JANATA PARTY
JANATA PARTY
CHARAN SINGH
JANATA PARTY
CHANDRA SHEKHAR
1980
JANATA PARTY
RAJ NARAIN
JANATA PARTY
CHARAN SINGH
JANATA PARTY
CHANDRA SHEKHAR
BJP
VAJPAYEE
1984
LOK DAL
CHARAN SINGH
LOK DAL (A)
AJIT SINGH
LOK DAL (B)
BAHUGUNA
1989
JANATA DAL
V.P. SINGH
1991
JANATA DAL
V.P. SINGH
JANATA DAL (S)
CHANDRA SHEKHAR
SAMAJWADI PARTY
MULAYAM SINGH
SAMAJWADI JANATA PARTY
CHANDRA SHEKHAR
TOWARDS
1996

known as the Lok Dal. Consequently there were six national parties on the eve of the seventh Lok Sabha elections in 1980 - the two Congress parties, the two Janata parties and the two Communist parties- the CPI and CPM.

After the Congress victory in 1980, the disintegration of the Janata Party continued. The two Janata parties split further. The Janata Party divide into the Janata Party led by Chandrashekhar and the Bharatiya Janata Party led by Atal Bihari Vajpayee. The Bharatiya Janata Party was essentially the same as the old Jana Sangh. Although the Jana Sangh had merged with the Janata Party in 1977, it had always maintained a separate identity and the break in 1980 was a relatively painless process. The old symbols - the umbrella and the lotus (earlier with the Jana Sangh) - were allotted to the two groups. Similarly, the Janata Party (S) broke into two groups - Janata Party (S)-Raj Narain and Janata Party (S)-Charan Singh. Their symbol farmer-ploughing-the-field was frozen and two new symbols, bicycle and woman respectively were allotted to the two parties.

However, after Raj Narain's death, the scene changed again and Charan Singh led the Lok Dal during the 1984 elections. The disintegration of the Janata Party was virtually complete by 1984 when its components contested as four separate national parties: Indian Congress (Socialist), Bharatiya Janata Party, Lok Dal and the Janata Party. In addition some of the break away groups contested as recognised State parties. The Congress faced a disunited opposition everywhere except in a few States either where strong State parties had emerged (as in Andhra Pradesh where N. T. Rama Rao's Telugu Desam swept the polls) or where the opposition had organised itself into a local coalition (as in Kerala).

An important development that has had a major impact on the nature of party politics in India was the Act commonly referred to as the 'Anti-Defection Act'. (The official title was The Constitution Fifty-second Amendment) Act, 1985). The aim of the Act is to stop members who are elected as representatives of one party 'crossing the floor' join another party after the election. Defections had become so frequent that it tended to undermine the party system, particularly since the reason for changing parties was often not related to ideological or policy differences but took place in response to other inducements. By preventing defections from the Congress, the Act was also intended to provide greater security to the Prime Minister Rajiv Gandhi and to help him to hold on to his 400 elected MPs. The Act was to prove of major importance in the party realignments of 1990 and 1991.

The Anti-Defection Act specifies that if a member of any house (Parliament or Legislative Assembly) votes or abstains from voting, contrary to the direction issued by the political party to which he belongs, he shall be disqualified from being a member of that house. However, if one-third or more of the members of a party break away, the Act recognises this as a 'split' in the party and does not disqualify the members of the break away faction. It also recognises the 'merger' of parties where not less than two-thirds of the members of a party have agreed to the merger. Finally, the Act states that no court shall have any jurisdiction over any matter connected with the disqualification of a member. The decision is entirely the responsibility of the Speaker of the house and only technical issues can be taken to court.

The Anti-Defection Act, which was brought in by Rajiv Gandhi only 15 weeks after coming to power, played a significant role in maintaining the stability of his government. During his five-year rule, although there was considerable dissent within the party, it never reached a point where one-third of the MPs could get together to cause a split. Before the Anti-Defection Act, individual MPs could leave a party without being disqualified. What would start as a trickle of defections would sometimes end up in a flood; this is now severely curtailed.

Nevertheless the Rajiv Gandhi government was shaken by a major loss when a senior leader, the popular Finance Minister, V.P. Singh, resigned.[1] In the run-up to the 1989 elections, V.P. Singh played a major role in uniting opposition parties to fight the Congress. He first persuaded several parties, the Janata Party, Lok Dal (A), Lok Dal (B) and others to merge under the label Janata Dal. The next step was the formation of a national Front against the Congress. Parties in the National Front, the Janata Party, DMK, CPI, CPM,

---

1 He resigned as Defence Minister after his portfolio was changed in January 1988.

Congress(S), AGP and other small parties retained their identity but agreed on a common platform to defeat the Congress. In the final process of opposition unity, the National Front came to an agreement with the BJP on sharing seats. The aim was to ensure that every constituency had only one opposition candidate facing the Congress. In some States the agreement was total (e.g.. Rajasthan, Gujarat); in many States only partial agreement could be achieved (Madhya Pradesh, Orissa) and in some States there was virtually no agreement (e.g. Maharashtra, Uttar Pradesh).

Despite the Congress winning 39.5 per cent of the vote in the 1989 general elections, it lost heavily in terms of seats. Although it remained the largest single party, the number of seats it won fell by more than half, from 401 in 1984 to 197 in 1989. This was seen as an overwhelming mandate for a change and all the opposition parties agreed to get together to form a government. V.P. Singh was sworn in as Prime Minister on 2 December, 1989, leading the Janata Dal which had won only 143 seats. The CPI, CPM and BJP agreed to support the government 'from the outside'. This meant they would not form part of a coalition government but would vote with the Janata Dal to ensure a majority in the Lok Sabha.

Once again the Anti-Defection Act played a role in keeping the Janta Dal together after serious inner party differences began to emerge. It was eventually the BJP withdrawing support, rather than a split in the Janata Dal, that brought the V.P. Singh government down on 7 November, 1990. However, immediately after the collapse of the government, the Janata Dal split. A group led by Chandrasekhar and backed by the former deputy Prime Minister Devi Lal gathered enough support from MPs to cross the one-third barrier and be recognised by the Anti-Defection Act as a separate party called Janata Dal (Secular).

The JD(S) was supported 'from the outside' by the Congress and formed the new government with Chandrashekar sworn in as Prime Minister on 10 November, 1990. However, the Speaker later disqualified 8 MPs who had left the Janata Dal to join the JD(S). After the Speaker's ruling, the party position on 11 January, 1991 is listed in Table 3.2.

Party Position in Lok Sabha on 11 January, 1991

Congress (I)	195	TDP	2
Janata Dal (incl. 2 associates)	77	Muslim League	2
		IPF	1
BJP	86	MGP	1
Janta Dal(S)	54	MCC	1
CPM	33	Congress(S)	1
CPI	12	Muslim Majlis	1
ADMK	11	KCM	1
Akali Dal	4	SSP	1
RSP	4	ABHM	1
Forward Bloc	3	GNLF	1
National Conference	3	Independents	10
BSP	3	Vacancies	29
JMM	3		
Shiv Sena	3	Total	543

Party Position in Lok Sabha as on 10 May, 1997

BJP	163	Indian National Congress	138
Janta Dal	45	CPI (M)	32
T. M. Congress (M)	20	DMK	17
Samajwadi Party	17	Telugu Desam Party	17
Shivsena	15	CPI	12
BSP	11	Shriomani Akali Dal	8
United Goa Demo. Party	1	BKKP	1
Independents	9	Nominated	2
		Total	545 (excluding HS)

Clearly, the survival of the JD(S) and of Prime Minister Chandrashekhar depended on the fragile support provided by the Congress. This did not last long. The Congress withdrew its support and India's tenth general election followed. the Parliament that finally emerged (after Punjab elections in February 1992) had a different but equally complex pattern (see Table 8.1).

Elections in India are normally spread over two or three days. This is partly to avoid special holidays which always occur in one

State or another but it is also to allow the Election Commission to redeploy its poll monitoring facilities. In 1991 the polls were scheduled for May 20, 23 and 26. But a few hours after he himself had voted in Delhi on 20 May, Rajiv Gandhi was assassinated. The polls due on 23 May and 26 May were postponed to 12 June and 15 June. It is a sad irony of 1991 that the Congress fared measurably better in the sympathy wave following their leader's death. In the votes cast on 20 May, there was a 5.7 per cent swing away from Congress. In the votes caste in June, there was a 1.6 per cent swing in favour of the Congress party.

This history of party splits and mergers shows how difficult it is to assess the evolution of support for a party over time. For example, what was the increase in the Congress party's popularity between the fourth and fifth general elections in 1967 and 1971? This question is not easy to answer, since there were two Congress parties in 1971, the 'Requisitionists' and the 'Organisation.'[2] Similar problems arise with the Socialists, with the Communists, and above all with the constituents of the Janata party after 1977. In six party-wise summary tables in chapter 10, we have tried to present the fortunes of the most important components or factions of parties before amalgamations and after splits.

The process of arranging the votes of altered parties within a single time-series must do some violence to the integrity of the series. For instance, obvious problems arise in presenting figures that show the evolution of support for the Indian National Congress since 1971. We have used votes of the dominant faction in the time series. The results of the 1971 and 1980 elections offer some validation for this approach. Using the principle we have taken the Indian National Congress(I) as the Congress from 1980 onwards.

---

2 The pro-Mrs Gandhi, Indian National Congress faction led first by C. Subramaniam and later by Jagjivan Ram has been known in popular parlance by various names such as Congress (J), Congress (R), etc. The Election Commission recognised this party simply as the Indian National Congress.

3 The part index in the Appendix lists in alphabetical order all the political parties that have ever been officially recognised in the Election Commission's records. It also gives the party code or abbreviated part name used in this book.

The Rajya Sabha

Under Article 80 of the Constitution, the Council of States consists of twelve members nominated by the President as representatives of literature, science, art and social services and upto 233 representatives of the States.[1] Seats are currently allotted to the States in the following manner :

Statewise Allocation of Rajya Sabha Seats

State	No. of Seats	State	No. of Seats
Andhra Pradesh	18	Orissa	10
Arunachal Pradesh	1	Punjab	7
Assam	7	Rajasthan	10
Bihar	22	Sikkim	1
Delhi	3	Tamil Nadu	18
Goa	1	Tripura	1
Gujarat	11	Uttar Pradesh	34
Haryana	5	West Bengal	16
Himachal Pradesh	3		
Jammu & Kashmir	4		
Karnataka	12	Union Territories	
Kerala	9		
Maharashtra	19	Pondicherry	1
Madhya Pradesh	16		
Manipur	1	Total Elected	233
Meghalaya	1	Nominated	12
Mizoram	1		
Nagland	1	Total	245

[1] From 1976 to 1987 the Rajya Sabha has 232 elected members. On 30 May, 1987 this increased to 233 as Goa became a State and was represented by one seat.

Members are elected by the members of each State Vidhan Sabha using the single transferable vote system of proportional representation. They serve for six years, with a third retiring every two years. Table 7.2 gives the break-up of Rajya Sabha seats party-wise since 1950.

References

In December 1929, the Congress gave its call for complete Independence for India instead of self-government within the British empire. The Independence resolution moved by Gandhiji and adopted by the Lahore Session of the Congress under the Presidentship of Jawaharlal Nehru (1989-1964) said : "The word 'Swaraj' in the article of the Congress Constitution shall mean complete independence." In August 1942, the All India Congress Committee at its session in Bombay then adopted a resolution demanding complete withdrawal of British rule from India. The Congress also launched a non-violent agitation for Independence which called the British to Quit India."

January 26, 1930 was observed throughout the country as Independence Day (That is how Indian Constitution was implemented from January 26, 1950). The Muslim League declared the 16th of August, 1946 as Direct Action day on which meetings were held to proclaim the determination to achieve Pakistan. The day witnessed wide spread Hindu - Muslim clashes and rioting in Calcutta and in Noakhali (then in East Bengal) and in Bihar. On August 24, 1946, Viceroy Lord Wavell announced the formation of an interim government in Delhi headed by Jawaharlal Nehru which the Muslim League joined in October, 1946. But the coalition was a divided house and could not function effectively. The Muslim League did not participate in the Constituent Assembly which formed part of the people for the transfer of power. In February 1947, Prime Minister Attlee made statement in the House of Commons that the Govt. has decided to transfer power to India not later than June 1948. As a consequence to this a new Viceroy Lord Mountbatten was appointed to implement the plan of India's Independence. He arrived in Delhi on March 1947. He tried to persuade Muhammad Ali Jinnah to agree to the federal scheme which could preserve the unity of India. But Jinnah insisted on the partition of India into a Muslim State to be called 'Pakistan. Early in June 1947, the Mountbatten Plan was announced which advanced the date of transfer of power from June 1948 to August 15, 1948.

After partition, Jinnah became the first President of Pakistan having its capital in Karachi. He died in 1949. Though he changed later but at the Lahore Session of the Muslim League in 1024, he said : "One essential requisite condition to achieve Swaraj is political unity between Hindus and Mohammadans. I am almost inclined to say that India will get dominion responsible government the day Hindus and Muslims are united." Gandhiji endorsed his view.

In March 1940, again at Lahore Session, the Muslim League under Jinnah got the resolution adopted asking for the partition of India.

ECONOMY GROWTH RATE

Economy Growth Rate

Plan	Year	Target	Actuals	Growth rate for
First Plan	1951-56	2.1	3.6	National income
Second Plan	1956-61	4.5	4.0	National income
Third Plan	1961-66	5.6	2.2	National income
Fourth Plan	1969-74	5.7	3.3	Net domestic product
Fifth Plan	1974-79	4.4	5.1	Gross domestic product
Sixth Plan	1980-85	5.2	5.5	Gross domestic product
Seventh Plan	1985-90	5.0	*	Gross domestic product

* Tentative growth rate of gross domestic product was 5.1% 1985-86, above 4.5% in 1986-87.

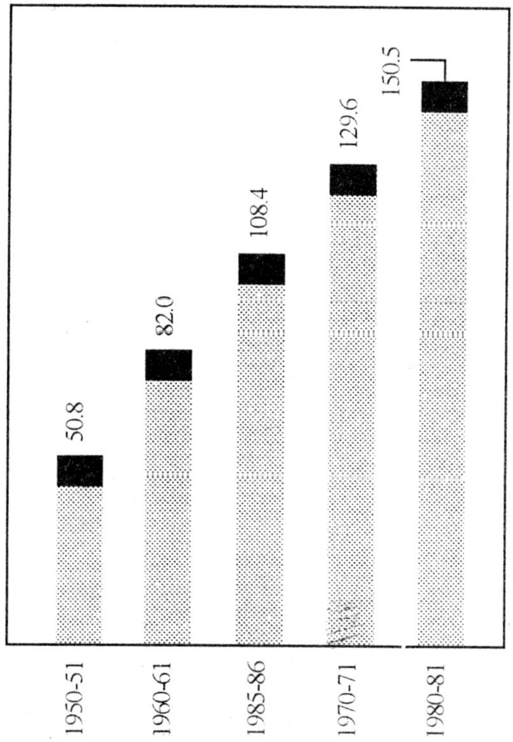

Selected Indicators 1950-51 to 1995-96

	1950-51	1960-61	1970-71	1980-81	1988-89	1989-90	1990-91	1991-92	1992-93	1993-94	1994-95	1995-96
1	2	3	4	5	6	7	8	9	10	11	12	13
Economic indicators												
GDP at factor cost :												
(i) At current prices (Rs. crore)	8979	15254	39708	122427	352706	408662	477814	552768	630772	731891	858340	98578#
(ii) At 1980-81 prices (Rs. crore)	42871	62904	90426	122427	188461	201453	212253	213983	225268	238864	256095	274209#
Per capita net national product, at 1980-81 prices (Rupees)	1127	1350	1520	1630	2059	2157	2222	2175	2243	2334	2449	2573#
Index of industrial production (Base : 1980-81 - 100)	18.3@	36.2	65.3	100.0	180.9	196.4	212.6	213.9	218.9	232.0	253.7	283.3(P)
Index of agricultural production (Base : triennium ending 1981-82)	46.2	68.8	85.9	102.1	140.0	143.0	148.4	145.5	151.5	157.3	165.0	164.3
Gross domestic capital formation (as per cent of GDP)	10.2	15.7	16.6	22.7	24.5	25.1	27.7	23.4	24.0	23.6	26.0	27.4#
Gross domestic saving (as per cent of GDP)	10.4	12.7	15.7	21.2	21.4	22.4	24.3	22.8	21.1	23.1	24.9	25.6#

	1950-51	1960-61	1970-71	1980-81	1988-89	1989-90	1990-91	1991-92	1992-93	1993-94	1994-95	1995-96
1	2	3	4	5	6	7	8	9	10	11	12	13
OUTPUT												
(a) Foodgrains												
(million tonnes)	50.8	82.0	108.4	129.6	169.9	171.0	176.4	168.4	179.5	184.3	191.5	185.1(P)
(b) Finished Steel												
(million tonnes)	1.04	2.39	4.64	6.82	12.84	13.00	13.53	14.33	15.20	15.1	17.8	21.4
(c) Cement												
(million tonnes)	2.7	8.0	14.3	18.6	44.3	45.8	48.8	51.7	54.7	57.8	62.4	69.3(P)
(d) Coal (including lignite)												
(million tonnes)	32.3	55.2	76.3	119.0	207.0	213.7	225.5	243.8	254.9	264.1	273.1	292.3(P)
(e) Crude oil												
(million tonnes)	0.3	0.5	6.8	10.5	32.0	34.1	33.0	30.4	27.0	27.0	32.2	35.1(P)
(f) Electricity generated												
(utilities only)												
(Billion KWH)	5.1	16.9	55.8	110.8	221.4	245.4	264.3	287.0	301.1	323.5	351.0	380.1(P)
Whole price index*												
(Base : 1981-82 = 100)	16.9	19.6	35.5	91.1	154.2	165.7	182.7	27.8	228.7	247.8	274.7	295.8
Consumer price index												
(Base : 1982 = 100)@@	17	21	38	81	163	173	193	219	240	258	284	313
Plan outlay (Rs. crore)	260##	1117	2524	15023	48645	55630	58369	64751	72852	88081	106204(RE)	119898(RE)
Centre's budgetary deficit												
(Rs. crore)	(-)33#	(-)117	285	2576	5642	10592	11347	6855	12312	10960	961	7600(RE)
FOREIGN TRADE												
(i) Exports												
Rs. crore	606	642	1535	6711	20232	27658	32553	44041	53688	69751	82674	106353
US$ million	2169	1346	2031	8486	13970	16612	18143	17865	18537	22238	26330	31797

	1950-51	1960-61	1970-71	1980-81	1988-89	1989-90	1990-91	1991-92	1992-93	1993-94	1994-95	1995-96
1	2	3	4	5	6	7	8	9	10	11	12	13
(ii) Imports												
Rs. crore	608	1122	1634	12549	28235	35328	43198	47851	63375	73101	89971	121678
US$ million	1273	2353	2162	15869	19497	21219	24075	19411	21882	23306	28654	36678
Foreign exchange reserves (excluding gold and SDRs):												
Rs. crore	911	186	438	4822	6605	5787	4388	14578	20140	47287	66006	58446
US $ million	1914	390	584	5850	4226	3368	2236	5631	6434	15068	20809	17044
SOCIAL INDICATORS												
Population												
Population (million)[a]	361.1	439.2	548.2	683.3	811.3	827.4	846.3	863.2[b]	880.4[b]	898.0[b]	915.9[b]	...
Birth rate (per 1000)[c]	39.9	41.7	36.9	33.9	30.6	30.2	29.5	29.2	28.7	28.7P	28.3P	...
Death rate (per 1000)[c]	27.4	22.8	14.9	12.5	10.3	9.7	9.8	10.1	9.3	9.3P	9.0P	...
Life expectancy at birth (in years)[d]												
(a) Male	32.4	41.9	46.4	50.9	57.7	58.1	58.6	...	60.4	...	...	...
(b) Female	31.7	40.6	44.7	50.0	58.1	58.6	59.0	...	61.2	...	...	...
Total	32.1	41.3	45.6	50.4	57.7	58.3	58.7	...	60.8	...	...	...
Education												
Literacy rate (percentage)*												
(a) Male	27.16	40.40	45.95	56.37	...	...	64.1	...	...	...	...	...
(b) Female	8.86	15.34	21.97	29.75	...	...	39.3	...	...	...	...	...
Total	18.33	28.31	34.45	43.56	...	...	52.2	...	...	...	...	...
Health & Family Welfare[f]												
Registered medical practitioners (RMP)												

1	1950-51 2	1960-61 3	1970-71 4	1980-81 5	1988-89 6	1989-90 7	1990-91 8	1991-92 9	1992-93 10	1993-94 11	1994-95 12	1995-96 13
(thousand)	61.8	83.7	151.1	268.7	368.6	381.9	394.0	410.8	...	...	...	...
RMP per 10,000 population	1.7	1.9	2.8	3.9	4.5	4.6	4.7	4.8	...	...	...	...
Beds (all types)** per 10,000	3.2	5.2	6.4	8.3	9.5	9.4	9.6	...	...	...	...	...

@ Relates to the calendar year 1950.

@@ Figures for the period up to 1988-89 derived by converting indices on earlier bases into base 1982=100.

\# Quick estimates.

\## Relates to 1951-52.

* Figures for the period up to 1980-81 derived by converting the indicates on earlier bases into base 1980-81=100.

** Includes beds in hospitals, dispensaries, P.H.Cs, clines, sanatoriums, etc.

RE Revised estimates

... Not avaliable.

P Provisional.

Notes :

a As on March 1, 1951 and so on up to 1980-81 and 1990-91 as per Census of India. Figures for the period 1988 to 1990 are based on adjusted projections of the Standing Committee of Experts on Population Projections.

b Relate to March 1, 1992, 1993, 1994 and 1995 based on projected estimates by Technical Group on Population Projections (August 1996) set up under the Chairmanship of Registrar General of India.

c Data for 1950-51, 1960-61, 1970-71 and 1980-81 are census estimates and relate to decades 1941-50, 1951-60, 1961-70 and 1971-80 respectively. The estimates for 1988-89 onwards are based on the SRS.

d Data for 1950-51, 1960-61, 1970-71 and 1980-81 relate to the decades 1941-50, 1951-60, 1961-70 and 1971-80 respectively, centred at mid-point of the decade, i.e., 1946, 1956, 1966 and 1976. The estimates for 1988-89, 1989-90 and 1990-91 refer to the periods, 1986-90, 1987-91 and 1988-92 respectively. For 1992-93, it is based on the extrapolated values of the Standing Commitee of Experts on Population Projections centred at June 1992.

e Data for 1950-51, 1960-61, 1970-71, 1980-81 and 1990-91 relate to the years 1951, 1961, 1971, 1981 and 1991 respectively. The figures for 1951, 1961 and 1971 relate to population aged 5 years and above and those for 1981 and 1991 relate to population aged 7 years and above. All India literacy rates exclude Assam for 1981 and J&K for 1991.

f Relate to calendar year e.g., 1950-51 pertains to December 1951 and so on.

Source : Economic Survey - 1995 - 1997 Government of India, Ministry of Finance.

PRESIDENTS
VICE PRESIDNETS
SPEAKERS
&
PRIME MINISTERS

Presidential Elections : 1952 - 1997

Date	Winner			Runner-up			Others	
	Name	**Valid Votes**	**(%)**	**Name**	**Valid Votes**	**(%)**	**Valid Votes**	**(%)**
1952 May 2	R. Prasad	507400	83.8	K.T. Shah	92827	15.3	5159	0.9
1957 May 6	R. Prasad	459698	99.3	N.N. Das	2000	0.4	1498	0.3
1962 May 7	S. Radhakrishnan	553067	98.3	C.H. Ram	6,341	1.1	3537	0.6
1967 May 6	Z. Hussain	471244	56.2	K. Subbarao	363,971	43.4	336	0.4
1969 Aug. 16	V.V. Giri	420077	50.2	N.S. Reddy	405427	48.5	10833	1.3
1974 Aug. 17	F.A. Ahmed	765587	80.2	T. Chaudhari	189186	19.8	—	—
1977 Aug. 6	N.S. Reddy	unopposed	—	—	—	—	—	—
1982 Jul. 12	Gaini Zail Singh	754113	72.7	H.R. Khanna	282685	27.6	—	—
1987 Sep. 7	R. Venkataraman	740148	72.3	V.R.K. Iyer	281550	27.5	2223	0.2
1992 Jul. 25	S.D. Sharma	675864	64.4	G.G. Swell	346485	33.8	3839	0.3
1997 Jul. 24	K.R. Narayan	—	94.79	T.N. Seshan	5	—	—	—

Prime Ministers and their Constituencies

Prime Minister	From	To	Constituency elected from	Largest margin of victory
Jawaharlal Nehru	15 Aug., 1947	27 May, 1964	Phulpur (1957, 1962) Allahabad (1952)	33.7% (1962)
Gulzari Lal Nanda	27 May, 1964	9 June, 1964	Sabarkantha	11.1% (1952)
Lal Bahadur Shastri	9 June, 1964	11 Jan, 1966	Allahabad	29.0% (1962)
Gulzari Lal Nanda	11 Jan., 1966	24 Jan., 1966	Sabarkantha	11.1% (1952)
Indira Gandhi	24 Jan, 1966	24 March, 1977	Rae Bareilly (1967, 1971)	49.3% (1980)
Morarji Desai	24 March, 1977	28 July, 1979	Surat	66.6% (1957)
Charan Singh	28 July, 1979	14 Jan., 1980	Baghpat	33.3% (1980)
Indira Gandhi	14 Jan, 1980	31 Oct., 1984	Medak	49.3% (1980)
Rajiv Gandhi	31 Oct., 1984	1 Dec., 1989	Amethi (1981, 1984)	77.3% (1981 by election)
V.P. Singh	2 Dec., 1989	7 Nov., 1990	Fathepur	27.8% (1989)
Chandrashekhar	10 Nov., 1990	6 March, 1991 (resigned)	Ballia	46.1% (1977)
	7 March, 1991	21 June, 1991		
P.V. Narsimha Rao	21 June, 1991	16 May, 1996	Nandyal (by-election)	82.8% (1991)
Atal Behari Vajpayee	May 16, 1996	31 May, 1996 (resigned)		
Deve Gowda	June 1, 1996	April 20, 1997		
I.K. Gujral	April 21, 1997			

Speakers

	LOK SABHA		SPEAKER		
	Date of first meeting after its constitution	**Date of dissolution**	**Name**	**From**	**To**
First Lok Sabha	13 May 1957	4 April 1957	Ganesh Vasudev Mavalankar	15 May 1952	27 Feb. 1956
			M. Anathasayanam Ayyangar	8 March 1956	10 May 1957
Second Lok Sabha	10 May 1957	31 March 1962	M. Anathasayanam Ayyangar	11 May 1957	16 April 1962
Third Lok Sabha	16 April 1962	3 March 1967	Hukam Singh	17 April, 1962	16 March, 1967
Fourth Lok Sabha	16 March 1967	27 Dec. 1970	Neelam Sanjeeva Reddy	17 March 1967	19 July, 1969
			Gurdial Singh Dhillon	8 August 1969	19 March 1971
Fifth Lok Sabha	19 March 1971	18 Jan. 1977	Gurdial Singh Dhillon	22 March 1971	1 Dec. 1975
			Bali Ram Bhagat	5 Jan. 1976	25 March 1977
Sixth Lok Sabha	25 March 1977	22 August 1979	Neelam Sanjeeva Reddy	26 March 1977	13 July 1977
			K.S. Hegde	21 July 1977	22 Jan. 1980
Seventh Lok Sabha	21 Jan. 1980	31 Dec. 1984	Bal Ram Jakhar	22 Jan. 1980	15 Jan. 1985
Eighth Lok Sabha	15 Jan. 1985	27 Nov. 1989	Dr. Bal Ram Jakhar	16 Jan. 1985	18 Dec. 1989
Ninth Lok Sabha	18 Dec. 1989	13 March 1991	Rabi Ray	19 Dec. 1989	9 July 1991
Tenth Lok Sabha	9 July 1991	—	Shivraj V. Patil	10 July 1991	21 May 1996
Eleventh Lok Sabha	22 May 1996	Till date	P.A. Sangma		

PRIME MINISTERS

PT. JAWAHARLAL NEHRU

V. P. SINGH

CHANDRASEKHAR

P. V. NARSHIMHA RAO

ATAL BEHARI BAJPAYEE

DEVE GOWDA

I. K. GUJRAL

1. Under Article 94 of the Constitution in case of dissolution of the Lok Sabha, Speaker does not vacate his office until immediately before the first meeting of the House after dissolution.
2. Dissolved 38 days before expiry of its term.
3. Died.
4. Dissolved 40 days before expiry of its term.
5. Dissolved one year and 79 days before expiry of its term.
6. Resigned.
7. Term of the Lok Sabha which was to expire on 18 March 1976 was extended by one upto 18 March 1977 by the House of the People (Extension of Duration) Act, 1976. However, House was dissolved after having been in existence for a period of five years, 10 months and six days.
8. Resigned.
9. House was dissolved after having been in existence for a period of two years, four months and 28 days.
10. Resigned.
11. Dissolved 20 days before expiry of its term.
12. Dissolved 48 days before expiry of its term.
13. House was dissolved after having been in existence for a period of one year, two months and 25 days.

Election Commissioners

1952	Sukumar Sen	1982	R.K. Trivedi
1958	K.V.K. Sundaram	1985	K.V.S. Peri Shastri
1967	S.P. Sen Verma	1990	T.N. Seshan
1972	Dr. Nagendra Singh	1995	T.N. Seshan
1973	T. Swaminathan		M.S. Gill
1977	S.L. Shakdhar		G.V.G. Krishnamurthy
		1997	M.S. Gill

Year of the Lok Sabha Elections

1952	1977
1957	1980
1962	1984
1967	1989
1971	1991

Anti-defection Act was passed in 1983 under the premiership of Shri Rajiv Gandhi. By the sixty-second Amendment to the Constitution in 1988, the voting age was lowered to 18. The country is divided into 4,061 Vidhansabhas and 533 Lok Sabha Constituencies.

The lowest percentage of votes had been 47.4 in 1962 and the highest recorded voting percentage was 64.1 in 1984. The average turnout in Indian polls has been 56.6%. In 1984 Elections, Shri Rajiv Gandhi won over 400 seats for the Congress Party in the Lok Sabha.

Size of the Lok Sabha

1952	489	1980	542
1957	494	1984	542
1962	494	1989	543
1967	520	1991	543
1971	518	1995	543
1977	542		

Two Members for the Lok Sabha are nominated by the President.

IMPORTANT DATES & EVENTS

August 15, 1947	Independence Day broadcast to the nation.
August 15, 1947	India wins freedom to became a free Nation.
January 30, 1948	Mahatma Gandhi was shot dead by an assassin in Birla Bhavan Grounds, New Delhi.
September 1948	Indian troops were sent into the State of Hyderabad in September 1948 to drive away the Razakars and the Communists and from controlling the residual State of Hyderabad.
December 31, 1948	End of Indo-Pak Conflict.
November 26, 1949	Constitution of India adopted.
1949	India became member of the Commonwealth.
January 24, 1950	In all 284 Members appended their signatures of the new Constitution.
January 26, 1950	Constitution of India comes into force. On this day the Constituent Assembly ceased to exist and transformed itself into the provisional Parliament of India until a new Parliament was constituted in 1952.
October 7, 1950	Chinese troops entered into Tibet on October 7, 1950.
1950	Planning Commission was set up. In 1938 Congress had set up a National Planning Committee with Nehru as the Chairman.
December 15, 1950	Sardar Patel died in Office
May 23, 1951	Tibetan leaders agreed to sign and agreement with China.
June 1951	First amendment to the Constitution was made to protect the laws relating to abolition of zamindari.
1952	The First General Elections were held in India.
October 24, 1954	Rafi Ahmed Kidwai died in New Delhi while in office.
November 1, 1954	France withdrew from Pondicherry

December 1954	Indian Parliament adopted the Resolution announcing Socialistic Pattern of Society as the objective of India's economic policy.
April 24, 1955	First Afro Asian Conference of 24 countries held at Bandung from 18th to 24th April 1955. This led to the creation of Non-Aligned Movement.
December 13, 1955	The First ever visit by the Soviet leaders Marshal N.A. Bulganin and N.S. Khrushchev when they came to India.
1956	States' reorganisation was done in 1956.
February 22, 1958	Maulana Azad died in Office in New Delhi
1959	Dalai Lama was forced to flee Lhasa (Tibet) and sought asylum in India.
1959	Indira Gandhi elected President of Indian National Congress.
November-December 1959	First visit to India by the President of the United States of America.
July 18, 1960	India became the sixth nation in the world to put a satellite in space using her own launch vehicle SLV-3.
1962	Nagaland became a separate State
October 20, 1962	Chineses Aggression
1963	Kamraj Plan - Some Congress leaders resigned from office.
May 27, 1964	Jawaharlal Nehru died in office in New Delhi.
1965 (Autumn)	Indo-Pak War over the Rann of Kutch which led to full fledged war in 1965
January 10, 1966	Signing to Tashkent Agreement between Lal Bahadur Shastri and President Ayub Khan - Death of Lal Bahadur Shastri.
1969	Split in the Congress Party took place when Mrs. Indira Gandhi was the Prime Minister.

August, 1971	Indo-Soviet Friendship Treaty was signed.
December 3, 1971	Pakistani forces again attacked India and a full fledged war took place and Bangladesh became a free country.
July 1972	Shimla Agreement was signed.
May 1974	India observed "World Population Year"
May 18, 1974	India's first underground test explosion was conducted at Pokharan in the Rajasthan Desert.
1976	First step towards normalisation of Sino-Indo relations was taken, diplomatic relations restored which had broken after the Chinese aggression of 1962.
June 26, 1976	Emergency imposed.
1977	Janata Party Government formed at the Centre
October 31, 1984	Indira Gandhi died at the hands of assassins
July 29, 1987	This historic India-Srilanka Agreement was signed by President Jayewardene and Rajiv Gandhi.
1988	India troops sent to help Maldive Government to suppress the rebellion by a handful of persons.
May 21, 1991	Rajiv Gandhi was assassinated at Sriperumbedur (Tamilnadu)

President's Rule was imposed in the State 89 times since the Constitute India has fifteen major languages and 844 dialects. Hindi is spoken by 45% of the population.

There were 565 princely States that were merged into the Indian Union and by August 1947, this process had almost been completed by Sardar Vallabh Bhai Patel.

Congress continued to rule at the Centre from 1947 to 1977.

Nehru remained Prime Minister for 17 years.

Maharaj of Kashmir acceded to India in October 1947. Before that raiders organised and equipped by Pakistan Army had attacked and advanced into the Kashmir Valley.

ASSASSINATION OF NATIONAL LEADERS IN THE SUB-CONTINENT SINCE 1947

Assassination of National Leaders in the Sub-Continent Since 1947

Mahatma Gandhi was killed by one of his own children; Indira Gandhi was gunned down by her personal body-guard team to whom she entrusted her life;

Rajiv was killed by a bomb planted by people for whose security he stood for.

All these are martyrs who died serving the country. In all the three cases the assassins had no personal enemity against the victims. But they were killed for what they stood for. Earlier, there were two unsuccessful attempts on the life of Rajiv Gandhi, the first at Rajghat on 2nd of October 1986 and the second on 30th July 1987, in Sri Lanka Rajiv was lucky the third time. Only Motilal Nehru and Jawaharlal Nehru died natural deaths. The assassination of Rajiv Gandhi is the tenth slaying of a national leaders in the sub-continent since 1947.

First was of Mohandas Karamchand Gandhi of India, on 30th January 1948 ;

Second was of Liaquat Ali Khan, the first Prime Minister of Pakistan on 16th October 1951 ;

Third was of Solomon Bandaranaike Prime Minister of Sri-Lanka on 25th September 1959 ;

Fourth was of Jigme Dorji, Prime Minister of Bhutan on 5th April 1964;

Fifth was of Sheikh Mujibur Rehman, President of Bangladesh on 15th August 1975 ;

Sixth was of Zia-ur-Rehman, President of Bangladesh on 30th May 1981 ;

Seventh was of Mrs. Indira Gandhi, Prime Minister of India, on 31st October, 1984 ;

A Troubled History of Pakistan

1947	–	Partition creates free India, led by Nehru and Pakistan – in two halves, East and West led by Jinnah.
1947-48	–	War with India in Kashmir.
1948	–	Jinnah dies.
1951	–	Prime Minister Liaqat Ali Khan murdered.
1956	–	Pakistan becomes an Islamic republic.
1958	–	President overthrows Constitution, brings in martial law under Ayub Khan.
1960	–	Ayub elected President.
1965	–	Ayub re-elected.
1965	–	Clashes with India in Rann of Kutch, then War in Kashmir, Foreign Minister Z.A. Bhutto resigns (1966) over peace terms.
1969	–	Ayub resigns, General Yahaya Khan takes power, imposing martial law.
1970	–	Elections (December) to constitutional assembly make East Pakistani autonomists largest party.
1971	–	East Pakistan breaks away (March) as Bangladesh. Pakistan army tries to suppress it, Indian troops intervene, Pakistan accepts defeat (December). Yahya resigns, Bhutto takes over, ending martial law.
1973	–	Under new Constitution, Bhutto becomes Prime Minister instead of President.
1977	–	Bhutto wins national elections, disorder follows, General Zia-ul-Haq deposes Bhutto, imposes material law.
1979	–	Bhutto hanged.
1985	–	National elections (February) go against Zia. Political Parties, banned since 1979, allowed to function, martial law ended (December).
1988	–	Zia dies (August) in air crash. Elections (November) bring Benazir Bhutto to power.
1990	–	Benazir's government dismissed (August). Her party loses in elections (October), Nawaz Sharif heads new government.

(Source : The Econamist November, 1991, London)